DISTANCES.

-TA to C. Passero .... 55'
    „ Tripoli .... 190'
    „ Benghazi .... 360'
    „ Taranto .... 325'
    „ Suda Bay .... 550'
    „ Tobruk .... 620'
    „ Port Said .... 1030'

TIC SEA

aples
Taranto
Brindisi
ssina
Calabria
Valona
St. of Otranto
Corfu
Salonika
GREECE
Ionian
Sea
C. Passero
MALTA
Athens
AEGEAN
Istanbul
Smyrna
ASIA MINOR
C. Matapan
Suda
CRETE
Rhodes
Scarpanto
CYPRUS
SYRIA
Bierut
Haifa
PALESTINE
Derna
Bomba
Benghazi
Tobruk
Bardia
Sollum
Sidi Barrani
P. Said
Suez
Alexandria
IBYA
EGYPT

The MEDITERRANEAN
BACKGROUND.

*Under
Cunningham's
Command
1940-1943*

ADMIRAL OF THE FLEET SIR ANDREW B. CUNNINGHAM, BT.,
G.C.B., D.S.O.**

Under Cunningham's Command

1940-1943

by

Commander
GEORGE STITT, R.N.

LONDON
GEORGE ALLEN & UNWIN LTD

First published in 1944

This Book is Produced in Complete
Conformity with the Authorized
Economy Standards

Printed in Great Britain by
W. S. COWELL, LIMITED, IPSWICH AND LONDON

INTRODUCTION

On the 10th June, 1940, Mussolini thrust his treacherous dagger into the prostrate body of France. War was automatically declared against Great Britain. Without an ally and deserted by France, on whose military forces we had principally relied for the defence of North Africa and the Middle East, the British Empire stood alone to face this new threat to the vital Mediterranean area. Our Army in Egypt was negligible, their equipment was out of date, and a mere handful of aircraft was all that could be set against the hundreds of winged demons possessed by Mussolini. To those who could appreciate these facts the outlook was grave, and it seemed as if nothing could arrest an Axis grip on the entire Mediterranean, their control of the Suez Canal and exploitation of the riches which lay beyond. Had this been achieved it is difficult to see how the war could have ended in anything but a compromise, if not a defeat for all we upheld.

But, while the whole world was paralysed by the shock of those tragic events which led up to Mussolini's ruthless action, there still flew in the Mediterranean one flag which proclaimed liberty, one flag whose strength had ever brought succour to the weak, one flag carrying a tradition of duty and service to humanity—the White Ensign of Britain's Navy, worn alike by warships belonging to all members of the great Commonwealth. While Mussolini mouthed bombastic threats and Hitler imposed his shameful terms on conquered peoples, Admiral Sir Andrew B. Cunningham, K.C.B., D.S.O., was metaphorically nailing that flag to the masthead of his ships. He knew one fact which many in the stress of anguish had forgotten—that none of these extravagant ambitions of the Axis could be realised until they had swept the British Navy from the Mediterranean. This, he resolved, would never be accomplished. That the British Fleet should be pushed out of the Middle Sea by a crowd of Italian jackals was unthinkable. Let them come and attack the Fleet if they liked—so much the better. But better still for him to use every opportunity, every means in his power, every device of ingenuity to seek out, harass and attack the enemy himself. Above all, he was determined to achieve, at the earliest possible moment, a moral ascendancy over the enemy. Europe lay in the ruins of despair, but on the edge of those ruins there burned a fierce faith—that faith, steeled by tradition, which has for ever inspired the ships of Britain's Navy.

No Naval Commander-in-Chief has ever been faced with a problem more complex, more vital, than that with which Admiral Cunningham had to contend during those anxious days. No victory could be won in Africa, no adequate protection could be guaranteed to the oil fields in the Middle East, no hope to the enslaved peoples of Europe until a powerful Army had been created in Egypt. And no Army could be created in those distant parts without the protection of the Navy which was also indispensable for its maintenance. That, therefore, was the first task—to enable military forces to be assembled in Egypt. A less resolute Commander might have concentrated everything on this one objective and been loath to risk his numerically inferior fleet until this had been accomplished. Not so Admiral Cunningham. He argued that there was only one strategy for a weaker force to adopt and that was NOT a defensive one. Attack, was his motto; attack and again attack. Only a determined policy of attrition and damaging the enemy at every possible opportunity would pave the way to final victory. The risks he took were colossal. They were not the risks of an irresponsible gambler, but the risks of a courageous and clear thinker.

Apart from numerical inferiority, we suffered from another severe handicap. The speed of each type of Italian warship was far in excess of that which could be reached by any of our ships. Hence, the enemy was in a position to choose where and when he should attack, and his advantage in speed enabled him to break off any action when and how he pleased. Had air power been available in any moderate degree it might have been used to counter this advantage by creating damage sufficient to slow up the Italian Fleet on those rare occasions when it put to sea; but for long, dreary months that power was sadly lacking.

For long past it had been accepted that, if war came to the Mediterranean *via* Italy, Malta would be untenable for the Fleet. It was all very well to risk ships in battle when they stood a chance of crippling the enemy, but to expose them to continuous and concentrated air attack when in harbour for rest and refit was naturally considered unreasonable. Though no one pretended to like the idea of leaving Malta—it seemed like deserting a friend—sentiment could not prevail against reality.

Alexandria, the only other base available, was more than 900 miles from the Italian mainland—a distance far too great to maintain an offensive against the enemy in the degree Admiral Cunningham desired. But there was no alternative. It was just another difficulty which had to be countered.

History will record the stupendous task which faced Admiral Cunningham, the grave menace which overhung the Empire and the disastrous prospect for a false strategical conception. It will record also a certain greatness in an unquenchable flame of faith which, in those early days of peril, was virtually the sole weapon to avert disaster.

The book gives detailed accounts of some of the more important naval Mediterranean operations in 1940-41 in an attempt to lift the veil on that thrilling and fantastic period. The last two years, up to the surrender of the Italian Fleet, are covered in an epilogue—not that the events during this time are less important, but because the size of the book had to be kept within limits. The accounts themselves do not pretend to be a detailed history of all the terrific happenings that occurred, for such a history would fill volumes. In fact, the story of our submarines alone would fill many hundreds of pages. Some of the accounts are plain, factual narratives, others I have treated more personally; but it is hoped that they will present the reader with a clear picture of the principal events during this unique period of Naval History.

G.M.S.S.

CONTENTS

ILLUSTRATIONS

Acknowledgment is due to the Controller of
H.M. Stationery Office for permission to use
some photographs and reproductions of paintings
by Lt.-Cmmdr. Roland Langmaid, R.N., which
appeared in the publication, *East of Malta, West
of Suez.*

Chapter 1

THE BATTLE OF CALABRIA — JULY 1940

THE world, and the Italians in particular, were soon to learn that the retirement of the British Fleet from Malta to the more distant base at Alexandria did not herald a defensive strategy. Quite the reverse. The entire fleet was inspired by Admiral Cunningham's policy of attack and his determination to keep open the sea lanes of the Mediterranean. It was, therefore, with the greatest enthusiasm that everyone entered into the game of tempting the Italians to issue forth from their sheltered harbours and give battle in the open sea. During the first four weeks of the Mediterranean war British warships swept the waters between Gibralter and Port Said, stamped on any submarines which dared to interfere and bombarded coastal positions in North Africa. Throughout this opening phase a few Italian destroyers, in addition to submarines, felt the lash of the British Fleet, but no important enemy unit attempted to exert that authority which Mussolini so blatantly proclaimed.

The evacuation of a naval base is not complete by the removal of warships. There are masses of material—stores of all kinds and men to establish a new dockyard organisation. All these had to be transported across the 900 miles of sea which separated Malta from Alexandria. In addition, there was a number of people to be evacuated from an island which would undoubtedly have to withstand a prolonged seige. This, then, was one of the first problems with which Admiral Cunningham had to contend—the sailing of important convoys with vital stores and personnel from Malta to Alexandria and their safe arrival.

It was finally arranged that two convoys—one faster and carrying personnel and evacuees; the other slow and transporting important naval stores—should leave Malta early in July while the protecting arms of the Fleet sought to cover their flanks. Here was an opportunity for the Italian Fleet to inflict a damaging blow and no one for a moment dreamt that they would not take full advantage of it. Here also was Admiral Cunningham's chance not only to prevent this blow, but also to give the enemy a taste of the avenging power of Britain's Navy. So, when the entire Mediterranean Fleet sailed from Alexandria on 7th July and the nature of the enterprise was divulged, a feeling of elation gripped every officer and man. They were convinced that, within the next few days, they would make decisive naval history, for it was only reasonable to suppose that the Italians would exert a very determined effort to frustrate the operation.

Warships sailed in three groups. Ahead was Vice-Admiral J. C. Tovey in *Orion*, leading the 7th Cruiser Squadron, *Neptune*, *Sydney*, *Gloucester* and *Liverpool*, and accompanied by the Australian Flotilla Leader, *Stuart*. The central group consisted of the Commander-in-Chief in *Warspite* screened by the destroyers *Nubian*, *Mohawk*, *Hero*, *Hereward* and *Decoy*; and some miles astern were the slower battleships *Royal Sovereign*— flying the flag of Rear Admiral H. D. Pridham-Wippell—and *Malaya*, the aircraft carrier *Eagle* and ten more destroyers.

The first event during the six days filled with incident occurred towards midnight on 7th July. *Hasty*, one of the destroyers screening the force with *Royal Sovereign*, suddenly sighted a submarine on the surface at a range of 1000 yards. She immediately altered course towards it and increased speed; but the 'U' boat dived, the wash from her conning tower passing close down the starboard side of the destroyer. A full pattern of depth charges was fired at once; part of the submarine was seen to break surface and this was followed by a strong smell of oil. About five minutes later four underwater explosions were heard in rapid succession, which could only have come from the submarine. She was, therefore, considered to have been destroyed.

On the way back to join her position on the screen forty-five minutes later, *Hasty* found another contact which indicated a second submarine, and she delivered a further attack with a full pattern of depth charges. There was again a strong smell of oil, and it is almost certain that this 'U' boat was, at least, damaged.

From these incidents it was clear that the Italians had a good idea of Admiral Cunningham's intentions and were determined to harass his fleet from the moment it put to sea. Information, however, regarding movements of the Italian Fleet was eagerly awaited, but it was soon forthcoming. Early next morning, news was received from the *Phoenix*, one of the British submarines on a patrol line stretched across the central Mediterranean. Two battleships, she reported, together with four destroyers were in a position half way between Benghazi and Italy, steering south. But they were at extreme range from the submarine and her attack with torpedoes proved abortive. The presence of this force, however, indicated that the Italian Fleet was either engaged convoying ships to Libya or else disposing itself across the Mediterranean to arrest the advance of the British. Flying Boat reconnaissance from Malta was, therefore, directed to watch the movements of these ships.

Meanwhile one of *Eagle's* anti-submarine air patrols had sighted two more submarines, one of which was bombed. The nearest bomb fell about seven yards on the 'U' boat's starboard beam as she dived and, from the quantity of oil which she then emitted from the stern, it was believed that the submarine had been damaged.

Now began a series of heavy and persistent air attacks as the British Fleet encountered a vast armada concentrated in the air to maintain a continuous hail of bombs upon the advancing ships. Seven attacks were delivered on *Warspite* between noon and 6.0 p.m., while eighty bombs fell round *Royal Sovereign* and her force in the course of six different raids. It was all bombing from a high level and, though no hits were caused, it was a trying experience for those on board. The aircraft were beyond the reach of guns, often too high to detect, and the first indication of attack was generally the high-pitched whistle of falling bombs. As day wore on, this whistling grew unpopular. Dive-bombing may be more spectacular and dramatic, but it was found that the high level variety, though less damaging, was more nerve-racking when continued hour after hour.

Admiral Tovey's cruisers were less fortunate than the battleships. They, too, had been subjected to continuous attack of the same kind and, up to late afternoon, had suffered only from near misses. In the last attack, towards evening, however, a bomb scored a direct hit on *Gloucester's* bridge. Captain F. R. Garside was killed instantly with six of his officers and eleven men, while a further three officers and six men were badly wounded; the whole bridge structure was reduced to a shambles together with the gunnery director and main steering position which necessitated both steering and gun control being carried out from aft.

There was now further news of the enemy force which had been sighted by *Phoenix*. Flying Boat reconnaissance had reported that two enemy battleships, six cruisers and seven destroyers were about 100 miles north of Benghazi and that they were now steering in a northerly direction.

This information, in conjunction with the intensive bombing the Fleet had received and the numerous submarines which appeared to be about, made it quite clear that the Italians intended to try and keep our Fleet from the central Mediterranean. The Commander-in-Chief, therefore, decided to postpone the sailing of the convoys from Malta and, instead, concentrate his own forces and move them at the best possible speed towards Taranto in order to get between the enemy and his base.

Six o'clock next morning found the Commander-in-Chief some sixty miles west of Navarin. In the van, eight miles ahead, were the cruisers; and the slower battleships, *Eagle* and destroyer screen were a similar distance astern. The Fleet was steering to the westward.

Presently reports began to arrive from aircraft of numerous enemy forces—battleships, cruisers and destroyers—almost right ahead and at a distance of about 145 miles from *Warspite*. Due to the inevitable difference of opinion between aircraft on their correct geographical position, and the similarity between an Italian 8-inch cruiser and a battleship when viewed from the air, the exact situation became somewhat confused. It seemed, however, that numerous enemy forces were spread over a large area and consisted of two battleships, 16 - 18 cruisers and 25 - 30 destroyers—as opposed to our three battleships, five cruisers and sixteen destroyers. Soon after 8.0 a.m. the course of our own ships was altered to starboard in order to work round to a position north of the enemy.

Towards noon it was estimated that the distance of the Italian battlefleet had been reduced to 90 miles, and orders were given for *Eagle* to fly off the first air striking force armed with torpedoes. Working round in order to deceive the enemy into believing that they were friendly aircraft approaching from the direction of Italy, the leader led his nine Swordfish in to attack at 1.30 p.m. Diving in sub-flights, they pressed home their attack in the face of heavy anti-aircraft fire, but the enemy was prepared. As torpedoes were dropped, the Italians turned at high speed, and the rapidity with which they altered course enabled them to comb all the tracks. This was disappointing, but for many of the pilots it was their first attack of this kind under action conditions at high speed targets. Although three of our aircraft received minor damage from splinters, there were no casualties, the pilots being agreeably surprised at the ineffectiveness of the enemy's gunfire.

About 2.15 it became clear from air reports that the Italians were effecting a concentration of their dispersed units, and that our own Fleet had now reached a position which effectively cut them off from Taranto. Course was then altered to west. In order to lend support to the cruisers who would be heavily out-numbered, *Warspite* had drawn ahead, leaving *Royal Sovereign* and *Malaya* 10 miles astern to catch up as best they could. *Gloucester*, because of the damage she had sustained on the previous day, was unfit to take part in serious action and had been ordered to fall back and provide close support to *Eagle*.

Surface contact could now be expected at any moment. At 2.50 a long line of white smoke was sighted to the westward by *Orion*, and through it were soon distinguished three destroyers and four cruisers. A few minutes later, the two enemy battleships were sighted and more cruisers; more destroyers. In fact, the horizon had suddenly become alive with an incredible number of ships.

Making enemy reports, Admiral Tovey led his cruisers round to the north-east in order to avoid getting himself engaged with a vastly superior enemy before *Warspite* was able to afford support. At the same time, he maintained his own position in the van.

Almost immediately the enemy opened fire, and shells from enemy battleships and cruisers straddled Admiral Tovey's ships with remarkable accuracy. At a range of 11 miles, *Neptune* and *Liverpool* replied, followed at once by *Orion* and *Sydney*. For a few minutes now—from 3.15 p.m.—our cruisers were in an uncomfortable position. Not only were they under a heavy and accurate fire from large units of the Italian Navy, but enemy destroyers had found the range and the firing from their 4.7's was most galling and irritating. Our own 6-inch armament was fully occupied in dealing with hostile cruisers, and the destroyers were out of range of the 4-inch guns. So they could fire without retaliation—neither could they be kept under sufficient observation to take avoiding action. One shot burst so close to *Neptune* that splinters damaged her aeroplane before it could take off, and the machine had to be jettisoned. Apart from this, however, no other damage was sustained in any of our ships.

Warspite, meanwhile, was coming into action and, at 3.10 p.m., the superstructures of two enemy warships began to rise above her horizon. Sixteen minutes later her main armament opened fire at a range of 26,400 yards, ten salvos being directed at a large 8-inch cruiser on which one hit was possibly obtained. Fire was then shifted to some 6-inch cruisers who provided a better target. They turned away under smoke and, for a few minutes, there was a lull in the action which gave a welcome respite to our own hard pressed cruisers.

Racing ahead of the slow battleship *Royal Sovereign, Malaya* was straining to join *Warspite* who made a short turn to the eastward in order to give her a chance to catch up; and at 3.40 the destroyer screens were released so that they could form up and be in a position to attack when the battle was resumed. Five minutes later, *Eagle* flew off her second striking force, and *Warspite* catapulted her own aircraft. By 3.50 all our advanced forces, including *Warspite* with *Malaya* a short distance astern, were again steering a north-westerly course to close the enemy.

Swiftly now, the enemy once more came into view, and at 3.53 *Warspite* sighted two battleships of the *Cavour* class at a range of 26,000 yards. This was the moment for which everyone had been waiting, and *Warspite* immediately opened fire. The enemy replied. *Warspite* was straddled, and our destroyers racing ahead on her disengaged side narrowly escaped being hit by 'overs' which were not intended for them. The Italians were straddled; and at 4.0 p.m. an unmistakable hit was observed at the base of the leading enemy battleship's foremost funnel.

That was quite enough for them. Ordering their destroyers to make smoke, the Italian Admiral reported that he was "constrained to retire," and the two battleships turned away under cover of a very effective smoke screen. *Warspite* had only fired seventeen salvos. *Malaya* had also fired, but the range was too great, and all her shots had fallen short.

In the meantime, the second air striking force was delivering an attack. Their objective was, of course, the battlefleet but, because of the smoke and cordite fumes, the confusion into which the enemy had been thrown and the general difficulty experienced in being able to differentiate ships from the air, the aircraft dived on a *Bolzano* class cruiser. Too late the mistake was realised, so the attack was continued. Showing

B

the scantiest respect for the enemy's anti-aircraft fire, the Swordfish pressed well home and, from a range of only a few hundred yards, dropped their torpedoes. This time they were more fortunate, scoring one hit and possibly two.

Our destroyers had now concentrated on the disengaged bow of *Warspite*, and both they and Admiral Tovey's ships were being hotly engaged by enemy cruisers trying to cover the retirement of their battlefleet. At 4.5 enemy flotillas were seen starting to move across, but the attack was very half-hearted and their torpedoes, obviously fired at long range, did no damage. Our own destroyers were ordered to counter-attack, while *Warspite*, by her fire, drove the enemy cruisers in to the cover of their own smoke.

From *Warspite* it seemed a most unconventional battle. Leaning over the bridge, the Commander-in-Chief laughingly indicated each enemy ship as it darted out of the smoke with a variation of the remark: "There's another b——! Shoot that b—— up!" *Warspite's* guns, therefore, engaged a variety of targets, but few of these waited for a second salvo. They preferred that bank of smoke.

All fire could now be concentrated on the destroyers who immediately broke up their formation, scattered and fled to the safety of their smoke screen which now hung heavily to the west.

For the next twenty minutes there was some more spasmodic firing as an enemy cruiser or destroyer darted out of the smoke screen and then rapidly disappeared again. By 4.40 p.m. all firing had ceased.

It was quite clear that the Italians had no intention of developing a close range gun action and, from signals intercepted, the idea was to draw our forces into the smoke where it seemed there was a concentration of 'U' boats. Admiral Cunningham, therefore, decided to alter course and work round to the northward and windward of the smoke. This was achieved by 5.0 p.m., but not a single enemy ship was then in sight.

To the west, the coast of Calabria was clearly visible at a

distance of 25 miles, and air attacks were, therefore, to be expected. They came rapidly. Between 5.0 p.m. and 7.0 p.m. six heavy attacks were delivered. *Warspite* and *Eagle* received the most attention, but many bombs fell near the cruisers and destroyers. Practically all the bombs were dropped from a considerable height, but there were no hits and only a few minor casualties from splinters.

The enemy were now making for the Straits of ·Messina as fast as they could go, and their movements were being reported by *Warspite's* aircraft. At first they all seemed to be in considerable confusion from which they could not sort themselves out until 6.0 p.m. There seemed a good deal of confusion also among their airmen because, at 5.5 and again at 6.7, *Warspite's* observer was amused to see Italian bombers attack their own fleet. Several bombs were dropped, but unfortunately there were no hits! That this actually did take place was confirmed by a signal intercepted from the Italian Admiral.

So ended the first encounter with the Italian Fleet in which we suffered neither casualties nor damage. To everyone its indecisive ending was a great disappointment, but it was felt that a moral ascendency had at least been gained over the enemy.

That the Italian Fleet was satisfied by their half-hearted and supine tactics was indicated by the following message from their Commander-in-Chief, in one of their battleships, to the Flag Officer in command of a cruiser squadron:

"For Admiral Paladini," it read. "I thank you with all my heart for the excellent aid you have given me."

To this Admiral Paladini replied: "I thank you on behalf of my squadron and send my admiration for the combat sustained by you."

The Chief of the Italian Armed Forces claimed the battle as a great victory in a special bulletin issued in Rome:

"On the 9th July, three groups of enemy units were sighted by our aircraft and submarines in the eastern Mediterranean, proceeding westwards. Violent attacks were carried out by

our aircraft, several enemy ships being struck, some set on
fire and one sunk. A submarine also attacked and sunk a
destroyer.

"Notwithstanding these attacks, the enemy advanced towards
the central Mediterranean when a strong Italian naval force
advanced to oppose them. An intense action took place until
the enemy broke away and retired. One Italian ship was
damaged, casualties amounting to 24 killed and 79 wounded.
Severe air attacks were then delivered until dusk, several units
being struck with bombs of heavy calibre."

·   ·   ·   ·   ·   ·

The action over, and there being no further possibility of
intercepting the enemy, the Mediterranean Fleet turned to the
operation for which they had originally sailed from Alexandria.
The convoys were sailed from Malta and, in spite of further
heavy bombing—on 12th July alone *Warspite* counted 300
bombs dropped round her during the course of seventeen
attacks delivered between 8.50 a.m. and 11.50 a.m.—the Fleet
provided that cover to ensure their safe and timely arrival
at Alexandria on 14th July.

Chapter 2

THE ACTION OFF CAPE SPADA
19TH JULY, 1940

DURING the early days of the war in the Mediterranean, considerable activity on the part of Italian 'U' boats was anticipated
in the Eastern Basin. The enemy had an important line of
communication to maintain with his outposts in the Dode-
canese, whereas British trade with the Balkans was by no means
negligible. Hence, the southern Ægean was expected to provide
a fruitful area of operations for our own offensive patrols.

On the 17th July, therefore, the Commander-in-Chief
ordered four destroyers to carry out an anti-submarine sweep,
leaving Alexandria at midnight, passing through the Kaso

Strait, west along the north coast of Crete and thence returning
to Alexandria *via* the channel between Crete and Antikithera.
The destroyers detailed were *Hyperion* (Commander H. St. L.
Nicolson), *Ilex*, *Hero* and *Hasty;* and *H.M.A.S. Sydney* (Captain
J. A. Collins) with the destroyer *Havock* was ordered to follow,
afford support to Commander Nicolson and intercept Italian
shipping in the Gulf of Athens.

July 18th was peaceful. Seven o'clock on the morning of the
19th found the destroyers nearing the western extremity of
Crete with *Sydney* some 45 miles to the northward. The weather
was fine and calm, but a slight haze made visibility very
variable. The destroyer force was in line abreast, ships one
and a half miles apart and steering a course of 240 degrees
at 18 knots.

During the normal bustle of dawn action stations there was
no anticipation of any excitement and no ship, submarine or
aircraft disturbed the view. Thus, when a misty sun began
to rise astern, the ships' companies secured from their action
stations. Soon the smell of frying bacon floated up the voice
pipes to the bridge.

Then, suddenly the look-out rivetted attention. "Two
cruisers on the starboard bow, sir!" he shouted, adding somewhat apprehensively, "They're Italians, too!"

Italians they were; steering south-east at a range of ten
miles. As the alarm rattlers rang and battle ensigns were
hoisted, disturbing thoughts passed through several minds.
Whether the cruisers were 6-inch or 8-inch, they hopelessly
outranged the destroyers over whom they also had a large
margin in speed. For them to continue, therefore, on their
present course might invite disaster, and Commander Nicolson's
obvious strategy was to try and draw the enemy towards *Sydney*.
He only had a very approximate idea of *Sydney's* position, and
estimated that he could not possibly make contact with her
before 9.0 o'clock. With a vastly superior enemy in sight
much could happen in an hour and a half, and it was not with
any high degree of confidence that he turned the destroyers

180 degrees to starboard—on to a course of 060 degrees—and ordered sub-divisions to concentrate.

To the enemy, the four destroyers should have appeared an

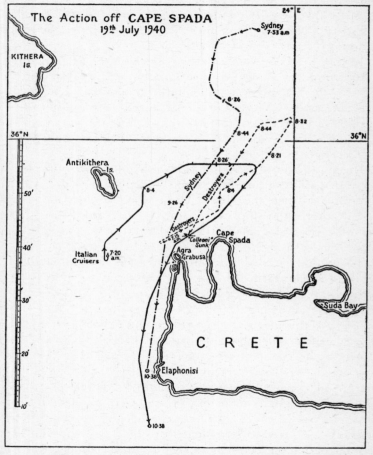

The Action off **CAPE SPADA**
19ᵗʰ July 1940

easy target, and had the Italians turned straight towards them to decrease the range as rapidly as possible, our ships might have suffered severely. On sighting, however, the two nearest destroyers—*Hyperion* and *Ilex*—opened fire. Although their salvos fell a long way short, they appeared to disconcert the enemy who first turned south and then right round to starboard to a course due north. Thus, the range could be opened.

As soon as they turned to their new course the enemy opened fire, but their shooting was slow and fortunately erratic. This was doubtless due to the fact that they were firing into the sun which increased the difficulty of spotting. The salvos from one cruiser threw up green splashes; those from the other were red, and some of them fell near enough to be unpleasant. The Italians had now settled down to a northerly course, thereby allowing Commander Nicolson, for some inexplicable reason, to open the range.

Surprised at increasing his distance to an unexpected extent, Commander Nicolson turned to the north at 7.47 in an endeavour to try and ascertain the class to which the enemy belonged, but they—apparently feeling more bold—made a sudden turn towards him which forced the destroyers back on to their original course of 060 degrees. At the same time, the enemy's fire was persistent, and Commander Nicolson anxiously scanned the horizon for a sight of *Sydney* whom he had kept fully informed about the movements of the Italian cruisers. But he still felt that 9.0 o'clock was the earliest time at which she could appear on the scene.

Meanwhile, all that the destroyers could do was to watch the enemy's fall of shot—a disturbing pastime, since the Italians frequently had the range, though they were out for line.

About 7.45 a dark shape loomed out of the misty horizon to the north. As the destroyers drew nearer it was identified as a Greek freighter tumbling lazily in the swell. Alarmed at this rude disturbance to their placid contemplation, and fearful lest one of those shells bursting round the fast on-coming destroyers should hit their own ship, the entire crew took to their boats. Then, as the battle passed into the haze, they pulled back to their peaceful ship and proceeded on their way.

Shortly before 8.0 o'clock, finding that his ships were still avoiding damage, and anxious to draw the enemy as far north as possible, Commander Nicolson again altered course to north to see how the Italians would react. Amazingly enough they conformed by altering in a similar manner, instead of seizing the opportunity to close the range. A little later, however, they came round to the east and headed straight for the destroyers. With the range now rapidly decreasing, the firing of the enemy grew more accurate. But help was at hand.

Suddenly, at 8.26, gun flashes were observed on the port beam of the destroyers, and it was first thought that enemy reinforcements were arriving. Then, out of the haze behind the flashes appeared two ships—*Sydney* and *Havock*. The relief to Commander Nicolson—indeed to all the destroyers—was immense, and they described this timely arrival of the supporting force as a most welcome sight.

As soon as *Sydney* had received the first enemy report, Captain Collins had at once increased speed and, led by the accurate information continually being passed by Commander Nicolson, proceeded to make contact. In order that the enemy should not suspect the presence of other warships in the neighbourhood, Captain Collins had maintained wireless silence and sacrificed the advantage he might have gained by passing his position to the destroyers. Thus, he was able to achieve surprise. At 7.45 the watch had been relieved a quarter of an hour early, and hands piped to clean into battle dress. Action stations had been sounded off at 8.15 and, only five minutes later, smoke had been observed on the horizon. By 8.26 the enemy had been identified, and the first salvo fired three minutes afterwards.

The enemy were now steering east. At a distance of about nine miles on their port bow were the destroyers, and *Sydney* had opened fire from the enemy's port beam at a range of 22,000 yards. As soon as she was within visual signalling touch of *Hyperion*, *Sydney* ordered the destroyers to turn and attack with torpedoes, but Commander Nicolson had anticipated this order and had already turned his force towards the enemy.

From a painting by Lt.-Cdr. Roland Langmaid, R.N.

H.M.S. DAINTY DESTROYS A SUBMARINE

By kind permission of the Admiralty

By kind permission of the Admiralty

BARTOLOMEO COLLEONI—STOPPED AND ON FIRE

About this time (8.40), however, the two Italian cruisers turned away to the southward, thus making a torpedo attack impracticable. Although there were two of them, each of gun power equal to *Sydney*, it was obvious from the way they made smoke and zig-zagged that they had decided to adopt evasive tactics. Perhaps they had mistaken *Havock*, who appeared with *Sydney*, for a second cruiser or, what was more likely to Captain Collins at the time, there was a strong Italian naval force in the neighbourhood towards which they wanted to lead our own ships.

The battle now developed into a chase, though there was no justification for such precipitate retreat. The enemy could have sunk *Sydney* and then dealt comfortably with the destroyers. *Havock* had joined *Hyperion*, and all ships were approximately in line abreast, pursuing at high speed an enemy fleeing to the south and subsequently hauling round to the south-west. Fire was concentrated first on the leading cruiser but, just when that was beginning to take effect, the target was obscured by smoke, and fire was shifted to the rear cruiser at a range of 18,000 yards. Meanwhile, the enemy's gunnery was fairly accurate: though mostly over, there were several straddles, but *Sydney* escaped being hit.

Shortly after 9.0 o'clock, the rear cruiser—now identified as *Bartolomeo Colleoni*—showed signs of being in difficulties. She had been hit in the boiler room; the range closed rapidly as her speed was reduced until finally she lay stopped within five miles of Cape Spada. During this time the enemy's fire had become more accurate and, at 9.21, *Sydney* was hit in the foremost funnel which caused only one minor casualty and little damage.

On seeing the danger to her consort, the leading cruiser had turned round—but only for a moment. Without apparently easing her wheel, she made a complete circle and, by 9.26, was rounding Agra Grabusa, off the north-western extremity of Crete, and steaming at high speed to the south. Ordering Commander Nicolson to finish off *Bartolomeo Colleoni*, *Sydney* continued to chase.

The stricken cruiser was a pathetic sight as *Hyperion* and *Ilex* approached. Here and there along her whole length, shell holes in the plating revealed the flames of fires raging inside her; at the foot of the bridge superstructure there roared a particularly large fire which compelled those on the bridge to leap for safety. On her foc's'le was the riddled wreck of her reconnaissance seaplane lying on a shattered catapult. It was learnt later that this machine should have taken off at dawn but, due to a defect in the catapult, had been unable to do so. Had it actually been able to make a reconnaissance at that time, the Italians might have been presented with a complete picture of all British forces in the vicinity, and the story might then have been different.

The Italian ensign still flew from the peak, and astern of her splashed or floated the vast majority of the ship's company. Her fore turrets appeared undamaged and were trained on the starboard quarter. As the destroyers approached it was impossible not to wonder whether some desperate officer or man was not waiting inside those ominous turrets to fire at point blank range. He could not have missed.

Although men on deck were waving sheets and towels in token of surrender, there was no alternative but to proceed with the cruiser's destruction because the ensign still flew. Listing on the turn, the sub-division fired torpedoes. A few moments later there was a thundering eruption under the foc's'le as a torpedo from *Ilex* struck, the hull of the ship before the foremost turret seeming to crumble away into the water. Some minutes later, *Hyperion's* torpedoes which had missed, burst on the rocks of the island of Agra Grabusa.

Bartolomeo Colleoni still floated. So Commander Nicolson, closing to point blank range, launched another torpedo. It hit amidships; a pillar of smoke and water rose over her and, to the crying of her company in the sea around and astern, she rolled slowly over on her starboard side and slid from view. The last that was seen of her was two of the giant propellors which had given such vaunted speed.

The sea was now littered with naked bodies. They had not even lowered any boats and this made the task of rescue more difficult. Picking up those in his immediate vicinity, Commander Nicolson wasted little time and proceeded with *Ilex* to rejoin *Sydney*. He left *Havock* who had joined *Hyperion* to rescue as many of the remainder as she could. Altogether 545 survivors were rescued, 51 of whom were seriously wounded, including the Captain. They were nearly all stark naked which made it difficult to differentiate between officers and men.

Meanwhile, the chase of the other cruiser was not going too well. West of Crete the typical Mediterranean haze helped to obscure the target who was herself making smoke, and this rendered the spotting of fall of shot most difficult. Although several hits had been obtained, none seemed to have burst in a vital part, and the enemy was steadily drawing away. Added to this, *Sydney* was now running short of ammunition and, by 10.20, there were only four rounds per gun of armour piercing shell left in 'A' turret and one round left in 'B' turret; so the situation seemed hopeless. The destroyers in company were unable to catch up and, at 10.38, the chase was finally abandoned. Course was then shaped for Alexandria. Altogether, *Sydney* had fired 956 rounds.

About noon a signal was received from *Havock* to say that a chaplain survivor reported that the Italians were expecting to meet large supporting forces that forenoon. This news, which had been suspected, was not welcomed by *Sydney* now that her ammunition was exhausted, but luckily for her no further encounter took place. The Commander-in-Chief at Alexandria had also foreseen this contingency, and heavy units of the Mediterranean Fleet were already at sea, steering for the western extremity of Crete. But nothing was ever sighted. If they had been at sea, the loss of *Bartolomeo Colleoni* had probably indicated to the Italians the advantage of returning to harbour.

The rescue operations being carried out by *Havock* were rudely interrupted at 12.37 when six Savoia bombers were seen approaching from the south. There was only one thing to do—leave the remainder in the water and proceed at full speed. With 250 survivors on board, some of whom were badly wounded, *Havock* opened fire on the bombers as the ship was straddled by several sticks, throwing up great columns of water which drenched everyone in exposed positions.

At 2.55 p.m., when south of Crete and steering towards a rendezvous with *Sydney*, nine more aircraft attacked. They bombed in threes, and large splinters from one near miss penetrated the ship's side below the water line and flooded No. 2 boiler room. Happily, there were only two minor casualties, but the ship lost her way. After five minutes, the situation was got under control, and *Havock* was able to proceed at 24 knots.

As soon as *Sydney* heard of *Havock's* misfortune, she detached *Hasty* and *Hero* to proceed independently to Alexandria and, with *Hyperion* and *Ilex* turned to make contact with the damaged destroyer. By 4.30 they were all in company, and one more bombing raid was experienced shortly before sunset. It proved abortive.

Thus ended a spirited and successful action described by the Commander-in-Chief as 'a very gallant affair.' Recognition was immediate, and a signal from the First Lord two days later announced that His Majesty had awarded Captain Collins with a C.B., and Commander Nicolson a bar to his D.S.O.

Chapter 3

STORIES OF OUR SUBMARINES
ACTIVITIES IN THE MEDITERRANEAN DURING
1940

FROM the commencement of hostilities with Italy—and, in fact, even prior to the actual declaration of war—our submarines maintained unceasing patrols in the Mediterranean. In the initial stages, our very meagre force of submarines—gathered from China, the East Indies and Malta—consisted of only

twelve boats and those, with the exception of the more modern
minelayers *Rorqual* and *Grampus*, were old, varying in age from
seven to ten years and not best suited for Mediterranean conditions. This small force was originally split into two equal
portions; those at Alexandria working directly under the
British Commander-in-Chief through Captain 'S' in the depot
ship, *Medway;* while the six at Malta were under the operational control of the French through Admiral Ven—the
Admiral in charge of submarines at Bizerta. Actually only
four were available at Malta as two—*Olympus* and *Otus*—were
taken in hand for refit in May and did not complete until
November. Thus, apart from the French forces, we had ten
submarines available when Italy declared war: the Italians
had 109.

With such a force it was manifestly impossible to do even a
fourth part of what was desired, and the problem of relieving
and maintaining a patrol in a particular area seemed almost
insoluble. On the evening before war was declared, the four
submarines available at Malta, *Odin*, *Orpheus*, and the minelayers *Rorqual* and *Grampus*, sailed for operations off the Sicilian
and Calabrian coasts, in the Gulf of Taranto and in the lower
Adriatic. *Rorqual* and *Grampus* successfully laid their mines in
the Adriatic and off Sicily, but the latter failed to return from
patrol. *Odin*, off Taranto, also encountered disaster, nothing
more being heard of her after leaving Malta; and *Orpheus*,
who was diverted to Benghazi, also failed to return to base.
This was a sad beginning. *Rorqual* duly arrived at Alexandria
after a most successful patrol, the first of many she was to
carry out.

From Alexandria, patrols set out round Crete, along the
African coast and up to the entrance to the Dardanelles.
Parthian (Lieut.-Commander M. Rimmington) started the ball
rolling at Tobruk. Tired of waiting for ships which did not
materialise, he accepted the risk of minefields and, keeping
within a few hundred yards of the shore, approached the
entrance from the eastward. The old cruiser, *San Giorgio*, who

was lying at moorings, seemed the most tempting target and, taking deliberate aim, he fired two torpedoes at 6000 yards. Before they were due to arrive at their mark, *Parthian* rose to periscope depth to observe. Two great columns of water were seen to rise as high as the *San Giorgio's* masts, but unfortunately they had exploded on the nets which Lieut.-Commdr. Rimmington had not seen. It was bad luck; but it must have caused what the army terms, 'alarm and despondency,' since it was over four hours before any retaliation matured. And that consisted only of a single aircraft and a destroyer who steamed hopefully up and down dropping twenty depth charges in a half-hearted manner. One or two were close, but none near enough to do any damage, and it was clear that the destroyer had not the remotest idea of the position of *Parthian*.

On the next afternoon, while in the same patrol area, *Parthian* was at periscope depth. Suddenly, the officer of the watch sighted a long low object on the starboard quarter. Calling the Captain, they quickly appreciated that this was an Italian submarine on the surface about 6000 yards away. She was steering in their direction, and they were in an ideal position to attack. In the swell and confused sea which was running, it was impossible to get an accurate range, but it was obvious that she would pass close.

Swinging *Parthian* round to a suitable course, Lieut.-Commdr. Rimmington fired a salvo of four torpedoes at a range of only 400 yards. Sixteen seconds after firing, the first torpedo hit and exploded: then, at regular three-second intervals, *Parthian* shuddered to the explosion of each of the remainder as they all found their target.

As the fourth torpedo exploded, the periscope was raised. An enormous column of water mixed with steam had risen to at least 150 feet into the air and, spreading from the top, were pieces of scattered debris, some of which were a considerable size. At the base of the column, and sticking up out of the water at an angle of about 70 degrees, was thirty or forty feet of the bow of the 'U' boat, showing the under-water curve and net-cutter. Then suddenly it disappeared beneath the waves.

Parthian then lost trim and went down to 70 feet, but a few minutes later regained periscope depth and began to examine the large area of dead-white effervescent water, covered with oil stains, which was now about 200 yards in diameter. In the hope of picking up survivors, a couple of strong swimmers were stationed in the conning tower, and *Parthian* was just about to surface when the whole boat was shaken by a sudden and heavy explosion, which felt to those in her like a blow on the back of their necks.

The thought of an air escort delivering a counter-attack was instinctive, and Rimmington immediately went deep, turning as he did so on to a suitable retiring course. Subsequent investigation, however, established that the explosion had undoubtedly come from below—in fact, from the wreck itself. As it was now more than likely that the patrols from Tobruk would have heard the five explosions, it was thought advisable for *Parthian* to move from this position.

Four days later, *Parthian* saw what she thought was another opportunity to repeat this most successful performance. They were closer inshore towards the end of the forenoon, when a long dark object was sighted through the periscope. To the Commanding Officer, it was undoubtedly another submarine. The attack started: first retiring and then advancing until an ideal position was reached and the boat steadied on the firing course. Then suddenly, Rimmington left the periscope in disgust. He had been carrying out an attack on a building situated on a low sand spit near Ras Assaz!

So ended an eventful seventeen-day patrol.

During the closing months of 1940, other submarines had varying degrees of success in the eastern half of the Mediterranean. On 3rd November, *Tetrarch* torpedoed two large supply ships escorted by destroyers west of Benghazi; *Pandora* sunk a 5000-ton merchant vessel off Ras Aamer on 28th September, and *Rorqual* carried out a successful attack on two transports off Ras el Hilal on 21st August; but these successes were only achieved after weeks of laborious and monotonous patrol.

Among other submarines who had exciting and sometimes alarming experiences, *Regent* may be quoted. Towards the end of September 1940, *Regent* (Lieut.-Commdr. H. C. Browne) sailed for patrol in the Ionian Sea and Adriatic. On the 30th she had a brief encounter with two Italian battleships which were heavily screened but, through a combination of circumstances, was unable to bring off a successful attack. After a very hectic twenty minutes, she broke surface accidently and trouble followed almost immediately.

She had, of course, been sighted, and a few minutes later a heavy explosion was heard and felt. It was too near to be pleasant, and the presence of destroyers overhead could be clearly detected. More depth charges were dropped—this time further away—and it became clear that the enemy had little idea of *Regent's* position. But the submarine was still in difficulties. She refused to settle down on an even trim, the stern became heavier and heavier in spite of continual pumping, and the angle on the boat was as much as 15 degrees.

The engine room became full of fumes, and oil overflowed into compartments where it had no business. The high level of oil and water in the bilge now made it unsafe to try and take the angle off the boat, and there was no means of pumping it out. A human bucket chain was then formed and, slowly but surely, 600 gallons of oil were moved and the situation got under control. At length, four hours after the attack, *Regent* could be brought to periscope depth. There was nothing in sight.

By nightfall, when it was safe for *Regent* to surface, a very high air pressure had been built up inside the submarine which it was intended to ease by opening up the conning tower hatch as slowly as possible. It was a dangerous process, and Lieut.-Commdr. Browne, therefore, decided to do it himself. But, once loosened, it was quite impossible to hold the second clip. A tremendous rush of air from the interior of the submarine passed up into the conning tower, burst the hatch open and carried Lieut.-Commdr. Browne partly through it. Fortunately he was able to hold on, but might well have been blown overboard.

Five days later, *Regent* had another exciting experience. It was very early in the morning when the boat was still operating on the surface, and the night was exceptionally dark. Sighting a single white light, Browne turned to investigate and, twenty minutes later, distinguished the masts of a small sailing vessel fine on the starboard bow. It appeared as if it had already crossed from port to starboard and, to give a wider berth, the submarine began to haul round further to port. Too late it was realised that the bow had been mistaken for the stern and, a moment later, a medium sized caique under auxiliary motor crashed into *Regent*, starboard side.

Terrified by what had happened, the entire crew of the caique disappeared below deck leaving the wheel unattended. Meanwhile, the caique's bowsprit slid up on top of *Regent's* jumping wire and tore away the loop aerial. The anchor, hanging over the bow, caught in the main aerial and broke the deck insulator; and the caique itself, swinging round, damaged the starboard hydroplane. By going astern, *Regent* eventually got clear. As the caique would now be in a position to report the submarine, every effort was made to locate and sink her but, in the darkness, she managed to escape.

Luck, however, was soon to turn, and *Regent* was at length rewarded. About 4.30 in the afternoon of 9th October when still operating in the southern Adriatic, two columns of smoke were sighted to the eastward. It proved to be a convoy consisting of two supply ships of about 6000 tons each, escorted by one armed patrol vessel, destroyers and smaller craft.

Pressing in to a favourable position to attack, *Regent* fired a torpedo at the leading ship from a range of 3000 yards. It hit amidships, and they had the satisfaction of seeing a column of smoke and wreckage thrown high into the air as the bow and stern of the ship rose as if her back had been broken.

When swinging back to fire at the second ship, however, the

C

patrol vessel was observed moving straight for *Regent* at full speed. There was no time to lose. Course was altered to 180 degrees and the submarine went deep. This time she held her trim, all machinery could be stopped and she was able to adopt the most effective tactics for evasion—remain still and silent.

A depth charge was dropped at once, and it was heard to explode unpleasantly close, shaking the boat and doing minor damage. Then, for the next hour, a consistent and disturbingly accurate hunt was carried out. Attacking vessels could be heard astern and on either bow. Then the one on the port bow would move in to let go a depth charge. Each time it seemed to move in a little closer than the last, and each time the submarine was shaken a little more violently by the explosion. Another light would go out—another rivet, perhaps, show signs of weakness—and those in the submarine began to feel distinctly uncomfortable.

Only fifteen minutes after the attack had started, *Regent* began to lose trim and sink fast with an angle of 20 degrees down by the stern. It was, therefore, essential to start a motor which steadied the boat and brought her under control at 380 feet. Half an hour later, the enemy ships seemed to lose contact, but they continued to hunt vaguely until 7.0 p.m. On surfacing at 8.40 p.m. no ships were found to be in sight.

But the day's adventures were not ended. It was a calm night with a brilliant moon nearing the first quarter, and on the side away from the moon a blue signalling lamp was observed flashing, 'SS'. *Regent* had undoubtedly been sighted by a patrol vessel as her silhouette crossed the path of the moon, so she was again forced to dive until hydrophone effects were no longer heard three hours later.

The moon set about 2.0 a.m., and it was hoped that the rest of the night would be peaceful. But at 3.40 a vessel was sighted on the starboard bow at a range of about 1500 yards. It was a small destroyer steaming directly towards the submarine. Slamming the conning tower hatch, *Regent* submerged as rapidly as possible. Above them could be heard the enemy destroyer dashing about at high speed: then six explosions in rapid succession, severely shaking *Regent* as she was sinking from 18 to 100 feet. Some of these were from depth charges; others were possibly gunfire. The destroyer was now joined by another and, for the next two hours, they both steamed madly about at high speed letting go depth charges indiscriminately. But no more fell close, although the enemy frequently passed almost overhead.

Next morning *Regent*, having probably experienced up to date more depth charge attacks than any other submarine in the Mediterranean, could almost treat with contempt another hunt for her which was carried out by two large M.A.S. boats. They detected the presence of the submarine, but seemed unable to pin her down nearer than 2000 yards. The depth charges dropped were all at a distance and had no effect.

At last, on 18th October, the patrol was ended, and *Regent* entered the Grand Harbour at Malta after twenty-three days at sea, many of which had been packed with excitement.

Meanwhile, since the commencement of hostilities, sub-marine activity in the western basin of the Mediterranean had been as intense as numbers allowed, and the first war patrol of *Triton* (Lieut. G. C. I. St. B. Watkins), carried out between 21st September and 12th October, was full of interest. Routed south of the Balearics from Gibraltar, she arrived in her patrol area in the Gulf of Genoa a.m. on 27th September. She first carried out a close inspection of Oneglia harbour, observing a medium sized tanker and two small ships berthed alongside quays.

For the next three or four days, further inspections of the coast were carried out, but there seemed to be little activity at sea. About 10.0 a.m. on 4th October, however, a large merchant vessel was sighted, and *Triton* was in a favourable position to attack. From a range of 1300 yards, Lieut. Watkins fired four torpedoes and had the gratification of seeing three of them hit. A column of brown smoke and water was thrown up into the air to a height of 200 feet, and the ship sank immediately.

There was a moderate sea running which made an accurate all-round observation difficult. Thus, when he raised his periscope again, about two minutes after the ship had sunk, Watkins received an unpleasant surprise. Barely 40 yards away was an M.A.S. hunting craft of the latest type, which had probably formed the escort for the merchant vessel. It was looking for him, but fortunately for *Triton* the entire crew were staring in the opposite direction. The speed at which the submarine went deep was phenomenal!

Two days later, just before dusk, *Triton* approached the ports of Vado and Savona, off which she observed a merchant vessel of about 3000 tons lying at anchor. She was unprotected, and a torpedo fired from 4000 yards hit her amidships. In a great cloud of white smoke, she blew up and sank.

The submarine immediately surfaced in order to follow this success with a bombardment of military objective ashore. First, the gas works at Vado were engaged, where several hits were observed; then, shifting target to a large factory at Savona, a further eleven rounds of high explosive were fired into it. Five minutes later, shore batteries opened fire on *Triton* and, though inaccurate, they were certainly persistent. The submarine was forced to dive and made off to the south-east pursued by various hunting craft. The hunt continued for some time and, although the depth charges which were dropped exploded at a distance and did no damage, *Triton* was compelled to remain submerged until 3.0 a.m., when she surfaced to re-charge her batteries. The rest of her patrol was without further incident, and she successfully completed the passage of the Sicilian Channel and arrived at Malta.

Not all patrols in 1940 were so full of incident as those described, and in many cases submarines went for their full three weeks without sighting the somewhat elusive enemy.

TARANTO — NOVEMBER 11TH, 1940

To cripple the enemy battle fleet has always been the principle object of the Naval Air Service. With our somewhat evasive opponent in the Mediterranean this was difficult to achieve, and after a few months of war it seemed quite likely that the fleet action for which everyone hoped would never materialise. On the other hand, the mere presence of powerful Italian surface forces—even if they remained inactive—necessarily contained many of our own battleships which were urgently required in other theatres of war. Could the Naval Air Arm by itself achieve a smashing blow at Italian numerical superiority which would take the place of a fleet action? Many were convinced that it could and, in fact, the idea had long been considered.

Before *H.M.S. Illustrious* (Captain D. W. Boyd), the new aircraft carrier destined for the Mediterranean, left a northern base on 22nd August, 1940 (wearing the flag of Rear Admiral A. L. St. G. Lyster as R.A.A.), a plan had already been formulated to attack the Italian fleet in Taranto harbour with torpedo carrying aircraft, and it was pursued with the utmost enthusiasm. Experience obtained from successful air attacks at Benghazi and Leros had disclosed the vulnerable points in Italian air defence, and air photographs of Taranto had already revealed the usual berths occupied by Italian battleships. But there was a mass of detail to be studied. The exact positions of the ships to be attacked and the direction in which they were lying had to be known by every pilot and observer taking part, as also the location of balloons, searchlights and A.A. defences. The most recent photographs taken from the air were therefore essential.

Suitable diversion from the chief objective—the torpedoing of the battleships in the outer harbour (Mar Grande)—had to be considered, and this was planned to take the form of bombing ships and other targets in the inner harbour (Mar Piccolo) just before the main attack. Then there were the

methods of approach for each aircraft to be decided. Moonlight
was essential, aircraft having the moon behind them as they
came in from the south-west before splitting up to make their
different attacks. Surprise was vital, and previous movements
of the fleet had to give no indication of what was intended.

To ensure some of these factors, the co-operation of the
R.A.F. at Malta was important. They alone could obtain the
necessary photographs, provide reconnaissance and perhaps
assist with a diversion. Finally, there was the question of
weather. If there was fog, thick cloud or rain, no organisation,
however perfect, could make the operation a success.

Fleet committments and the necessity for subordinating
offensive action to the primary task of ensuring the safe passage
of convoys until reinforcements had arrived, prevented an
opportunity for an attack on Taranto from taking place for
some weeks. This was just as well. It gave time for the pilots
concerned to become more proficient in night flying, and also
enabled the R.A.F. to perfect their reconnaissance of the enemy
base, their later photographs revealing the existence of balloons
and anti-torpedo nets.

Early in November the chance occurred. Naval reinforcements were being passed through the Mediterranean from
Gibraltar, and the fleet left Alexandria on November 6th to
cover both the new arrivals and the movement of convoys to
and from Malta, the Piræus and Suda. One night on the return
passage was to be set aside for the attack on Taranto.

It had been the original intention for both aircraft carriers,
Illustrious and *Eagle*, to take part in this enterprise, but *Eagle*
had suffered from so many near misses by bombs that her
petrol tanks were defective and she had to be left behind. She
was, however, represented, five of her Swordfish and eight
crews being embarked in *Illustrious* which brought the number
of those available to take part in the raid up to twenty-four.

On passage westward searches were carried out deep into
the Ionian Sea, and so successful were the fighters flown off
Illustrious that no enemy aircraft came within 29 miles of the

fleet. On the 8th November three hostile aircraft were shot down by the air patrols, and a further nine were forced to jettison their bombs long before they came within sight. Similar successes were recorded on the two following days, but two of our own Swordfish were unfortunately compelled to force-land in the sea. This was not due to enemy action but was caused by contaminated petrol. Both crews were picked up by destroyers and taken to Malta; then, subsequently returned by air to *Illustrious*.

The reinforcements from Gibraltar joined the fleet on the 10th when south of Malta. An easterly course was then set, and the attack on Taranto was arranged for the following night.

The usual patrols were flown off at dawn on 11th November, but there was another accident. A third aircraft force-landed in the sea, thus reducing the available striking force to twenty-one. The crew were picked up by the cruiser *Gloucester*. Both the pilot and observer were detailed to take part in the Taranto raid, and they were so keen to return to *Illustrious* that they prevailed upon the Captain of *Gloucester* to fly them back in the cruiser's Walrus amphibian plane. They had been injured in the crash earlier in the day and the pilot's face was swathed in plaster, but their enthusiasm to take part forced the Captain of *Illustrious* to yield to their pleading.

On the previous evening the R.A.F. had taken final photographs of Taranto and it was essential for these to be studied. A machine from *Illustrious* was accordingly flown to Malta and returned later in the day with copies of these precious photographs. The final positions of the enemy battleships and defences were plotted and preparations were complete. One question only remained unsolved. Would the weather remain suitable? As the afternoon wore on, doubts on this point were set at rest and, at 6.0 p.m. *Illustrious*, with an escort of four cruisers and four destroyers, was detached from the main fleet.

Two hours later the flight deck of the carrier became a scene of activity, as one aircraft after another emerged from the lift shaft and was wheeled into position for taking off. The machines available were to fly in two separate groups and, by 8.35 p.m., the first twelve were ranged and ready to start. *Illustrious* turned into the wind, the signal was given to commence and the gently throbbing engine of the leader—Lieut.-Commander Williamson—increased to a roar as his machine started forward and rose into the night. Swiftly the others followed, and within a space of a few minutes they were all in the air. *Illustrious* turned to the eastward and began to prepare the second force.

It took a few minutes for the aircraft to form up, but shortly before nine o'clock they took their departure and shaped course for Taranto, 170 miles distant. A quarter of an hour later they encountered a heavy bank of cumulus cloud in which four aircraft unfortunately got separated from their leader, thus preventing them from arriving simultaneously over the target. Continuing with eight machines—five torpedo bombers, two flare droppers and one bomber to distract attention to the inner harbour—the Squadron Commander approached Taranto.

Gradually the coast line of Southern Italy loomed into view; objects were identified and each observer fixed his position. The time had now come to release the flare droppers and, a few minutes before eleven o'clock, the first indication of the attack was given by a series of flares dropped at half-mile intervals along the eastern edge of the harbour. At the same moment the five torpedo carrying aircraft split into sub-flights. With a machine on either quarter, Lieut.-Commander Williamson led at a height of 4000 feet over the island of San Pietro to the centre of the Mar Grande. At this point the two following aircraft broke away and started their dive, while intense fire from the defences burst all round them. That was the last either of these aircraft saw of their leader—he did not return.

Following each other in their mad dive between the bursting shells and in the face of continuous machine-gun fire, the two aircraft, piloted by Sub-Lieutenants Sparke and Macaulay, flattened out at only 30 feet above the water. Sweeping over the breakwater, they sighted the floating dock to starboard and then tried to identify their target—the southernmost of the two

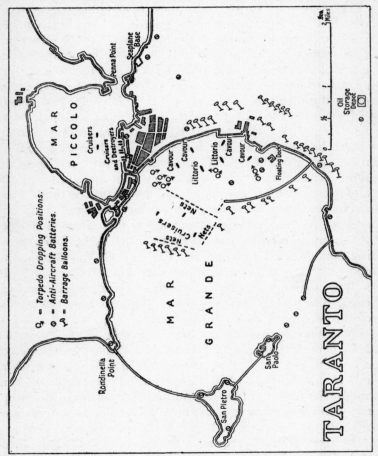

Littorio class battleships. In the excitement of the moment they failed to distinguish this vessel among the shadows now looming all round them. Instead, they saw a *Cavour* battleship right

ahead. Deciding instantly to make that their target, Sparke dropped his torpedo at 700 yards followed by Macaulay who pressed in 100 yards nearer.

Executing quick turns to port, they twisted their way between the protecting barrage balloons, gained height and managed to escape damage from the terrific volume of fire which seemed to be coming from every direction. It was, of course, quite impossible to observe accurately the results of their attack but, one minute after dropping, Sparke's observer saw a large explosion in the direction of the *Cavour* at which they had aimed.

Meanwhile, the two machines in the other sub-flight were slightly separated. Lieutenant Kemp in one, passing over the western breakwater at 4000 feet, began his dive for a position in the centre of the Mar Grande. From batteries along the shore, from cruisers and small merchant vessels, a terrific pandemonium of fire broke out, and it was noticed that several merchant vessels were struck by projectiles fired from the cruisers. As Kemp flattened out a few feet above the water the gunfire seemed to pass overhead and he was able to steer direct for the northern *Littorio*. The torpedo was dropped at 1000 yards, the aim appeared accurate and the observer could see it was running correctly. Then, turning rapidly to starboard, Kemp made his 'get-away', unscathed by the terrific volume of fire to which he was again subjected.

Lieutenant Maund in the other machine of the sub-flight passed over the land north of Rondinella Point. Here he dived, encountering fierce fire from the shore batteries and cruisers until he flattened out when the fire passed overhead. Steering straight for the southerly *Littorio* he made an accurate 'drop' and, turning to starboard, doubled back among the merchant ships off the commercial basin, getting away unharmed.

The sixth aircraft carrying a torpedo and piloted by Lieutenant Swayne had become detached from the leader soon after leaving *Illustrious*, and had actually arrived off the harbour entrance a quarter of an hour before the others. Here Swayne waited until he saw the first flare when he came in at 1000 feet, gradually losing height until a suitable position for approaching the most northern *Littorio* was reached. Picking up his target, Swayne pressed in until he was only 400 yards from the battle-ship. At this point he released his torpedo but, instead of turning, passed right over the *Littorio* from which a column of smoke was suddenly seen to rise directly abaft the funnels. The aircraft then gained height, passed over the cruisers and through their intense barrage of fire, over San Pietro island and so to seaward.

The two machines detailed for flare dropping were piloted by Lieutenants Kiggell and Lamb, but so effective were those released by Kiggell that none were dropped by the other aircraft. With the flares providing satisfactory illumination, both pilots then looked around for their allotted bombing target which was an oil storage depot. Standing out with reasonable clearness Kiggell suddenly saw the tanks and, followed by Lamb, dived down towards them. Releasing their bombs from a height of a few hundred feet, they turned rapidly and crossed the coast. Of the success of this attack neither aircraft was able to observe any positive result.

The four remaining aircraft which had composed the first striking force had as their objective the bombing of ships in the Mar Piccolo, or inner harbour. Each pilot selected his own target. At a height of 8500 feet Captain Patch, Royal Marines, swept over San Pietro island in the face of intense fire, crossed the Mar Grande and dived down to 1500 feet from which height he let go his bombs across two cruisers. From pom-pom fire at numerous points he escaped damage, and avoided further opposition by diving behind neighbouring hills before crossing the coast.

Sub-Lieutenant Sarra followed a similar course to Patch, but found great difficulty in identifying a suitable target. Cruising along the southern shore of Mar Piccolo and paying scant attention to the shells bursting all round him, he suddenly sighted the sea-plane base. Immediately putting the nose of his machine down to a steep angle, he swooped to 500 feet scoring hits with bombs on the slipways and one hangar from which a large explosion was observed. Pom-pom and other anti-aircraft fire was now more intense than ever, but Sarra managed to get away unharmed.

Sub-Lieutenant Forde and Lieutenant Murray had both become separated from the leader in cloud and arrived independently, the former reaching the harbour a few moments after the first flare had been dropped. Once over Mar Piccolo, Forde saw two cruisers which he immediately selected as his target. The first bomb was observed to fall just short, but no immediate result was seen from the remainder. Possibly they hit, but Forde was uncertain whether they had actually been released. In spite of the volume of gunfire which rocked his machine as he gained height and circled for a second dive, he gallantly repeated his attack, but his bombs had already fallen. Then, carrying on to the north-west, he gradually turned and made out to sea.

Lieutenant Murray arrived while the attack was in progress, flew along the southern shore of Mar Piccolo and dropped his bombs from 3000 feet in a line across a number of cruisers and destroyers lying fairly close together. He then made a sharp turn to port and retired along the same route on which he had arrived. . . . .

Three-quarters of an hour after the first striking force had taken off, eight of the remaining aircraft were ranged on the flight deck of *Illustrious*. The ninth had been unfortunate, accidently sustaining damage to the wing fabric. The pilot of this machine—Lieutenant Clifford—happened to be the one who had been unlucky earlier in the day, having force-landed in the sea, subsequently returning in *Gloucester's* Walrus. Having overcome that difficulty, he was determined not to allow this second misfortune to stop him. He sent his observer, Lieutenant Going, to the Captain at once. The machine, Going insisted, could be repaired within ten minutes and he was quite confident that he could catch up with the remainder and find Taranto on his own. Captain Boyd was dubious, but he was so

impressed at the enthusiasm shown by this young observer and
his pilot that he gave his permission. Working as they had
never worked before, the crew of the aircraft repaired the
damage, but it took longer than ten minutes. It was, in fact,
twenty minutes after the others had started before Clifford was
able to take off.

He had scarcely gone when suddenly a red vereys light
appeared in the sky a short distance to the northward.
Although this was the usual signal for an aircraft in distress
none of our own were expected, and it was immediately concluded that hostile planes were about to attack *Illustrious*. The
carrier and escort at once opened fire. A moment afterwards
came the shout of, 'friendly,' as the special secret recognition
signal of our own aircraft was displayed in the sky. One of the
machines which had been flown off with the second striking
force had encountered difficulties, the external overload petrol
tank having fallen off. It was quite impossible for her to
continue, and the pilot had reluctantly been forced to return.
As a measure of his disgust, the pilot cruised around out of
gun range for another fifteen minutes before he landed on.

The narrative of the second attack on Taranto closely
followed that of the first, Lieutenant-Commander Hale, the
Squadron Commander, leading all five torpedo bombers over
Rondinella Point as soon as the flare droppers had started to
illuminate the harbour. He himself then glided down from
5000 feet, encountering heavy fire particularly from the shore
batteries, and headed straight for the northern *Littorio*.
Dropping his torpedo at a range of 700 yards, he turned to
starboard and successfully escaped.

Immediately following Hale over Rondinella Point, Lieutenant Bayly commenced his dive. Whether he flattened out
and released his torpedo is unknown, for this gallant officer
failed to return and no one saw his machine again after this
point.

Lieutenant Lee, breaking away from the other quarter of
the Squadron Commander, glided down untouched by the

projectiles flying all round him, picked up the northerly *Cavour* battleship and dropped his torpedo at a range of 800 yards. Then, turning sharply to starboard, passed between two cruisers and away to seaward.

Lieutenant Torrens-Spence was the next to follow and, as he dived, it is possible he became silhouetted to the cruisers by the light of the flares. Whatever the reason, he encountered fire which came unpleasantly close, but he persevered towards his objective which was the northern *Littorio*. Also turning to starboard for his 'get-away,' he again encountered heavy fire from all directions but managed to escape unharmed.

The last torpedo bomber piloted by Lieutenant Walham had an even more exciting time. Soon after he commenced his dive, he nearly came to grief on a barrage balloon. Avoiding it by only a few yards, his machine was hit by bullets in several places, causing damage to the outer aileron rod and putting the aircraft temporarily out of control. With great skill Walham managed to regain command and pressed in to a position about 500 yards on the port bow of one of the *Littorios* where he released his torpedo. During his retirement he was again hit in the port wing, but managed to return in safety to the carrier.

Lieutenants Hamilton and Skelton, in the two flare droppers, had each laid lines of successful illumination along the eastern edge of the harbour. Then, following each other down in a shallow dive, they both straddled the oil fuel depot with sticks of bombs before making their retirement.

It was about this time when Lieutenant Clifford arrived. Although he had left the carrier twenty minutes after the remainder, he had made such good time that he reached Taranto while the attack was still in progress. From some miles to seaward he had spotted the flares and the firing, so it was easy for him to make an accurate landfall. Passing over the coast to the east of the harbour entrance, he made straight for the far side of Mar Piccolo. Then, swinging to port, he dived down through the anti-aircraft barrage and laid a stick of bombs across some cruisers he had clearly identified. He gained height, turned rapidly to starboard and disappeared along the same route as suddenly as he had arrived. . . . .

By 1.0 a.m. those in *Illustrious* were filled with acute expectation. Soon, now, the first aircraft would be returning, and the carrier was approaching the pre-arranged position where it was intended they should land on. Not a spark had disturbed the ether to indicate what success had been achieved, since wireless silence was imperative, and the planes were to return relying on their own navigation to pick up the *Illustrious*. How many would return ? That was the anxious question because the enterprise had been fraught with great hazards. Everyone on board shared the enthusiasm of those who had carried it out so gallantly and each, in his own way, felt he had taken a share—however humble—in the daring operation.

A few minutes later the drone of aircraft was suddenly heard approaching. Powerful binoculars swept the night to pick up the red and green navigation lights shown by the returning planes: then there tumbled from the sky the recognition signal. At once the carrier turned into the wind, switching on the landing lights which illuminated the flight deck from the air while screened to seaward. Then from astern there swooped a shadow as the first machine glided down, touched the deck and finally came to rest in safety.

At frequent intervals now the others arrived, and as each one was wheeled away it seemed as though one personal load was lifted from the minds of those on board. How anxiously the planes were counted! Would they all return ? For over an hour they came back in their ones and twos until, at 2.30 a.m. it was realised that there were no more. Twenty had set out (excluding the one which had been forced to return minus its external petrol tank)—two were missing. *Illustrious* then turned with her escort to rendezvous with the Commander-in-Chief at daylight.

From accounts of those who had taken part it was impossible to tell what measure of success had been achieved. One thing was clear—in each case attacks had been pressed home with

the utmost gallantry and resolution, and there was every ground
for reasoned optimism. But until further photographs had been
obtained by the R.A.F. the actual extent of the damage
inflicted could not be assessed.

These photographs were not long in coming, the R.A.F.
from Malta making a reconnaissance soon after day-break.
A few hours later the eagerly awaited signal was received.
Two *Cavour* class battleships were beached and heavily damaged
—one so badly that it had apparently been abandoned—and
one of the *Littorios* was down by the bows with a heavy list to
starboard and numerous auxiliaries alongside. In the inner
harbour it was difficult to determine what had happened, but
two cruisers appeared to be listed to starboard and surrounded
by oil fuel.

That night it had been hoped to repeat the attack, but
those concerned were bitterly disappointed when the weather
started to deteriorate making this intention quite impossible.
But with the magnificent success which had been gained, the
Fleet Air Arm had more than justified its existence and con-
founded its critics. The crippling of half the Italian battlefleet
with such small loss to ourselves was a remarkable achievement,
and its immediate result was the release of two of our own
battleships for urgent service elsewhere. No finer tribute could
be paid than the Commander-in-Chief's signal:

"Illustrious manoeuvre well executed."

Chapter 5

MATAPAN — MARCH 1941

BY the beginning of 1941 the nucleus of a great army had
been built up in Egypt. Though it numbered considerably
less than 100,000 men and the equipment was not all to be
desired, the spirit of the troops and the ability of the Royal
Navy to give support enabled General Wavell to launch his
victorious African offensive across the Libyan desert to
Benghazi. Meanwhile, Italy had also experienced a defeat in

From a painting by Lt.-Cdr. Roland Langmaid, R.N.

APPROACH TO TARANTO— *ILLUSTRIOUS AND DESTROYER SCREEN*

By kind permission of the Admiralty

ITALIAN SUBMARINES LYING AT MALTA AFTER THEIR SURRENDER

Greece which so threatened her position that Germany was forced to go to her assistance.

The success, therefore, achieved by General Wavell's Army in the Libyan desert was offset by the growing danger to Greece and the corresponding threat to our whole position in the Middle East if the Germans acquired complete control of the Balkans. Hitherto, she had been stoutly, and successfully resisting the Italians, but the whole situation had become transformed by the German attack on Jugo-Slavia and Greece. There was only one possible course of action for the British, and that was to rush reinforcements to the Greek front in order to stem the tide of German invasion. But, with the inadequate forces and material at our command, it meant running a grave risk in North Africa and the loss of hard won territory. However, there was a real chance that this stiffening in Greece might enable a line to be held beyond which the Germans could not penetrate; but as a strategical conception the whole policy was open to criticism.

In the wardroom of one of the great battleships lying in Alexandria a discussion took place concerning the dramatic possibilities beginning to materialise in the Balkans.

"I contend," exclaimed the Captain of Marines, "that, from a military point of view, it is unsound to weaken our position in North Africa at the present time. I don't believe we can possibly hope to do any more than delay the Germans for a few days if they really intend to over-run Greece."

"On the other hand," declared the Gunnery officer, "I don't see what else we can do. Militarily it may be unsound, but from a political and moral point of view it is, without doubt, essential. There can be no two opinions on that point."

"That may be, but surely, when we're fighting a war, military expediency should come above every other consideration."

"That's just where you're wrong. It may produce local successes, but in the long run neglect of moral and political considerations must invite disaster. That is why, in spite of

D

their astonishing victories so far, I am confident that the Germans are bound to be defeated. Their concentration on the military aspect of every situation blinds them to the political consequences of their actions, and they thus create an ever stronger opposition."

"Didn't they nearly succeed last year?"

"Yes, they did. I will grant you that if you have sufficient power to ensure a short war, political considerations can be swept aside. But if you foresee a prolonged conflict, then they must be a paramount factor in all strategy."

"I suppose you're right," the Captain of Marines conceded. "We're really not in a position to form a clear picture of all that's going on. I wonder, though, if these convoys we're running to Greece will tempt the Italian fleet to try and have a crack at them."

"Shouldn't be surprised," the Gunnery Officer agreed. "They bloody well ought to, considering their numerical superiority to us, and all the advantage of being able to attack within a reasonable distance of their home bases. How do the distances compare, Pilot, say from Taranto to Crete and Alex to Crete?"

The Navigator, who had been listening to the argument with interest, replied promptly. "The western corner of Crete's about half way—four hundred miles as near as dammit. But as you say, the advantages of being able to operate from a number of home ports are enormous compared with a place like Alex."

From the Commander-in-Chief downwards, everyone was alive to the possibilities of a sortie being made by the Italian fleet, and hoped ardently that it would materialise. Aircraft patrols, operated both from Malta and Maleme aerodrome in Crete, scoured the seas as far as their limited numbers allowed, and every means was employed to acquire intelligence concerning the movements of the Italian warships.

Very soon there came a hint that powerful Italian surface units were, indeed, at sea with the object of attacking a particular convoy approaching Crete from the south-east, and due to pass through the Antikithera Channel—between Crete and the mainland of Greece—during the afternoon of the following day. There was nothing very firm in the intelligence, but it was sufficient to decide the Commander-in-Chief, Admiral Sir A. B. Cunningham, to go to sea. Suppose, it was thought, that instead of a convoy of merchant vessels only lightly covered by our forces, the Italians found the entire British Mediterranean Fleet.

The convoy, was, therefore, ordered to alter course to due east, and Admiral Pridham-Wippell, the Vice-Admiral Light Forces (V.A.L.F.) who happened to be at the Piræus in his cruiser flagship *Orion*, with *Ajax*, *Perth* and *Gloucester* forming the remainder of his squadron, was instructed to sail forthwith for a position south of Crete. Four destroyers completed his force. The battlefleet, meanwhile, led by *Warspite* flying the flag of the Commander-in-Chief, accompanied by the aircraft carrier *Formidable* and more destroyers, raised steam and sailed from Alexandria at 7.0 p.m. on 27th March, with the intention of contacting V.A.L.F. about noon on the following day.

Dawn found the two forces some 150 miles apart: V.A.L.F. steering a course slightly east of south and the battlefleet bearing up to the north-west. The night had been quiet and no further indication had been received of the presence of Italian surface ships.

As the report, "*Formidable* hauling out of line," was made in each ship, the aircraft carrier turned into the wind and proceeded to fly off five reconnaissance machines, one after the other, to search the area between Crete and Africa.

There was still no sign of the enemy, but shortly after 6.0 a.m. the force with *Orion* received the first confirmation that there *was* something in the report which had galvanised the British fleet into activity. Two hostile aircraft were suddenly sighted and a study of their type brought an obvious conclusion. They belonged to a class which was only used by the Italian navy for catapulting from ships. But V.A.L.F. did not feel justified in breaking wireless silence to inform the Commander-in-Chief.

It was over an hour later that the first report was received from one of *Formidable's* reconnaissance machines. Four enemy cruisers and four destroyers had been sighted steaming on a south-westerly course. Twenty minutes later another aircraft gave a similar report. Throughout the Fleet interested officers studied the Plot.

"How do the reports compare?" was asked in one battleship.

"There's a difference of fifteen miles between the two positions and I calculate that V.A.L.F. is in the same area." The Plotting Officer demonstrated with a pair of dividers.

"They're undoubtedly the same force," said the Navigator, "as an error of fifteen miles between two aircraft reports is quite common."

"Isn't that the composition of V.A.L.F.'s force—four cruisers and four destroyers?" The Captain had followed the Navigator into the Plotting House.

"Why, yes sir, it is." The Navigator looked disappointed. "Do you think the aircraft could have made a mistake, sir, and reported our own ships."

"Looks rather like it, but we'll soon see." The Captain turned and took a message handed to him by a signalman. "The Commander-in-Chief apparently thinks so. Here's a signal he's just made to *Formidable*: 'Why have the aircraft reported V.A.L.F.'?"

In the mind of V.A.L.F. himself the same question had arisen and so certain did he feel that *Formidable's* aircraft had reported him by mistake that he began seriously to consider the advisability of making a signal to the Commander-in-Chief. But events suddenly happened to clarify the situation.

Away to the north the smoke of ships travelling fast was seen to rise above the haze on the horizon. Quickly they took form and were identified as four Italian 8-inch cruisers and four destroyers.

Making an immediate report, V.A.L.F. hauled round to a

similar and slightly opening course. Both in gun power, range and speed, the enemy ships were superior, and the only chance of their destruction lay in drawing them on towards the fleet and within easy range of torpedo bombing from *Formidable*.

At 8.13 the enemy, though still out of range from our own ships, opened fire and *Orion* was straddled immediately. Snaking the line to avoid being hit and proceeding at their utmost speed, the British cruisers continued to lead the enemy towards *Warspite*. *Gloucester*, who was on the port (eastern) wing and therefore nearest to the enemy, opened fire; but it was at extreme range, her shots fell short and, after the third salvo, she desisted. So the action continued with shells falling round our own ships who were unable to reply. But the enemy was being steadily drawn towards the battlefleet racing at full speed to make contact.

In each ship careful plots were being kept of all the movements and it was calculated that if the rate of closing was maintained, the enemy would be sighted from *Warspite* about 10.0 o'clock. Then came a disappointment. Fifteen minutes after firing their first shot, the Italians suddenly reversed their course, and began to steam at the same high speed towards the north-west. Their own reconnaissance aircraft had possibly reported the presence of British battleships and inspired the manoeuvre. V.A.L.F. countered in the only possible way. Turning his own cruisers round, he sought to follow and keep touch with the enemy who had now ceased fire and were rapidly increasing the range.

By 9.40 the enemy were out of sight, but V.A.L.F. pressed on. Twenty minutes later they were re-sighted from the masthead and gave the impression that they had altered course to port. This revived the hope that they would be held until conditions were more favourable for a successful action.

When the news was received hope rose again that the battlefleet would arrive on the scene in time, but it was realised that, unless something was done to slow them down, the superior speed of the Italians would allow them to escape. It was, therefore, with a feeling of intense satisfaction that *Formidable* was seen to haul out of line and fly off a striking force of six Albacores armed with torpedoes and accompanied by two *Fulmars* as escort. Their orders were to attack the enemy cruisers.

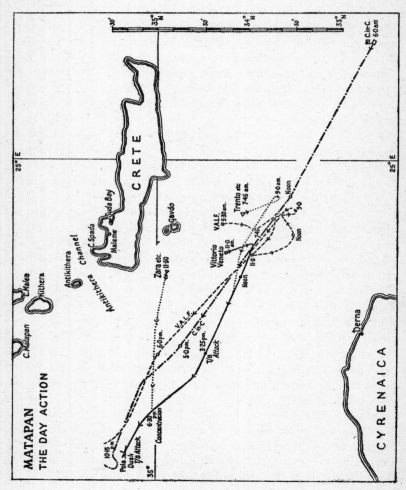

Even if the battlefleet could not arrive in time, it was considered that V.A.L.F. was in an excellent position to administer the *coup de grace* to any damaged Italian warship which was left behind.

Then suddenly a signal was made by V.A.L.F. which transformed the entire tactical situation. It was made on full power and flashed round the world. It must have stirred Whitehall, it certainly thrilled warships on monotonous escort duties in the west Atlantic, where the charts in use were hastily replaced by one of the eastern Mediterranean.

"Enemy battleship," it read, "bearing 002 degrees, sixteen miles."

The moment for which the Navy longed had arrived—the Italian battlefleet (if there was one battleship there were probably more) was at sea, and there was every prospect of a decisive encounter.

But V.A.L.F. was now in a most uncomfortable position, because the battleship had opened fire immediately and was closing our cruisers at terrific speed, cutting a huge bow wave with a good 30 knots. He had only one alternative, and that was to turn his ships together to a course of 180 degrees, directly away from the approaching enemy.

With remarkable accuracy, the Italians quickly found the range, and great fountains of spray rose up between the British cruisers, as big 15-inch projectiles plunged into the sea. On the light armoured vessels one hit from those shells would have caused great devastation, resulting probably in the total loss of the ship concerned. For the next ten minutes, *Orion* was singled out as the principal target, and shells fell about her; one so close that her decks were drenched and slight damage sustained in the superstructure.

At the same time as V.A.L.F. turned southward, he had ordered all ships to make smoke, and as the smoke screen became effective, *Orion*—now to leeward and thus well screened —ceased to be the focus for this embarrassing gunfire.

The cruisers were steaming south at full speed in line abreast;

the wind was from the east, and it was therefore inevitable that the port wing ship (to windward) should receive no protection from the great clouds of smoke pouring from her funnels. This windward ship was *Gloucester*, and the enemy—now recognised as one of the latest and most powerful Italian battleships, *Vittorio Veneto*—immediately began to concentrate on her. In vain the destroyers who, after the sudden turn, found themselves on the western flank, struggled to pass ahead and screen *Gloucester* by their own smoke, but the speed was too great for them to draw ahead except very slowly.

The speed of V.A.L.F.'s cruisers was high, but that of *Vittorio Veneto* was higher. Range closed steadily, and the enormous bow wave of the giant battleship as it bore down on them was anything but re-assuring to observers in *Gloucester*, and though for the first half hour she miraculously escaped unscathed, it was regarded as a matter of time only before she received a hit.

Watching the drama unfold by carefully plotting all reports received from V.A.L.F. those in the British battlefleet chafed impatiently at the delay, while the ships themselves strained every ounce of steam to reach the scene of action.

Would they be too late, and find only the shattered remnants of the cruiser force which it might be impossible to avenge? The political consequences of such a disaster were incalculable. Against such a formidable opponent, backed by powerful cruisers, destroyers and probably more battleships, V.A.L.F.'s small force could achieve little, however heroically they fought.

Prospects were by no means bright, and it was now impossible to divert the air striking force which had been flown off *Formidable* before the Italian capital ship had been sighted. The machines were out of range for communication.

But relief came. The Commander of this air striking force found the cruisers which he had been directed to attack, but he also saw a large single ship, screened by destroyers, heavily engaging the British cruisers. A closer inspection revealed to him exactly what it was, and he at once decided to attack the battleship—an action which was to transform the entire situation. The depth settings of the torpedoes were rapidly changed, swift instructions were passed to the leaders of sub-flights and the *Albacores* went in to make an attack, which was skilfully and daringly executed. One sub-flight approached from the port side of the battleship forcing her to turn to starboard; the remainder met her while she swung, pressed in to within a few hundred yards and released their torpedoes in such a manner that they were almost impossible to avoid. In spite of a terrific barrage of anti-aircraft fire none of the aircraft were damaged, and at least one hit was scored near the stern of *Vittorio Veneto*, while one of the escorting *Fulmars* shot down a *Junkers* 88 which tried to interfere.

This sudden blow which reduced the speed of his flagship by at least eight knots caused the Italian Admiral to break off the action and retire as fast as he could towards his base. He had lost a freedom of movement which had given him a superiority over the British forces, and he now ran a great risk of losing more.

By this dramatic intervention V.A.L.F. was saved from an unpleasant position and, when *Gloucester* reported that the enemy had ceased fire, he ordered ships to stop making smoke. When it had cleared, there was no enemy in sight. Instead, to the eastward, he saw the dim shapes of the British battlefleet hastening towards him. It was now noon.

Though the cruisers were saved, a chance of catching up with the Italian fleet retiring to the west appeared remote.

"There's only one way to bring them to action," the Captain of a battleship declared as he studied the strategical plot with his Navigator and one or two other officers, "and that's to inflict more damage on them by air attack. We must reduce their speed, otherwise we haven't a hope. How far do you reckon the *Vittorio Veneto* is?"

The Plotting Officer measured the distance with his dividers. "About sixty-five miles, sir."

The Captain performed a rapid calculation. "Even if she's

only capable of twenty knots, that means we cannot get within range before dark." He turned to the Gunnery Officer. "Do you know, Guns, exactly what aircraft *Formidable* has available ?"

"Very few, sir, I'm afraid. I think she only has two *Albacores,* four *Swordfish* and thirteen *Fulmars.* It'd be impossible for her to launch a really powerful attack with so few, and at the same time keep the necessary reconnaissance machines in the air."

"There're five *Swordfish* in Crete, sir," the Fleet Air Arm Pilot of the battleship's Walrus broke in. "Here's a signal saying one of them has just flown down from the Piræus with the only aerial torpedo in Greece." He handed a signal to the Captain.

"And I see the Commander-in-Chief ordered them to attack at 10.30," the Captain announced, studying a sheaf of signals which a Yeoman thrust into his hands. "But," he added, "only three appeared to be available. Anyhow, *Formidable* ought to be able to launch another attack soon."

Shortly afterwards, news was received of the result of the attack from Crete. The enemy had been located but had managed to avoid all torpedoes dropped from the aircraft.

Meanwhile the fleet was still steaming at full speed to the north-west—the cruiser squadron ahead and within vizual signalling distance of *Warspite*—and *Formidable* was seen preparing a second striking force. The situation was confusing. Varying wind conditions had caused the positions reported by aircraft to differ considerably; poor visibility made it difficult to determine the exact composition of the enemy, and the presence of numerous *Junkers* 88 made the task of the few aircraft, which could be spared for reconnaissance duty, infinitely harder.

Shortly after noon, information was received that there was another enemy force consisting of three cruisers and two destroyers, steering west from a position about 20 miles south of the western corner of Crete. Another report stated that there were two battleships with this group and placed them all further south.

About this time the Commander-in-Chief signalled his appreciation.

It read as follows: "The enemy appear to be in two groups, the southern consisting of one damaged battleship of the *Littorio* class, three cruisers and seven destroyers, last seen steering north at 11.30 about 60 miles to the west of *Warspite*. The northern group appears to consist of two battleships, three cruisers and four destroyers."

To show the confusion that existed, even in the mind of the Commander-in-Chief, the actual composition of the enemy was quite different. With *Vittorio Veneto*, who was flying the flag of Admiral Lachino, there were three 8-inch cruisers, *Trento*, *Trieste* and *Bolzano;* two 6-inch cruisers, *Garibaldi* and *Abruzzi*, and seven destroyers. In the northern group there were three 8-inch cruisers, *Zara*, *Pola* and *Fiume*, escorted by four destroyers.

The battleship in the southern group had been damaged and her speed probably reduced. If her speed could be reduced still more, the rest of the force would have to keep with her to afford protection, and the contact for which everyone longed might be achieved. It was, therefore, essential for the limited air striking force to concentrate on *Vittorio Veneto*.

Thus it was with the highest expectations that *Formidable* was seen to fly off her second striking force a few minutes before 1.0 o'clock, but, as she turned to regain station in the line there was a sudden cry of enemy aircraft. Two Italian *Savoias* 79 had appeared coming in low to attack the carrier, but the volume of fire they encountered from all ships caused them to drop their torpedoes from a distance, and then retire as rapidly as they could. *Formidable*, therefore, had little difficulty in combing the tracks and so avoided being hit.

Much now depended on the success of the second striking force, but it was not until late in the afternoon that the machines returned to the carrier and made their report which was broadcast to the fleet. Unfortunately the aircraft piloted by the leader of this gallant attack, Lieut.-Commander Dalzell-Stead, failed to return. No one saw him crash. This was, in fact, the only casualty sustained by the British forces throughout the entire operation.

After searching round for an appreciable period, the Squadron Leader had finally located the target and the attack was delivered at 3.25. Diving out of the sun unobserved, the machines had pressed home before dropping their torpedoes. One destroyer who opened a withering fire had been shot up by the fighter escort and forced to turn away, while the attacks on the battleship had been made from different directions and were well synchronised. At least two hits had been obtained on *Vittorio Veneto*.

This news produced a thrill of elation throughout the fleet and the Commander-in-Chief, voicing the feelings of all those under his command, immediately made a congratulatory signal:

"Well done—give him another nudge at dusk."

By how much had the enemy's speed been reduced? That was the question. Conflicting reports were received from reconnaissance aircraft. Some said she had been reduced to nine knots, others to twenty. The latter appeared more correct, because it soon became obvious that the British fleet was only overhauling the Italians very slowly, and it was highly improbable that they would be within range before dark. Sunset was at 6.45 p.m.

At 6.0 o'clock a study of the plot indicated that a good fifty miles still separated the two fleets. Responsible officers looked grave.

"Well, it all depends," was a typical remark, "on what the aircraft can achieve in a dusk attack. If only we had a few more planes!"

A signal was received to say that all enemy forces appeared to be making a concentration and that the northern group had joined up with the others.

The largest possible striking force was prepared and flown off *Formidable*—six *Albacores* and two *Swordfish*. Two aircraft from Maleme in Crete also participated. There were unavoidable delays, and it was not until 7.30 that the squadron leader led in to attack the heavily screened battleship under poor conditions of light and visibility. On closing to 3000 yards they were received by a terrific barrage. Flaming onions, antiaircraft and short range weapons from every ship in the now powerfully constituted Italian fleet opened up over a wide arc, forcing the aircraft to turn to starboard, break up formation, and attack independently from widely different angles.

In the smoke and confusion it was very difficult to see, and there were many narrow escapes from collision between different machines. All the pilots pressed home their attacks with great gallantry, and the majority of them were under the impression that they aimed at the battleship. But in the poor light and the blinding effect of the great volume of fire, it was impossible to assess results, though many pilots reported that *Vittorio Veneto* had again been hit, and that at least one cruiser had been severely damaged.

To the advanced British surface units, who could see the vast pyrotechnic display, it was a wonder that any of the aircraft could live through such a hail of fire. Yet not one was lost, all returning safely to the carrier.

A night shadowing aircraft who had observed the attack, reported at 7.50 that the enemy force had divided, and that the battleship, surrounded by six other vessels, had stopped with smoke pouring from all parts of her. This aircraft remained in the vicinity for another twenty minutes, observing the battleship the whole time, until it was forced to return on account of diminishing petrol supply. Even in the light of subsequent events, the pilot very definitely maintained that he had been observing the battleship and not a cruiser. It was unfortunate that no machine was available to relieve this night-shadower on escort duty.

In reality, the only hit that could afterwards be claimed was that on the cruiser *Pola*. The damage she sustained had brought her to a standstill, and caused all electrical power to fail. She was left a drifting hulk.

Subsequently the Captain of the *Pola* is reported to have said: "I have never seen such courage as was displayed by the aircraft attacking me."

II

Previous to the dusk attack by the air striking force, there had been considerable uncertainty among members of the fleet concerning the tactics which the Commander-in-Chief would adopt. Everywhere there was a general feeling of anxiety that the Italians would elude them and that the British ships would return to harbour with only the negative achievement of having, by their sortie, saved another convoy to Greece from annihilation.

In one of the battleships the situation was being discussed.

"If any of them are badly damaged," the Captain remarked, "it's possible we may sight them at dawn. If we don't, then, we might as well return to Alex. With the few aircraft *Formidable* can put up, the Commander-in-Chief won't run the fleet into waters where the Italians can get cover from an air umbrella."

"What are the prospects of a night action, sir?" The Navigator put the question hopefully.

"Very few, I should think. Anyhow, conventional tactics do not encourage capital ships to indulge in night action. It's far too chancy." The Captain raised his binoculars and watched eight destroyers forming up on the flotilla leader *Jervis*, gaining distance on the battlefleet and speeding away towards the west in the direction of V.A.L.F.'s squadron some forty miles ahead.

"I presume they're going to work independently as a night striking force. It doesn't leave many for A./S. protection of the battlefleet. Who's left?"

The Chief Yeoman of Signals studied the remaining destroyers in company through the telescope. "*Stuart* and *Havock* to starboard, sir, and *Greyhound* and *Griffin* to port."

"Our forces are obviously being used to the absolute limits of prudence." The Captain's jaw set grimly.

A messenger thrust a handful of signals at the Chief Yeoman, who thumbed rapidly through them arranging the messages in order of priority for the Captain.

"Commander-in-Chief's night intentions, sir."

"Good; that'll be interesting." The Captain took the pile of signals and began reading aloud.

" 'If the cruisers gain touch with the damaged battleship, the 2nd and 14th destroyer flotillas'—that's the striking force, I presume—'will be sent in to attack. If she is not then destroyed, the battlefleet will follow. If she is not located, intend to work round to the north and west by dawn'."

The Navigator nodded his head understandingly. "That's clear enough, sir. It'll be grand if we're to the west of them by dawn."

"I imagine we'll be closed up at action stations all right, sir ?" The Gunnery Officer was naturally interested on this point.

"Yes, of course. We may be involved in a night action after all."

The wind died down to a gentle breeze singing in the rigging. It grew dark rapidly and, overhead, the stars broke through the scattered wisps of cirrus fanning out in the sky. A new moon had showed itself for a few moments—then dipped below the western horizon. But the haze had cleared, and it was possible to see distinctly for some distance through the high powered glasses, especially adapted for night work, with which ships are supplied.

Then the report of the air attack was received. It implied that the *Vittorio Veneto* was probably lying helpless in their track. Every officer and man was stimulated by this news. A ship like that would not be left by herself; therefore, the night held the promise of startling, and perhaps, decisive events.

Meanwhile, in the cruisers ahead, there was even more excitement. On them lay a big responsibility, and to them would probably fall the first contact with the enemy. A hundred pairs of highly trained eyes peered into the darkness, sweeping round in a wide arc from right ahead to either beam, getting more accustomed to the gloom at every moment, and seeing objects with greater distinction. Suddenly, about 8.30, *Ajax* on the port wing detected a ship ahead, which resolved itself into a big ship stopped on her port bow. It was too dark to make out details, but V.A.L.F., who was immediately told, at once decided that this must be *Vittorio Veneto*. According to the Commander-in-Chief's orders the destroyers were to finish her off. Her position was fixed, she obviously could not move, so, making the necessary report, V.A.L.F. turned his cruisers away to search for other enemy forces which, he felt certain, must be in the vicinity. But he was out of luck, and this manoeuvre led him directly away from the action which subsequently followed. His signal was picked up by the Commander-in-Chief in *Warspite*, but unfortunately was not received in *Jervis* or in any of the destroyer striking force, who continued their sweep. The ship, however, which had been detected was not *Vittorio Veneto*, but the helpless *Pola*.

Everyone in the battlefleet was now filled with expectancy, and, on the bridge of each ship there was a silence of suppressed excitement among the concentrated watchers. Only the voice of the Officer of the Watch ordering a change in revolutions or a slight adjustment of course to maintain station on the next ahead broke the stillness. *Barham* was at the end of the line. Ahead of her steamed *Formidable*, then *Valiant* who followed close astern of Admiral Cunningham in *Warspite*. On their starboard side were the destroyers *Stuart* and *Havock;* to port were *Greyhound* and *Griffin*.

Swiftly they closed the position where they believed the Italian battleship lay stopped, expecting at any instant to see the darkness stabbed by great explosions as destroyers of the

ZARA   FIUME

From a painting by Lieut.-Cdr. Roland Langmaid, R.N.

THE CLIMAX AT MATAPAN

BARHAM   VALIANT   WARSPITE

By kind permission of the Admiralty

DESTROYER NIGHT ACTION

striking force fired their torpedoes. But the night remained silent, for the destroyers concerned, missing V.A.L.F.'s signal, had hauled away to the north.

In the *Barham*, about 10.0 o'clock, the Navigator paid a quick visit to the plot. "I reckon, sir," he said, on returning to the Compass Platform, "that she's about on our port beam now." He did not explain what he meant by 'she'; they were all thinking of the one ship—*Vittorio Veneto*.

"Alter course together, sir, 40 degrees to port, Executive signal." The Chief Yeoman interpreted sudden flashing from a pin-point of light on the flagship.

"The C.-in-C. seems to be of the same opinion. Over you go. Stand by all guns." The Captain slipped from his stool in the corner of the bridge, and gave the orders crisply.

The Navigator leapt to the voice pipe, taking over from the Officer of the Watch, and followed carefully the movements of *Formidable* on whom it was of vital importance to keep accurate station. With the fighting of the ship or the location of the enemy—however tantalizing it was to look around—he was not concerned. He had to concentrate solely on handling the ship in the manner ordered by the Commander-in-Chief.

For a few minutes ships steadied on this new course, then suddenly there occurred a series of dramatic incidents.

"Flashing light bearing red nine-oh."

"Alarm red nine-oh!"

The guns of *Barham* swung round to this bearing as eyes were focussed on a speck of light which had suddenly broken the darkness and was flashing a 'general call.' Then, from behind the light, a red rocket shot into the air, and it was possible to distinguish the shape of a great vessel lying stopped! She, too, had seen the British vessels, but doubtless thought they were friends coming to her assistance.

But the Captain had not time to order, *open fire*, for other events were occurring with startling swiftness. The Commander-in-Chief had ordered ships to turn together 40 degrees to starboard, which brought them back in line ahead on to

E

their original course. As *Barham's* wheel was put over, the Captain was puzzled by this alteration away from the enemy. Should he report to the C.-in-C. or open fire on his own initiative?

He had scarcely time to frame these questions in his mind

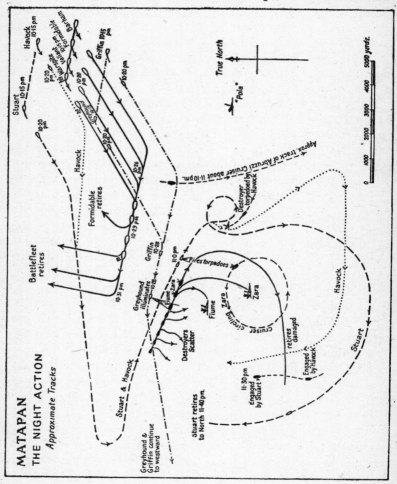

MATAPAN
THE NIGHT ACTION
Approximate Tracks

when, with ships barely steady on their new course, the reason became apparent. *Greyhound*, slightly ahead, and on the port bow suddenly exposed the beam of her powerful searchlight to reveal a most dramatic situation. Scarcely 3000 yards away and steaming towards the helpless *Pola* were three large Italian cruisers in line ahead followed by a string of destroyers; and *Greyhound's* searchlight was focussed on the third ship in the line, thus perfectly silhouetting the two leading vessels. In that first glimpse it was quite clear that they were in complete ignorance of the presence of British warships, for their guns were still trained fore and aft.

Instantaneously an inferno broke loose. 15-inch broadsides from the battleships ahead of *Barham* crashed into the cruiser caught in the questioning beam of *Greyhound's* searchlight. It was the 8-inch cruiser *Fiume* of 10,000 tons. Hits were obtained with all broadsides, and the stricken vessel turned away, a blazing wreck, to sink a few hours later.

Above the din of gunfire and explosions the Chief Yeoman shouted that the destroyers on the port beam of the battlefleet had been ordered to clear the line of fire—a bold move, for it also exposed the capital ships to unrestricted torpedo attack. But there was no time to reflect on these consequences in the height of the melee.

"*Open fire*," the Captain of the *Barham* yelled as soon as *Greyhound* disclosed the enemy. But nothing occurred.

"What is the delay?" he fumed impatiently.

"Turrets have to be trained round from the after bearing, sir." The Gunnery Officer was able to remind him that only a few moments before they had been trained on to the ship they had found lying stopped.

Although it only took a matter of seconds for the guns to be swung round on to the bow, the time seemed interminable, especially as it was realised that this marvellous opportunity could only be fleeting and that every moment was therefore precious. At length the guns were round, and those on the bridge were momentarily blinded by the flash of a full broadside and shaken by the blast. The Captain had given orders to engage the leading enemy cruiser, and a brilliant sheet of flame underneath her bridge told that the shells were going home while other bursts were observed along the whole length. A second salvo was fired, scoring more hits; the enemy turned away and was last seen retiring on a westerly course with smoke and flames pouring from her sides.

"Shift target right!" *Barham* swung her guns and *Zara*, the second ship in the Italian line, came under the concentrated fire of all the battleships. She was quickly stopped and left a flaming beacon.

"*Formidable* hauling out of line, sir." Yelling to make himself heard, the Chief Yeoman reported the sudden movement of the aircraft carrier to the Captain.

"Don't worry about her," he managed to shout.

It was quite obvious that *Formidable* had decided that a night meleé was the last sort of action in which a vulnerable, but invaluable, ship like herself should be involved. So her Captain was doing the right and only possible thing—getting well out of it.

Now that the cruisers had been dealt with, there were the enemy destroyers to consider. A destroyer was suddenly reported on the port side of *Warspite*, whose secondary armament of 6-inch guns straddled her with shells.

Griffin, originally stationed on the port beam of the battle-fleet, had been drawing ahead on *Greyhound* for the reasons already explained, but, due to the swiftness of the action, she was still a long way from the position she was striving to reach. It was, therefore, with considerable alarm that the Commanding Officer found himself being straddled with shells from his own battlefleet. Fortunately none actually hit, but some fell so close that he and those with him on the bridge were drenched by the fountains of water thrown up by near misses.

The Commander-in-Chief was sympathetic (?) when the mistake was discovered.

"Get out of the way, you damned fool!" he signalled.

The Italian destroyers had also been caught unawares, and it was quite clear that they were in considerable confusion from the sudden turn of events. But they were now a definite menace to the battleships, and no one was surprised when a signal flashed down the line ordering ships to alter course together 90 degrees to starboard—directly away from the scene of carnage. With the heavy cruisers crippled and on fire, it was now a destroyers' battle and not a place for heavy ships.

But, as they turned, the battleships opened a heavy fire with their secondary armament, and the sea was alive with fountains of spray thrown up by the barrage of plunging shells. In the light of the gun flashes and flames from the burning cruisers in the background, long, low shapes of enemy destroyers could be seen turning towards, dodging the avalanche of shells. But the attack was half-hearted, they swung away to starboard, releasing torpedoes on the turn and disappeared in the darkness to the west. There were a few moments of breathless suspense. In the churned up water it was impossible to discern the tracks, and those on board the battleships could only hope that their own swing to starboard would enable them to avoid the peril. Moments passed; then it was clear that all torpedoes had passed safely between the ships, and it was judged that the enemy destroyers were no longer an immediate menace.

Ordering the four British destroyers to counter-attack, Admiral Cunningham led the battlefleet away, though they were now without any anti-submarine escort.

After the *cease fire* order had been given, the astounding fact was revealed that from the time of the first salvo to the battle-fleet's turn away was only three minutes.

It seemed incredible. During that short time they had dealt the death blow to three large cruisers and probably damaged or sunk one or two destroyers.

From *Warspite* a light flashed: "Form single line ahead."

Together *Valiant* and *Barham* swung to port, then turning in succession, followed astern of the flagship. A great darkened shape loomed to starboard which was immediately identified as *Formidable* edging in to resume her station in the line. A zig-zag was ordered and the sounds of action being carried on by the destroyers gradually faded away. But for hours afterwards, gun flashes continued to break the night over a large area to the south-west.

The battlefleet steamed on to the northward. To return would invite disaster, because in the darkness, with scattered forces it would be impossible to distinguish between friend and foe. The battleships had staged a situation which was now a picnic for destroyers.

When the battlefleet turned away, the four destroyers which had been their escort during the early part of the night drove hard at the enemy destroyers trying to escape. Repeated hits were definitely scored on the fleeing Italians who displayed a remarkable enthusiasm for firing Breda bullets in the air, possibly in the belief that bursting star shells fired by the British ships to illuminate them were, in reality, flares dropped by aircraft. Whatever the cause, these Bredas made excellent aiming marks for the gunners, but the Italian destroyers with their superior speed, gradually drew further ahead until they were lost in smoke and darkness.

About this time the destroyers received a signal from the Commander-in-Chief ordering them to return and finish off with torpedoes the damaged Italian cruisers. *Greyhound* and *Griffin* were too far to the west to take immediate action, but *Stuart*, the flotilla leader, led *Havock* round to port and observed the blazing *Zara* about two miles to the south, and in the light thrown by the flames an undamaged cruiser could be seen circling round. Here was a most desirable target—much more so than the already helpless vessel, and *Stuart* immediately fired her full outfit of torpedoes.

At least one hit was scored on the undamaged cruiser—later seen to be stopped and burning heavily. The two destroyers then closed and engaged both cruisers with gunfire. It was returned by a few small calibre guns, firing wildly, but the destroyers went unscathed.

The scene was eerie. Flames and explosions from the burning cruisers made the surrounding darkness more profound, and the night seemed full of strange, elusive shapes. A tongue of flame or the flash of a gun might momentarily reveal the outline of an unknown vessel lurking in the background in a state of uncertainty and confusion. To *Stuart's* alarm one of these darkened shapes suddenly appeared close on the port bow bearing rapidly down on her from the north-east. It was so close that those on board were able to identify it as an *Abruzzi* class cruiser who, at that range, with one broadside, could have blown both destroyers out of the water. Breathlessly they watched the cruiser pass, and could hear shouting on her upper deck, but the flash of flame which would have spelt their destruction never came, for the cruiser doubtless thought the two destroyers, if indeed she saw them, were friendly.

Furious at having no torpedoes left for this easy target (*Havock* was in no position to fire hers) *Stuart* led round to attack with gunfire, but a sudden diversion upset this intention. An Italian destroyer appeared unexpectedly, passing close ahead from starboard to port and, to avoid collision, *Stuart* was forced to put her wheel hard over. *Havock*, with more freedom of manoeuvre, was able to fire a torpedo which caught the enemy in the stern, sending up a shower of flame and water and causing her to stop. *Havock* then turned round, firing her guns, until the enemy finally blew up and sank about twenty minutes later.

During this time *Havock* lost touch with *Stuart*, who had moved over to the south-west to continue her interrupted action with the cruiser she had already torpedoed. She was found listing badly, and *Stuart*, opening fire, scored many more hits, but her shells were not large enough to cause destruction. It was a lonely situation for *Stuart*, and she felt uncomfortable, too, without torpedoes; so the destroyer decided to work round to the north-west. Dark shapes continually passed close by, and another undamaged cruiser loomed to starboard. Regardless of consequences, fire was immediately opened, but so shaken was the enemy, that there was only an ineffectual reply. Then, observing that a small fire had been started on board as a result of her shooting, *Stuart* finally hauled off to the northward.

When the enemy destroyer she was engaging had sunk in a cascade of flame, *Havock* decided to move over in the direction of most intense gunfire. It was to the south-east, and the Commanding Officer came to the conclusion that either V.A.L.F.'s cruisers or the destroyer striking force had made contact with some enemy units. In point of fact, the remaining British light forces were well to the northward, so some Italian ships must have been indulging in a scrap among themselves!

The firing ceased before *Havock* had proceeded very far, so she turned round to finish off the burning *Zara* in accordance with the Commander-in-Chief's original orders. But, as she approached, the inferno of raging fire sweeping the decks of the Italian cruiser showed clearly that it was only a matter of minutes before she would sink. Under these circumstances, it seemed a pity to waste torpedoes on her. *Havock* was drawn towards a more tempting target by the sight of a single fire burning near the bridge of a large ship. Approaching slowly and silently, *Havock* discovered that the ship in question was a cruiser—probably the second which *Stuart* had engaged, the first having disappeared.

Turning to the requisite course, the destroyer fired her remaining torpedoes, but something went wrong, and they all unfortunately missed. Thoroughly exasperated with this bad luck, *Havock* closed to engage the cruiser with gunfire, and scored several hits. But the demoralisation of the enemy was so complete that the few shots fired in reply fell astern.

It was now *Havock's* turn to feel lonely and uncomfortable. Surrounded by enemy ships, and with no sign of any friendly forces in the neighbourhood, she might at any moment receive the undivided attention of those mysterious shapes which kept passing and re-passing in the darkness. Her sting had been removed with the discharge of her last torpedo, and there was little she could really effect with gunfire; so the Commanding Officer decided to retire at high speed to the northward.

But when clear of these ghostly vessels moving about amid the scene of devastation, he paused, amazed that no one had attempted to engage his ship. *Zara* and *Fiume* still burned, their flickering flames casting a lurid glow over the sea, and he had been ordered to sink them. So turning round and reducing speed to make his approach less conspicuous, *Havock* proceeded again towards *Zara* and fired star shells to illuminate the area all round.

As the balls of fire burst in the sky, and slowly fell lighting up more and more of the area, the Commanding Officer suddenly saw what he imagined to be the primary target for which the whole fleet had been searching. Stopped, silent and very dark, with her guns trained fore and aft, lay a large ship with a heavy list. It must, he thought, be the *Vittorio Veneto* which his own battlefleet had missed.

Thrilled and elated by his discovery, he immediately broke wireless silence and broadcast the necessary report. Captain D 14 in *Jervis* some miles to the north heard it, and led his destroyers round and proceeded at full speed towards *Havock*: *Greyhound* and *Griffin* still pursuing Italian destroyers to the westward also turned and raced back. Realising that help would soon arrive, *Havock* eased speed and stood off, while the Commanding Officer seized the opportunity to study silhouette cards of Italian warships. Then, to his horror and disappointment he suddenly appreciated that the ship he had reported as *Vittorio Veneto* was, in reality, the 8-inch cruiser *Pola*. Though he made a second signal amending his first report, the other destroyers continued in his direction.

Bored with the inactivity of waiting, *Havock* now decided to approach *Pola*, at whom she fired a few rounds. Much to the surprise and perplexity of those on board, the fire was not returned, and the destroyer closed until she was virtually nosing the stern of the Italian cruiser. An astonishing sight awaited them. A large number of men were in the water clinging to rafts or wreckage, and shouting to be taken on board, while the upper deck of the cruiser was thronged with excited and hysterical sailors who rushed aft and kept shouting pathetically to be rescued by *Havock*.

Apparently on seeing the fate of her sister ships, who had been despatched to her assistance after dark, *Pola* had jettisoned all the ready use ammunition near the gun positions in order to avoid the risk of explosions on deck. The Captain had then given the order to abandon ship, but he later rescinded this order, though many men were unable to get back on board.

It was now 2.0 a.m. and the Commanding Officer of *Havock* was faced with a situation which he had never conceived in his wildest dreams. His first inclination was to prepare a boarding party and capture the cruiser, but he was saved from his quandary by the opportune arrival of Captain D. 14 in *Jervis*.

"Am hanging on to stern of Italian cruiser *Pola*," signalled *Havock*. "Shall I board her or blow her stern off with depth charges?"

Captain D.'s reply was crisp: "Get clear."

So ended *Havock*'s adventures. Both she and *Stuart* had been exceptionally fortunate in escaping disaster. Against a less demoralised and more attentive enemy they would almost certainly have been sunk. Each destroyer, however, carried Italian Breda guns, and it is possible that the firing of these caused the enemy to mistake them for their own ships.

As *Jervis* arrived, *Fiume* blew up and sank. *Zara* was still burning fiercely, and four torpedoes were fired into her to complete her destruction, while more destroyers picked up survivors who littered the sea in the vicinity. *Jervis* then proceeded towards *Pola*, circled round to inspect her and, ordering other destroyers to rescue survivors from the water, proceeded alongside. A close view of the upper deck revealed a scene of incredible chaos. Many of the men were half drunk, and the deck presented a shambles of clothing, bottles and rubbish.

Two hundred and fifty-six prisoners, including the Captain, were embarked and *Jervis*, satisfied that no one was left, cast off. Then, from close range, two torpedoes were fired into the hull, and, heeling over, *Pola* sank shortly after 4.0 a.m.

When questioned as to why *Pola* had not opened fire on the destroyers as they approached, a prisoner is reported to have replied: "Well, you see, we thought that if we did you would fire back and sink us!"

While on board *Jervis*, the Captain of *Pola* removed all his badges of rank, saying that they were the outward and visible signs of his command, and now ceased to have any significance. It was pointed out kindly that they still held meaning for his British captors but, though obviously touched by the thoughtful remark, he persisted in his decision. All were most profuse in gratitude for their rescue, and in appreciation for what was done for them on board the destroyers.

Survivors from *Zara* stated that it was probably the intention of the Italian Admiral to sacrifice their division, if necessary, to allow *Vittorio Veneto* to get back to her base. They described the scene on board after the British battleships had opened fire, as an inferno. When lying stopped, their own Admiral (*Zara* was a junior flagship) and Captain went to the quarter-deck and addressed those of the ship's company who had not jumped overboard. Cheers were then given for the King and Italy, and these were followed by the order to abandon ship. The Admiral is believed to have jumped overboard without a lifebelt. He was not seen again.

An Italian Yeoman of Signals, when asked for an account of what had happened, stated that he was asleep at the time and was roused by heavy gunfire. On seeing and hearing explosions all round him, he made the Sign of the Cross, invoked all the Saints he knew, and leapt overboard. There were many stories similar to his.

With numerous survivors on board, the British destroyers formed up and then proceeded to the north-east to rendezvous with the Commander-in-Chief at daylight. The Battle of

Matapan was over at the cost, to the British, of only one aircraft and its gallant crew of two.

. . . . . .

Dawn broke, calm but misty, and disclosed the British battlefleet some fifteen miles to the south of Cape Matapan. From the bridge of the flagship anxious eyes swept the horizon through high powered binoculars. No enemy ships were suspected of being in the vicinity, but apprehension was felt for the safety of British destroyers who were known to have been engaged in night action.

"There they are!" Someone had spotted a low small speck looming larger every moment in the haze to the south.

Every pair of glasses was immediately focussed in this direction. How many destroyers would there be? All started to count as one shape after another emerged from the mist, steaming in two divisions towards the battlefleet as signals winked from search-light projectors across the intervening distance.

"One, two, three, four." They were counted aloud. "The whole twelve are there." The exclamation was made with unashamed relief. A feeling of immense elation gripped every one.

"*Formidable* reports, sir," the Chief Yeoman interrupted, "that she has only three machines serviceable for reconnaissance." He put up his telescope to study the carrier. "She's preparing to fly them off now."

"Hopelessly few," was a muttered remark.

Some two hours later the aircraft returned, having searched to a depth of 80 miles and only discovered wreckage to which numerous survivors were clinging near the scene of action. Risk of submarine and air attack made the question of rescue quite impossible, so the fleet shaped course for Alexandria.

Presently the Commander-in-Chief ordered one of the aircraft to pass a signal to Malta for re-transmission to the Italian Chief of Naval Staff. It read:

"A number of Italian sailors are believed to be on rafts in an area round position 35″ 20′ N.: 21° E. A fast hospital ship is needed to pick up these survivors whom I have not found."

Later in the day, the C.-in-C. called for reports from destroyers of the number of survivors they had on board and how many of them were wounded. To everyone's amusement, Captain D.14's signal from *Jervis* finished with the statement: "The Captain of *Pola* has piles."

"We are not surprised," was the immediate retaliation from the Commander-in-Chief.

Thus ended the Battle of Matapan. It was brought about by the action of one torpedo fired by a Fleet Air Arm aircraft at the *Vittorio Veneto* during that critical period about 11.0 a.m. when the Italian battleship had our cruisers at a disadvantage. Matapan was the probable reason why the Italian Fleet declined to take an active part in subsequent operations off Greece and Crete. Had it done so, the entire war in the Mediterranean might have turned very much to our disadvantage. It is fascinating, therefore, to speculate on the relationship between the course of that one torpedo and the course of the whole war in the Mediterranean.

Chapter 6

A GALLANT EFFORT

ATTEMPT TO RESCUE BRITISH AND ALLIED PERSONNEL FROM KOTOR

THE collapse of official resistance in Yugo-Slavia towards the middle of April 1941 was more rapid than had been anticipated. Events had moved so swiftly that the situation had become utterly confused. No one knew what was happening; whether the entire Dalmatian coast was in enemy hands or what had occurred to units of the Yugo-Slav Navy. One thing only was abundantly clear—the British Minister and other important British and Allied personnel were cut off and, if they were to

be rescued, some drastic action had to be taken. The only
means which promised the smallest chance of success to effect
this rescue was a submarine actually going to the Yugo-Slav
port of Kotor, where the Minister and his staff were believed
to be, and embarking all those with whom it was possible to
get in touch . It was not known whether Kotor was in enemy
hands, and the risks attending such an enterprise were immense,
but Lieut.-Commander H. C. Browne in the submarine *Regent*
was determined to achieve success if it were possible. He was
fully alive to the hazards involved and to the importance
attached to the safe evacuation of the people concerned. Yugo-
Slav authorities were told of the project, but it was considered
doubtful if the message would get through to the proper
quarters.

Leaving Malta on the 17th April, *Regent* passed through the
Straits of Otranto on the 21st, arriving off the Gulf of Kotor
at dawn next day. Apart from distant rumblings and the noise
of a wire striking the hull of the ship while diving through the
Straits of Otranto, the passage had been uneventful. Browne
had no information at all about local minefields off Kotor, the
positions of shore batteries, defence booms or signal stations, so
it was necessary for him to proceed into the Gulf with the
greatest caution.

It seemed quite fantastic to think that in broad daylight
Regent might be entering an enemy port where hitherto friendly
warships might now be flying hostile colours. The unpleasant
consequences that could happen were innumerable and Browne
was determined to be ready for any eventuality. The submarine
was partially trimmed down and the crew at diving stations
prepared instantly to submerge; the bridge personnel were
armed, men were stationed to leap to the gun' at a moment's
notice, and all torpedo tubes were kept at the 'ready.' So that
there could be no doubt whatsoever about his identity the
largest white ensign which could be found flew from the mast.
The risk from mines had to be accepted, and the selection of
the track taken was based on the desire to be sighted at the

earliest possible moment.

Entering the channel between Ostri Point and Mamula Island it was noticed that the former was crowned with a building and masts, obviously indicating the presence of a signal station. At once the Aldis was brought into action and the station was repeatedly challenged. But no notice was taken and the place appeared deserted. That looked ominous.

Regent continued past the small town of Ercegnovi lying apparently peacefully at the foot of the towering mountains on the northern shore, and then up the Gulf as far as Gjenovic where the passage narrows to about 700 yards. At this point a double boom, stretching from shore to shore, barred further progress. There was no alternative but to stop and try to attract attention.

It would have been thought that the sudden arrival of a British submarine would have commanded instant curiosity, but the people ashore were probably too stunned by the dramatic sequence of events and tragedies to which they had been subjected during the previous few days that they were unable to take much interest in *Regent*. Whatever the reason the submarine lay off the boom for an hour and a half, and within hailing distance of the shore, trying vainly to get someone to take notice. The situation was almost ludicrous.

At length a group of Yugo-Slav naval officers were observed approaching along the water front. By dint of frantic waving and shouting they were finally prevailed upon to pay attention and, much to Browne's relief, were seen to commandeer a small boat in which two of their number and a civilian pulled off to the submarine. The civilian was apparently a local pilot and he, with one of the naval officers—a Lieut.-Commander— climbed on board. They were most friendly, but their news was disturbing, conversation being carried on in a mixture of French and English.

"We are no longer at war," the Naval officer disclosed. "Five days ago an armistice was signed between my country and the Axis. Now, everywhere, there are Italians."

So *Regent* was in an enemy-occupied port after all. The armistice had apparently been signed on the very day they had left Malta after which the Germans, who had first occupied

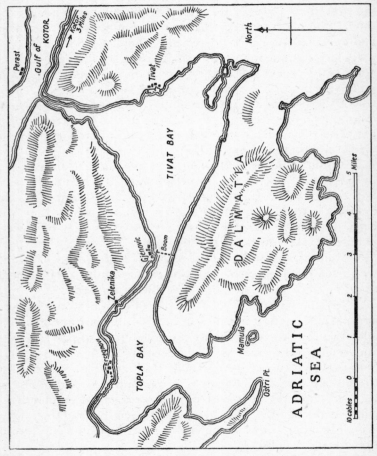

the Kotor area, turned over the whole district to the Italians. With the exception of a submarine and a few smaller craft which had managed to get away, the Yugo-Slav Navy was now lying under Italian control at Tivat, about four miles further up the Gulf. Though the Italians themselves had sent no ships to Kotor after the occupation, there was an Italian Admiral in charge.

"And what is your business?" the Yugo-Slav Lieut.-Commander enquired.

Browne told him that he wanted to get in touch with the British Minister and, in view of what he had heard, felt no surprise when he was told that they had no knowledge that a submarine might be expected. But news about the Minister was encouraging. He was, they stated, at Ecergnovi, the little town three miles to the westward and nearer to the entrance of the Gulf. If *Regent* would go towards Zelenika—half-way towards Ercegnovi—where there was a suitable jetty, the pilot would return to the beach, phone the Minister and suggest he came to this point where boats were available. This he did, the Lieut.-Commander remaining on board to give local advice as the submarine turned round and steered for Zelenika.

The Yugo-Slav naval officer was most communicative. Infuriated by the armistice which had been signed, he was anxious to go on fighting, emphasising how much he loathed the Germans and Italians. Could he possibly escape in *Regent*? Lieut.-Commander Browne willingly agreed to take him and a few of his friends. The Slav then pointed out on the chart the positions of the minefields off Ostri Point, and Browne noticed with considerable interest that he had dived in the middle of one!

On arrival off Zelenika another Yugo-Slav Lieutenant-Commander came on board, while an Italian Army Captain, who was understood to be in command of the troops at Gjenovic, appeared on the jetty.

"Will you please place your ship alongside the jetty?" requested the new arrival.

But Browne emphatically refused. Once alongside it would be difficult to get away in a hurry, and the submarine would be placed in a more hazardous position.

F

"Well, if you won't do that, will you please accompany us ashore and discuss with my Commanding Officer what arrangements you wish to make for the British Minister?"

Again Browne refused. Under no circumstances would he leave his ship, but he was quite prepared to receive the local Commanding Officer on board. With this decision they had to agree and both visitors proceeded ashore to telephone. But, on getting into touch with their Commanding Officer, they were informed that the Italian Admiral had given orders that Lieut.-Commander Browne was to interview him before he was allowed to see the British Minister. When the Yugo-Slavs returned on board with this report, Browne reiterated his decision not to leave the submarine and it was then suggested that he might allow an officer to represent him. Again he refused and a deadlock seemed to be reached. At length, after further argument, Browne agreed to let one of his officers go provided he was given an Italian officer to hold as hostage. Both Yugo-Slav officers then went ashore to get approval for this arrangement, after warning Browne that *Regent* would be fired on by shore batteries if she attempted to move.

As soon as they were gone, Browne reviewed the situation. It was quite clear that the submarine was in imminent danger from land, sea and air attack and that the Italian Admiral was probably prevaricating. On the other hand, he argued, those who had given him his orders knew that Kotor might be in enemy hands, but they attached so much importance to the embarkation of the British personnel that they were prepared to risk losing a submarine. It was therefore his duty to make every effort to get in touch with the British Minister who, according to Browne's information, had been signalled to expect him. To do this, the chance he took of losing an officer and the risk run by waiting for him to make the relatively long journey to Kotor and back was fully justified. At the same time he considered it advisable to destroy all secret books and papers except those necessary for current signals and recognition. This occupied two officers and two men for an hour and a half.

From the bridge of the submarine which remained stopped about 200 yards from the landing jetty, officers and men watched the second Yugo-Slav officer and the Italian Captain conferring on the jetty, from time to time disappearing into what appeared to be the local post office—presumably to telephone. During this time it was strange to see considerable movement of Italian mechanised infantry taking place along the road past Zelenika.

At length, about 12.30, the two Yugo-Slav officers returned with their own Commanding Officer—a Commander—and shortly afterwards another boat pulled out bringing Second Lieut. Bonetti Amando of the 94th Infantry Regiment as a hostage. Lieut. D. Lambert, R.N., then prepared to land, the Yugo-Slav Commander assuring Browne that he had the authority of the Italian Admiral to promise safe conduct of this officer who would be allowed to see the British Minister after being interviewed by the Italian Admiral. As an idea it was sound, but the promise seemed to lack sincerity.

Lambert was warned to be very reticent over what he said, but to make every effort to see the British Minister, find out the diplomatic position and point out Browne's intention to sail that night at the latest. Finally he was told that he would only be left under stress of circumstances—a contingency which it was hoped would not arise.

In case anything untoward happened, Browne now considered it imperative that the Commander-in-Chief should be given some idea of the situation. So he prepared a signal saying that Kotor was in enemy hands, that every effort was being made to find the British Minister, that *Regent* was threatened but that he hoped to leave by nightfall. He then added a list of secret publications which had not been destroyed. At 3.0 p.m. the transmission of the signal was commenced, but difficulty was experienced because of the high mountains surrounding the Gulf of Kotor. Eventually the message was made on full power.

During the afternoon Italian aircraft had from time to time flown round *Regent* performing different aerobatics without taking any offensive action, so when two planes suddenly dived on the submarine about 3.30, no one imagined that the display was any more unfriendly than those previously carried out, and the men on *Regent's* bridge merely watched with idle curiosity. Then something fell. Suddenly Lieut.-Commander Browne realised that this was no demonstration, but a definite hostile act. Ordering men below with the exception of the Officer of the Watch and one Petty Officer, he remained on the bridge to watch this new and unpleasant development. The water was shallow—50 to 60 feet—and very clear, so he instantly decided not to dive, appreciating that a direct hit on the surface would cause less damage both to the submarine and to personnel.

At that moment the first bomb struck the water, exploding on impact about 30 yards on *Regent's* starboard bow, scattering a shower of fragments in all directions and seriously wounding the First Lieutenant. Then, for the next few minutes, there seemed to reign a concentrated fury. At least six more heavy bombs were dropped, all of which fell within 15 feet of the submarine and burst under water in rapid succession. One, indeed, dropped about three feet from the hull, but *Regent* miraculously escaped a direct hit, though she was severely shaken and, at times, positively leapt in the water.

The movement of the submarine upwards and then downwards, in conjunction with the great column of water thrown up, convinced Browne that she had actually been hit forward and was sinking so he gave the only possible order under the circumstances—"Abandon Ship." A moment later, finding that all was well, he cancelled it.

Down below, the experience for everyone was more than unpleasant, but Sub-Lieutenant Anderson, R.N.R., though young and inexperienced, assumed the duties of the wounded First Lieutenant and took over in a most cool and determined manner, restoring the confidence of some of the younger men.

The Engineer Officer, Lieutenant (E.) H. G. Southwood, coolly moved from compartment to compartment looking for defects, helping by his manner to keep up the spirits of the ship's company. On the order to abandon ship, he calmly arranged for the destruction of the remaining secret publications which was actually commenced before the order was cancelled.

Typical of the conduct of the crew was the action of Leading Telegraphist W. Diggins who was still transmitting the important wireless signal when the attack started. Though badly shaken, he remained in the W./T. office and finished making the message which was received complete. The Coxswain, Petty Officer F. A. Young, was outstanding in his coolness and determination, while the engine room ratings concerned calmly set the demolition fuzes when 'abandon ship' was ordered, returning to make them safe in spite of continual bombing, when it was cancelled. E. R. A. Starrett remained quietly at the main blowing panel, even when the order to 'abandon ship' had been given in case he should be required to flood or blow any tanks, and Stoker Petty Officer A. A. Penfold set a fine example by his cheerfulness.

As soon as they had dropped all their heavy bombs, the aircraft swept low and carried out machine gun attacks, at the same time letting go a number of small bombs which burst at the height of the bridge throwing out numerous small fragments, including explosive bullets which burst with a noise like squibs. Meanwhile, machine gun and rifle fire was directed on the submarine from the shore. During this period both Lieut.-Commander Browne and the Petty Officer on the bridge received nasty wounds.

When the attacks were completed, it was quite obvious that, if *Regent* was to be saved, she must leave at once. Though she had miraculously received only superficial damage, the aircraft were bound to return until they had destroyed her. So reluctantly abandoning the British Minister and Lieutenant Lambert, the submarine dived, setting course for the entrance

of the Gulf. From time to time Browne brought her to periscope
depth in order to have a look round, and each time there were
noises indicating that there was firing at the periscope. But
it was singularly ineffective.

Having got clear of the Gulf after about an hour and sighting
no surface ships, *Regent* went deep and shaped course for the
Gulf of Otranto. That night she surfaced. On throwing open
the hatch, Second-Lieutenant Amando, who seemed quite
bewildered by his shattering experience, picked up his cap
and enquired if he could now go ashore! He thought they
were still in Kotor harbour.

The voyage to Malta was uneventful, but trying. Having
lost one officer ashore and with the First-Lieutenant dangerously wounded, the only ones left qualified to keep watch,
were Lieut.-Commander Browne himself and a young Sub-
Lieutenant—and Browne was suffering from a painful wound
in the leg which was rapidly going septic. Then the weather
was bad, and this delayed *Regent* who did not get back to
Malta before 10.0 p.m. on 26th April.

Thus ended a very gallant and daring attempt to rescue
our own people from the grasp of a treacherous enemy.
Though abortive, it had fortunately not ended in disaster.

Chapter 7

THE EVACUATION FROM GREECE
(APRIL 1941)

WHEN our military forces were rushed to the aid of a Greece
threatened by the Nazi hordes who were massing on her
northern frontier, there were many experts who shook their
heads in apprehension. It was regarded as a military mistake,
especially with the small amount of equipment which was
available to us in the Mediterranean theatre of war. But
whether it was a military mistake or not, there were few to
deny that it was a political and moral necessity.

There was, at first, a sporting chance that the Germans

could be held, but the early collapse of Yugo-Slavia, followed later (April 21st) by the capitulation of the Greek army in the Epirus, made the threat to the left flank of the British forces so great that evacuation was the only alternative. Military commentators may say that if this capitulation had not taken place, the Thermopylae line might have been held indefinitely.

Throughout the entire Greek campaign, our greatest disadvantage lay in the inadequate numbers of aircraft available to support our forces. With the German advance these numbers dwindled, and by April 19th there were only seven fighters effective in the whole of Greece—after the 23rd there were none. The fact that there was, therefore, no air support to assist evacuation was to make it all the more difficult and hazardous.

During the second week in April, shipping was held in readiness, and Rear-Admiral H. T. Baillie-Grohman, C.B., D.S.O., was sent to Athens with a small staff to make preliminary arrangements. On his arrival, he was horrified to find the port of Athens almost unusable—in fact, it was barely functioning as a port at all. During the evening of the 6th April a terrific mining blitz and bombing raid had been carried out by the Germans on the Piræus. Most of the damage had been caused by one bomb which had struck a wharf setting fire to the ammunition ship, *Clan Frazer*, which was lying alongside.

This vessel was loaded with 800 tons of explosives which she was in the act of discharging. She had caught fire at 11.30 p.m. and heroic efforts had been made to fight it—all to no avail. At 4.30 in the morning she had blown up with a deafening explosion, and it was this that had wrecked the harbour. Enormous masses of incandescent steel were hurled for considerable distances, starting fires in ships in harbour and in buildings ashore; houses collapsed like packs of cards, tugs and small craft of all sorts were destroyed, cranes and all electric power were put out of action, and many of the ships on fire burnt out and sank where they were. Only a few berths were thus available for shipping.

Because of all this damage and the extensive mining in the harbour, many merchant vessels in Salamis Bay were unable to obtain coal or water, and the majority of them were subsequently sunk by dive bombers. As a port for the evacuation of large numbers of troops, Athens could no longer even be considered.

As soon as Admiral Baillie-Grohman arrived—his correct title was Flag Officer Attached Middle East, and he was therefore known as F.O.A.M.—he started to take control of shipping. Naval officers were despatched to reconnoitre the beaches in order to decide which of them would be suitable for evacuation, while special beach parties, provided by the Commander-in-Chief Mediterranean and consisting of 12 officers and 100 ratings, began to arrive. A caique and local craft committee was also formed to charter and fit out as many local vessels as possible, but the difficulties facing F.O.A.M. were immense.

The news of the collapse of the Greek army in the Epirus made an enemy landing at Patras, in the rear of our forces, a real possibility. The date for the first day of evacuation was then immediately fixed for April 24th. Taking advantage of the confusion into which the country had been thrown, the enemy now advanced with unexpected rapidity, and it was appreciated that the main evacuation would have to take place from the Morea. Beaches to the east of Athens, however, were to be used for the withdrawal of the rear guard.

On the 21st April, and again on the 22nd, the Germans carried out mass air raids on shipping. Except for a small volume of anti-aircraft fire, they were entirely unopposed and succeeded in sinking twenty-three vessels, including two hospital ships and a Greek destroyer. This did not augur well for a successful evacuation, and it was therefore decided that ships must arrive off the beaches after dark and leave not later than 3.0 a.m. Even so, it was realised that, by the light of flares, aircraft could make the operation extremely hazardous.

Special motor lighters capable of accommodating large

numbers of men and running up on low shelving beaches, arrived on the 23rd. Known officially as 'A' lighters and originally designed for the landing of tanks, they were now to prove invaluable for evacuating troops. Six were employed— all except one were eventually lost during the operation. During the day, they were to lie hidden at secluded points on the coast, proceeding to the different evacuation beaches after dark.

Meanwhile, all the light naval forces available, under the command of Vice-Admiral H. D. Pridham-Wippell (V.A.L.F.) flying his flag in the cruiser *Orion*, were being mobilised to operate from Crete. These included six cruisers, nineteen destroyers, three escort vessels and two corvettes. In addition, there were the three 'Glen' liners with their specially equipped landing craft, and eight transports.

The urgent need of all destroyers for the evacuation left none for screening battleships, and there was, therefore, no protection if powerful enemy surface forces chose to interfere. The fact that Taranto was only twelve hours steaming from the scene of operations was always present in the minds of Commanding Officers and added to the hazards of the whole enterprise.

On April 24th—officially described as *Day One* for the operation—the King and Government left for Crete, although this was not disclosed until a few days later. F.O.A.M. in Athens had informed V.A.L.F. of the beaches going to be used that night, but he had so far been unable to make adequate arrangements for the evacuation of the remnants of the British community who still remained in Athens, and numerous wounded.

The sudden appearance of a large Greek yacht, *Hellas*, in the Piræus was, therefore, a welcome surprise, especially when she reported that she had accommodation for 1000 and could steam 18 knots. She was berthed alongside, and about 500 of the British community—mostly Maltese and Cypriots—were embarked together with a number of walking cases from the

Australian hospital. As soon as it became dark *Hellas* was ordered to sail.

Unhappily, as dusk approached, the ominous drone of aircraft was heard approaching. They could only be hostile because there were no others. In the sharp concentrated attack which followed, two bombs struck *Hellas* and she burst into flames, setting fire to the jetty alongside and destroying the only gangway to the shore. With the port already in a state of chaos, no hoses could be made to work for over two hours, and the yacht was totally destroyed. Practically everyone on board, amounting to about 600 persons, perished in the diaster.

The principal evacuation that night was to take place from the Gulf of Nauphlia, the head of which lies about 20 miles due south of the Corinth Canal. A large number was also to be embarked from Raphtis—one of the beaches to the east of Athens.

The force detailed for Nauphlia consisted of the cruiser *Phoebe*, *Glenearn* with her special landing craft, the destroyers *Stuart* and *Voyager*, the corvette *Hyacinth* and the transport *Ulster Prince*. The A.A. cruiser *Calcutta* and another Glen liner —*Glengyle*—were to be detached for Raphtis.

On passage during the late afternoon of the 24th, misfortune occurred. Diving out of the sun, two Heinkels concentrated on *Glenearn*, straddling her with a stick of bombs one of which struck the foc's'le, penetrated the deck and exploded in the paint store. The port anchor and hawse pipe vanished completely, tearing away a great sheet of side plating; the windlass was smashed and fires broke out in some of the forward compartments. These were brought under control and *Glenearn* was able to proceed with the remainder of the force. There were only four men wounded and the valuable landing craft were undamaged.

On arrival off Nauphlia about 10.0 p.m., *Ulster Prince* proceeded to berth alongside, but when about half a ship's length from the mole she grounded. All efforts to refloat her failed and she had to be abandoned. This was doubly unfortunate.

Not only was the force now deprived of her troop accommodation, but she had effectively blocked the harbour, thus making it impossible for a destroyer to berth alongside. Next day she was heavily bombed and left ablaze fore and aft.

About an hour after the force had arrived, one of the Tank Landing Craft—'A' 5—suddenly appeared, and the expeditious way in which she was handled, embarking large numbers of troops at a time and ferrying them to waiting ships, made up for the unfortunate loss of *Ulster Prince*. The landing craft, too, from *Glenearn* were most efficient and all those awaiting passage —amounting to 6685—were successfully embarked.

Besides troops, *Voyager* took off 160 nursing sisters, one of whom had an unpleasant experience. She slipped and fell into the sea between the ship and the caique from which she was disembarking. Weighed down by her equipment she was soon in difficulties, which were increased by the darkness and the moderate sea which was running. A young Ordinary Seaman from *Voyager* jumped in to her assistance. Both were in grave danger of being crushed between the two vessels which were moving awkwardly in the swell, but the sailor was able to hold her up until they were hauled to safety.

Finally, at 3.45 in the morning, the force proceeded out of the Gulf—*Glenearn* having to slip her starboard cable because she had no windlass. They later met *Calcutta* and *Glengyle* who had, between them cleared the beach at Raphtis of 5700 troops. With the help of another 'A' lighter, their embarkation had proceeded smoothly.

The returning convoy was only attacked once from the air, about noon, but all the bombs dropped ahead of the ships, and they reached Crete without damage during the late afternoon of 25th April.

On the second night evacuation was arranged to take place from Megara, a beach due east of the Corinth Canal and twenty miles from Athens. Meanwhile, F.O.A.M. and the joint planning staff left Athens and, passing in to the Morea soon after midnight, established themselves near military

G.H.Q. at Myli on the Gulf of Nauphlia.

Two 'A' lighters had been detailed to work from Megara but, during the day, one was bombed and sunk without casualties. The other—'A' 19—though bombed, was still serviceable and managed to be present for the evacuation on the night of the 25th.

The A.A. cruiser *Coventry*, three destroyers, *Wryneck*, *Diamond* and *Griffin*, with the transports *Pennland* and *Thurland Castle* were sailed from Suda so as to arrive Megara after dark. At 3.10 in the afternoon, two Junkers 88 suddenly attacked, scoring an unlucky hit on the foc's'le of *Pennland*. But the Master of that transport refused to allow a thing like that to interfere with his objective. Shoring up the damaged bulkheads, he reported that he could still steam at 7 knots, and continued with the remainder of the force.

There was a fresh wind blowing from the north, and it was soon discovered that the damage sustained was more extensive than was at first thought. *Pennland's* speed grew less and less until, at 5.0 p.m., the Master regretfully reported that she was no longer seaworthy. There was no alternative but to leave her and, with *Griffin*, to stand by and escort her back to base, she turned to the south while the remainder proceeded towards their destination.

An hour later, *Pennland's* difficulties seemed to increase and *Griffin* was requested to close within hailing distance. The destroyer had just reached a position about 50 yards on her beam when a Junkers 88 suddenly glided down out of the sun and with its engine shut off. Although *Griffin* opened fire immediately, two bombs were dropped, one of which fell between the two ships and the other struck *Pennland* abaft the funnel.

There was now no hope of salvage as the transport burst into flames, heeled over and began to sink. Boats were lowered and the ship abandoned by all those who were alive, *Griffin* eventually rescuing 250 survivors.

Meanwhile, at Megara, things were going well. The force

arrived at 10.0 p.m. All the ships' boats available were immediately lowered into the water, and with the help of the 'A' lighter and a number of local caiques, 5900 troops were embarked without interference. This was 900 more than the number expected. By 4.0 a.m. the beaches were reported clear, boats hoisted and the ships ready to sail.

The expected air attacks began soon after daylight and persisted throughout the day. At 7.30 a.m. six machines dived on the force, and *Thurland Castle* suffered from near misses but had no casualties. Three hours later, twelve of the deadly Junkers 87 were observed, but the concentrated fire of the cruiser and destroyers caused their bombs to fall wide. Then, to everybody's amazement, three Blenheims appeared from Crete, shot down at least one of the enemy and damaged others. A half-hearted attack from more Junkers 87 occurred about noon, and a final one at 1.15 was equally ineffective.

II

A few hours after F.O.A.M. and his staff had crossed the bridge spanning the Corinth Canal and entered the Morea, an event of unpleasant consequence occurred. Following a dive-bombing attack of unusual intensity, large numbers of German parachute troops were suddenly dropped near the Canal and rapidly gained command of its approaches. This unexpected success on the part of the enemy transformed the whole operation into one of extreme urgency, and made it imperative to strain every effort to evacuate the maximum numbers possible that night. Myli in the Gulf of Nauphlia, Nauphlia itself and Tolon were now threatened from the land, and by the following morning would undoubtedly be occupied by the Germans. The military rear-guard, cut off from retreat across the Corinth Canal, could only be evacuated from the beaches east of Athens.

For the night, therefore, of the 26th/27th April, three big

evacuations were arranged—from Raphina and Raphtis east of Athens, from Nauphlia, and from Kalamata in the extreme south. At Raphtis the evacuation was completely successful, *Carlisle* and two destroyers—*Kandahar* and *Kingston*—and the transport *Salween* clearing the beaches of 4720 men, although only about 3000 were expected. An 'A' lighter again proved invaluable.

Glengyle and three destroyers stood off Raphina a little further up the coast where a swell hampered embarkation alongside. The beach was well organised and another 3500 were embarked, but owing to the vital necessity of leaving up to time, a further 500, including the naval beach party, had to be left behind. Most of these were rescued on the following night.

In the early afternoon of the 26th, *Calcutta*, with the destroyers *Isis*, *Hotspur*, *Griffin* and *Diamond* escorting *Glenearn* (who was still serviceable after her bombing on the previous day although she had no anchors) and the troopships *Slamat* and *Khedive Ismail*, left Suda for the Gulf of Nauphlia.

A stiff northerly breeze was blowing, but otherwise there was nothing to disturb the serenity of the afternoon. Indeed, as the sun began to dip towards the horizon, it was hoped that, by hugging the east coast of the Morea—the route chosen to minimise the chance of detection—the *Luftwaffe* might be avoided. But there was no such luck.

"Here they come!" someone shouted about 6.0 p.m.

As *Calcutta* hoisted the red flag to indicate the alarm and men rushed to their positions at the guns, two waves of *Junkers* 87 and 88 were observed approaching at a great height. Almost immediately they broke formation and the air suddenly filled with the shriek of diving planes, the bursting of shells, the crackel of machine guns and the whine of falling bombs. The noise was terrific, and it was at once obvious that the aircraft were manned by crack pilots of the *Luftwaffe* who were both determined and skilful in attack. Around practically every ship bombs fell within a few yards, scattering spray and splinters and causing several casualties: *Slamat* and *Khedive Ismail* were slightly damaged by near misses, but it was *Glenearn* who again suffered most. A near miss punctured her already damaged hull in several places and flooded the engine room, putting main engines and the dynamo out of action. The ship was helpless and could not possibly proceed to Nauphlia. Her invaluable landing craft would not be available to assist with this important evacuation and, in addition *Griffin* had to be detailed to tow her back to Crete. She did, however, lower and send her landing craft inshore to the beach at Monemvasia where a subsequent embarkation was planned.

With the fall of darkness, danger from air attack decreased, but the knowledge that the enemy must be fully aware of the composition and probable destination of the force was by no means re-assuring. Though the night was dark, the towering cliffs and forbidding mountains were visible on either side, closing in on the ships as they proceeded at high speed up the Gulf. Two nights before these wild regions had appeared deserted—dark and very still. But now they seemed to be alive with dancing lights; tongues of dull red flame from numerous small fires; sweeping rays from the head lamps of many vehicles.

In one of the cruisers officers were puzzled.

"There seems a lot of activity ashore tonight, sir," the officer of the Watch remarked.

"If you want my candid opinion," his Captain announced after studying the phenomenon for a few moments through his glasses, "all these lights are coming from the enemy who seem to be in occupation of the entire countryside. Our men would never give away their position like that, but to the Germans it makes no difference. They must know we haven't got the aircraft to disturb them."

It was an eerie sensation to realise that those lights, twinkling on the mountain sides above the darkened ships were, in truth, the visible signs of an enemy whose purpose was to destroy the troops they were proceeding to rescue. It emphasised the hazards of the enterprise, showing only too clearly how it was in the power of the enemy to thwart it. A light carelessly disclosed in one of the ships, a star shell fired at random from the shore, the sweep of a questioning searchlight or a flare dropped by some inquisitive plane—any of these might reveal

the ships and provoke the concentrated fire of shore batteries
or devastating attacks from the air against which the ships
would be helpless.

Officers alternately shivered in the fresh breeze and discussed
the situation on the bridge of a cruiser.

"I've just seen a signal," the Captain announced, "to say
that V.A.L.F. himself is proceeding at full speed with *Perth*
and *Stuart* to give us a hand. I presume he wants to try and
make up for the loss of *Glenearn*."

A sharp gust of wind, blowing down the Gulf, whistled
through the rigging and flecked the sea with angry wavelets.

"Boat work won't be too easy in this, sir," the Navigator
remarked.

The Captain shook his head. "I'm afraid not. Those
landing craft in *Glenearn* are the only answer for these conditions."

About 10.0 p.m. land loomed ahead, speed was decreased
and, as quietly as possible ships crept to the anchorage off
Nauphlia. Anchors had scarcely touched the bottom when
boats were swung out and lowered, tossing alongside in the
choppy sea, and throwing up a fine spray which beat coldly
in the faces of the crews.

"Warn all coxn's," the Captain told his Commander, "not
to overload their boats."

In a few moments the boats had disappeared in the darkness,
made more dense by numerous lights from the enemy in the
hills above.

A large shape nosed its way round the stern of the cruiser.

"Thank goodness, we've at least got one 'A' lighter!" The
Captain heaved a sigh of relief.

Presently the Commander appeared. "Practically all the
officers and men in that 'A' lighter are wounded from a
bombing attack," he said. "It was as much as I could do
to make them accept quick medical attention. Fortunately
none of the wounds are serious, but they must be suffering a
lot."

G

"Good chaps." The Captain stared to seaward through his glasses. "This looks like *Orion*."

From astern, the black waters of the Gulf were parted by the white waves of oncoming cruisers. The disturbed waters subsided and the shape of ships coming to rest loomed in the darkness. Immediately, the creek of davits and the purr of motors starting up, indicated that no time was being lost in sending boats inshore.

For a good half hour there was silence. To those waiting on board the time seemed longer, and it appeared as though the lights flashing among the wooded hills above were growing more numerous. Surely, was the unvoiced opinion, it was only a matter of minutes before the enemy realised what was taking place immediately below them! Then somebody hailed from the upper deck, shouts were heard in reply, and small boats, thrashing their way through the spray and crowded with huddled figures, were seen approaching. Willing hands leapt to the gangways and jumping ladders to help files of soaked, weary figures on board.

As each man stepped on to the upper deck he was given a packet of cigarettes, paid for out of the ship's canteen fund. The troops were then led below to the mess deck where sandwiches were waiting for them, and sailors drew cocoa and soup from the galley, but, for the most part, all that the soldiers wanted was a hot drink and sleep. Breakfast next morning was more difficult, but each man was provided with a couple of boiled eggs, tea and bread.

Meanwhile, as soon as the boats were empty they turned round and proceeded at their best speed back to the shore. It was slow laborious work with the boats available, and the gusty weather conditions prevailing. It held dangers, too, apart from what the enemy could do. Early in the proceedings a whaler full of troops in tow of *Calcutta's* motor boat capsized. The soldiers, disliking the cold spray had suddenly surged to the lee side of the boat with inevitable disaster. Fortunately, no lives were lost, but the delay was aggravating.

A destroyer's motor boat broke down inshore and had to be abandoned. The crew escaped in a local caique with a Brigadier-General they had contacted, and sailing down the coast all next day, finally landed at Monemvasia, where they were rescued two nights later.

A few more local caiques—slow unhandy craft—did their best to assist, but difficulties were immense, and the time taken to embark and transport troops to the waiting ships was painfully slow. Indeed, the transport *Khedive Ismail* eventually had to sail without a single soldier because there were insufficient boats to bring any to her.

It was of vital importance to sail no later than 3.0 a.m. so as to be out of sight of land, and beyond the reach of dive bombers by daylight. This had been carefully impressed on all ships beforehand. As the hour approached it was realised that many men would have to be left ashore, but it would be certain suicide for all to delay, and it was hoped that those left behind would be able to find their way down to the next beach further south, at Monemvasia, where it was intended subsequent evacuations should take place. This the majority of the 3000 troops left behind, actually did; passing within hailing distance of the Germans.

Shortly before 3.0 a.m. when only about 4500 soldiers had been embarked, orders were received to hoist all boats and prepare to get under way. But an unforseen delay occurred.

Dawn was awaited with trepidation; and when the day actually broke land was still in sight and the whole force within easy reach of dive bombers.

Almost immediately the 'Red' air raid warning was sounded and three *ME*. 109 were observed skimming out from the lee of the land flying low. Shortly afterwards the air was full of diving planes, and the whole force was subjected to a continuous series of attacks. Though towering columns of water showered on the decks of practically every ship, only one really suffered and that was the transport *Slamat*. Within the first ten minutes a large bomb struck her just before the bridge and the ship was soon a mass of flames.

Two destroyers—*Diamond* and subsequently *Wryneck*, who had been carrying out anti-submarine patrols during the night and therefore had no troops on board—were detailed to proceed to her assistance and rescue the unfortunate survivors. The rest of the convoy proceeded at full speed towards Crete, pursued by more planes who were fortunately unable to achieve any further success.

As the day wore on and darkness settled over the harbour of Suda Bay, anxiety was felt for the two destroyers who had proceeded to the rescue of *Slamat*. Shortly after 12 o'clock a signal had been received to say that about 500 survivors had been picked up and that they were proceeding to Crete. By steaming at full speed they should have arrived hours before dark, but, as time went by, anxiety deepened into a real fear that they had met with some further disaster. Accordingly, V.A.L.F. ordered the destroyer *Griffin* to proceed at once to sea and find out what had happened. But not until two days later did the grim story come to light.

For *Diamond* to proceed alongside a blazing ship in a heavy swell was no mean task, but the destroyer managed, after great difficulty, to embark the majority of troops. Others had jumped overboard or pulled away on boats and rafts, a few of which proceeded to *Diamond;* and one boat full of troops capsized alongside. Jumping in to the rescue, sailors hauled the soldiers inboard, but it was all a long and tiresome business. By this time, however, *Wryneck* was there to assist, and succeeded in picking up all the men clinging to wreckage in the water or drifting in boats and rafts.

By noon the rescue work was complete. The troopship was still afloat and, despatching her with a torpedo, *Diamond* formed astern of *Wryneck* and proceeded at 28 knots towards Crete.

About an hour later disaster occurred. Unseen and unheard, dive bombers suddenly swooped low out of the sun with their engines cut off. There was scarcely time to press the alarm rattlers before the decks were riddled with machine gun bullets, causing many casualties, and bombs had found their marks. In *Diamond* a near miss forward made a large hole in her side and another bomb hit amidships, exploding in the engine room and bringing down the mast and after funnel.

Steam began to blow off in all directions, but a Stoker Petty Officer heroically leapt to the upper deck emergency valves to release it. He then helped to get men up from below and assisted to free the carley floats, as all boats were smashed. Those who could abandoned ship, and in a few moments the sea was littered with men clinging to wreckage. The enemy, not satisfied with his success, again swooped low and machine gunned the men as they struggled in the water. The planes then made off as *Diamond* suddenly rose perpendicular in the air and disappeared stern first. On one carley float was the Commanding Officer with a number of men, but in order to make room for others he plunged over the side. He was not seen again.

Wryneck, meanwhile, had been equally unfortunate. Taken unawares in the same way as *Diamond*, a bomb had struck the foc's'le near 'A' gun, killing or wounding everyone at the gun, on the bridge and in the sick bay, shattering the stokers' mess deck and killing numbers of stokers and soldiers. Another fell down the engine room hatch bursting all the steam pipes, and a third bomb struck aft setting an ammunition locker on fire. With the ship moving at about 18 knots, with a heavy and growing list to port, and with steam pouring from the engine room, an E.R.A. managed to open the safety valves; then, with others, he got a whaler away which was practically undamaged, and released the rafts before abandoning ship.

The only officer to survive of the two ships was the Engineer of *Wryneck*. After having put an army officer survivor to bed in his bunk, he was changing in his cabin when the ship was struck. Though wounded in several places by splinters, he proceeded on deck to ensure that the boilers were made safe and to assist with the fire and repair parties; but when he saw the hopelessness of the situation he returned to his cabin to find the army officer lying in oil fuel with both his legs injured. Assisting him to the upper deck, he adjusted his lifebelt and left him by a raft while he went forward to examine the ship.

The Engineer's own pneumatic life-belt had been damaged by splinters, but someone fortunately strapped a cork belt round him as he made his way forward. By now the deck port side was awash, and the list and oil fuel which made the decks slippery, coupled with weakness from his own wounds, caused him to lose hold, and he slid overboard. Floating clear of the propeller as the ship still moved ahead, he saw the list grow steeper until *Wryneck* finally rolled over and disappeared. After half an hour, he was assisted on to a raft and eventually hauled into the whaler with twenty-three others.

It seemed incredible that the boat could keep afloat, but men sat in the holes made by bomb splinters, and tin hats were used to bale the water out. At first it was decided to take all the rafts in tow so as to keep everyone together, but towards dusk, the wind freshened and there was a grave risk of each one damaging the others which necessitated the tow being cast off. Later that night *Griffin*, who had been sent to discover what had happened found all the rafts—but the whaler was some miles away.

The party in the whaler consisted of eighteen men from *Wryneck*, four from *Slamat* and one Sergt.-Major R.F.A. Most of them were in a bad state from wounds and exhaustion. There was nothing with which to construct a sea anchor, so the stern of the boat was turned into the wind, and relays of men on the oars kept her from broaching-to.

At night the wind was cold, so the men who were worse clad took frequent spells at the oars and, when not pulling, huddled close together and clasped each other to maintain circulation. Dawn on the 28th found the boat thirty miles from Milo, when an *Ajax* class cruiser was sighted about six miles to the east. The firing of Vereys lights failed to attract attention and she passed them by. A little later, two destroyers were sighted and three *Blenheims* passed close overhead; but again they were not seen and their spirits began to fall. They were lucky enough, however, to pick up one orange which was carefully divided and augmented the meagre water ration provided from a damaged barricoe half full of contaminated water.

At noon they appeared to be closing Ananes Rock, which lies about sixty miles north of Suda and, as everyone was practically exhausted, it was decided to make the rock and rest in its lee. As they approached a small cove about 4.0 p.m. after having paddled and drifted some forty miles, they were amazed to see people waving at them from the shore off which a caique was lying. To their great relief they turned out to be army officers, some other ranks and a few Greek families, all of whom had escaped from Athens and were lying hidden during the day.

By removing ballast from the caique, room was made for the survivors, but it was decided, in case of accidents, to tow the whaler with the caique's skiff inside it.

After dusk they set course for Suda making a speed of about five knots under sail and with the auxiliary motor running. They arrived safely next morning when they were overtaken by an 'A' lighter and towed into harbour.

Thus ended one of the most tragic features of the evacuation from Greece. Out of over 1000 officers and men in the three ships, only one officer, forty-one sailors and eight soldiers were rescued.

III

The evacuation from the shores of the Gulf of Kalamata, which is contained by the sweep of the coast to the north and west of Cape Matapan, had been successful. It was understood that there would be about 8000 men to be embarked from Kalamata itself, the small port at the head of the Gulf. Accordingly a force consisting of the cruiser *Phoebe*, the escort vessel *Flamingo*, the destroyers *Hero*, *Hereward* and *Defender*, and the transports *Dilwara*, *City of London* and *Costa*

Rica arrived off the port about 10.0 p.m.

There was nobody there. Although troops were in the neighbourhood, they had not received information that the Navy would be coming for them that night, due to telephone communication and army W./T. having broken down. Thus, precious minutes were wasted while contact was made with the military authorities. Then things moved swiftly. Berthing two at a time, the three destroyers, carrying 1200 or more each trip, ferried 8650 troops to the waiting transports. If it had not been for the initial delay they might have collected another 3000, but they had already remained for longer than was wise and it was after 4.0 a.m. when the convoy finally sailed.

From 8.0 a.m. onwards, the day was full of excitement as one attack after another developed from the air. First, ships were subjected to high level bombing, during which one soldier in *Defender* was killed by a splinter, but no damage was caused. One aircraft was shot down. Twenty minutes later, eighteen *Junkers* 87 dived out of the sun, but encountered such heavy fire that their bombs missed; one aircraft was destroyed and at least one other seriously damaged.

The *Junkers* 87 were followed at intervals by two more high level attacks and, at 12.15 twelve *Junkers* 88 made a second attempt at dive bombing, followed by another wave of *Junkers* 88 an hour later. Although there were several near misses, intense anti-aircraft fire put the bombers off their aim and no damage was inflicted on any ship.

At 2.45 the seventh and last attack was delivered—again by *Junkers* 88 diving out of the sun. In spite of sustained opposition from the ships' guns, a near miss damaged *Costa Rica* who had on board some 2400 troops. She immediately stopped, took on an alarming list and reported that her engine room was flooded and that the boiler room was rapidly filling up.

Defender immediately went alongside, followed in turn by *Hereward* and *Hero*, although *Costa Rica* gave every indication that she would roll on top of them at any moment. Together they embarked everyone on board while, on her other side—where the swell precluded a destroyer from berthing—the transport lowered boats and rafts in which a few soldiers pulled away. Except for one man who dived overboard and cracked his skull on a raft, every single man was saved—a tribute not only to the skilful and courageous handling of the destroyers, but also to the discipline of the troops, who assembled on the upper deck and quietly waited their turn to disembark into the rescue craft.

On the off chance of being able to salve *Costa Rica* at dusk, *Hero* remained in the vicinity while the rest of the convoy proceeded. But, within a short time, the damaged vessel rolled over and sunk, and *Hero* rejoined the other ships, all of whom reached Suda Bay in safety without further opposition.

Throughout that day—Sunday, 27th—F.O.A.M. was busy at Monemvasia. On the night previous he had been at the different beaches in the Gulf of Nauphlia and had hoped, himself, to get on board a destroyer which would land him further down the coast. But matters were confused and as time went on, he commandeered a caique. Apprehensive that its slow progress would never give him time to see that the beaches were properly organised at this new point of evacuation, he was relieved when he saw a destroyer moving down the coast. Signals from the caique were answered and F.O.A.M. soon found himself on board *Havock* who landed him at Monemvasia before dawn. There he met the landing craft which the damaged *Glenearn* had thoughtfully sent ashore at this point, and arranged for them to be scattered among the beaches. Fortunately they were not observed by enemy aircraft.

News was received that the retirement on Monemvasia was going according to plan, but that the troops would not be ready for evacuation until the next night—28th/29th. This also applied to Kalamata where a further operation was intended. A final evacuation had, however, been arranged on Sunday night for the rear guard from the beaches east of Athens.

Here the cruiser *Ajax* and three destroyers—*Kingston, Kimberley* and *Havock* arrived soon after 10.0 p.m. It was reported

that 800 men were at a beach eight miles to the north of
Raphina, surrounded by the enemy and unable to move either
up or down the coast. *Havock* was immediately detailed to go
there and managed to rescue every man without a single
casualty.

Meanwhile, at Raphina the embarkation proceeded smoothly
and rapidly, the presence of an 'A' lighter being essential to
success. *Ajax* herself embarked 2500 troops.

By 3.50 a.m. the beach was cleared and, with a total of
4640 troops on board, the four ships shaped course for Suda
Bay at high speed. No air attacks developed and they reached
their destination in safety.

The night of Monday, 28th, was the fifth, and last, day for
the main evacuation. Throughout that day air attacks were
persistent all along the beaches. 'A'5—the lighter which had
performed such invaluable work in the Gulf of Nauphlia and
had now moved south—was discovered, bombed and sunk,
but not before she had shot down at least two of the enemy.
Fortunately there were no casualties. The landing craft from
Glenearn, however, remained undetected and, after dark they
were moved down to the points of embarkation.

At 10.0 p.m. the warships were expected; but the time
passed and nothing happened. Had communication failed, or
had the ships gone to the wrong rendezvous? F.O.A.M. was
anxious and at 10.30 sent one of *Glenearn*'s craft out to try
and make contact. A few minutes later she was able to distinguish a long shape to seaward. It was the destroyer *Griffin*.
Ajax and three other destroyers—*Havock*, *Hotspur* and *Isis*—
followed and were quickly led to the beaches.

The embarkation was remarkably well carried out from five
different points and, by 3.0 a.m. the beaches were clear. To
F.O.A.M. the army organisation in the rear and the discipline
of the troops was magnificent, especially in view of the long
rear guard action they had been fighting all the way from
Salonika. This undoubtedly contributed to the success of the
operation.

F.O.A.M. then embarked in *Ajax* with military headquarters staff and, leaving behind a mass of burning motor transport, the force sailed for Suda with 4320 troops. They arrived safely without incident.

Another small and successful evacuation had been taking place that night from the island of Kithera where a number of troops had been reported. Between them, the New Zealand escort vessel, *Auckland*, and the corvettes *Salvia* and *Hyacinth* had rescued 810 men belonging to miscellaneous units.

Meanwhile, a force of cruisers and destroyers had proceeded to complete the evacuation from Kalamata. As wireless communication had been unsatisfactory, the destroyer *Hero* was sent on ahead to make the necessary preparations.

But that day, disturbing events had been taking place in and around Kalamata. As waiting troops lay hidden in the olive groves and in the light cover on the slopes behind the town, wave after wave of hostile aircraft bombed and machine-gunned them mercilessly, attacked the shipping in the harbour, dropped mines off the entrance, smashed up the quays and did considerable damage to the town.

Then, in the early afternoon, there fell an ominous silence. As a small party of Hussars were meditating whether they should emerge from the wood in which they had taken cover and make their way towards the sea, they suddenly heard the noise of engines coming down the road. A sergeant, sharing the pleasant prospect of a lift, stepped out and held his hand up to stop an armoured car which had just turned the corner. To his horror he was greeted by a burst of fire. An enemy motorised column was approaching the town! Diving rapidly into the woods again, the Sergeant and his companions made a difficult dash across marshy country to the beach eastward of Kalamata, where they were fortunate enough to find a boat in which they put to sea and—after various hardships and adventures—were picked up by *Isis* two nights later.

Meanwhile, the German column swept into the town taking everyone by surprise. They burst into the offices of the Naval

Captain who had arrived as Sea Transport Officer, captured him, his staff and the embarkation officers and, hurrying them into a car, sent them inland.

On the beaches and in the neighbourhood, fifth column activities spread rumours and alarms. Germans were reported everywhere; their numbers were grossly exaggerated and the general situation was so conflicting, that clashes frequently occurred between parties of our own troops who consisted of details belonging to many different units.

At length, about 9.0 p.m., a Lieut.-Colonel of the R.A.S.C. decided that the strength of the German force was much weaker than was previously conjectured—actually there were only 300 with two 60-pounder guns. Collecting parties of Australian and New Zealand troops and some R.A.S.C. details, he organised a counter-attack and drove the enemy out of the town, taking over 100 prisoners and putting one of their guns and an armoured car out of action.

At this moment *Hero* was approaching the port. From ten miles off big fires had been observed raging in the centre of the town, and as she closed, tracer bullets in profusion indicated that heavy fighting was in progress. Suddenly from a position to the east, an army signalman began to flash: "Bosche in harbour."

After passing this message to the approaching cruisers, *Hero* proceeded to investigate and, steaming close inshore, landed the First Lieutenant to try and contact the army to the south-east of the port. As the situation was so confused and firing frequently broke out from positions thought to be friendly, this officer was as likely as not to find himself landing on a beach held in strength by the enemy. But he persevered, found the Brigadier and immediately began to arrange for a beach evacuation to take place.

Because of the mines off the harbour entrance, numerous sunken caiques and the damaged quays, it was considered quite impracticable to embark troops from the harbour—even when the Germans had been driven from the town—and for this, and other, reasons, the cruisers did not approach. Previous embarkation arrangements had been thrown into complete chaos by the capture of the Naval S.T.O. and his staff.

Soon after midnight, however, *Kandahar*, *Kingston* and *Kimberley* joined *Hero* and, with their own boats, the four destroyers embarked as many troops from the beach as time and their inadequate transport permitted. The numbers rescued were pitifully small in comparison to those it had been hoped to bring off, but the 400 who did actually embark represented the utmost effort on the part of the destroyers under most difficult and unexpected circumstances.

At dawn next day, the Germans arrived in force, and the Brigadier believed that he had no alternative but to surrender. To expose troops to another day of intense bombing, surrounded by superior forces, and with no ammunition or food, invited annihilation. Small parties, nevertheless, refused to heed the order to lay down their arms, and made off down the coast. Some found boats in which they put to sea by night, and laid up during the day; others assembled on beaches north of Cape Matapan; all experienced alarming adventures and endured considerable hardship, but their firm conviction that the Navy would not let them down provided them with that urge to keep on going. Their trust was justified for, on the two succeeding nights, destroyers swept the waters where they were likely to be found, picked up many caiques full of escaping soldiers and proceeded to lonely beaches where small parties had gathered in the blind faith that they would be rescued. The Navy will come, was their contention: and—the Navy came.

IV

Apart from the sweeps into the Gulf of Kalamata, one more minor operation took place. It was reported that about 2000 troops had managed to reach the island of Melos—about 65 miles north of Suda—where they were holding out in the hopes of being rescued. The destroyers *Hotspur* and *Havock* were accordingly despatched to collect them on the night of April 30th.

Detailed information was, however, vague, and, on arrival, *Hotspur* lowered an armed boat's crew with orders to proceed inshore and discover if the troops were really there or if the island had already fallen to the Germans. The boat soon made contact with officials ashore who gave the crew a great welcome. Two days before, a German aircraft had landed and demanded the surrender of the island, threatening severe bombing reprisals if it was refused. The islanders did refuse, and they had since been subjected to intensive air raids. A large number of magnetic mines had also been dropped and numerous wrecks were said to encumber the harbour. Yes: there were troops to be rescued, but nothing like two thousand.

The destroyers then got busy. Because of the reported mines and wrecks it was considered unwise to approach too close. So they lay off while ships' boats, assisted by local craft, did all the ferrying. By 3.30 in the morning they had embarked 700 which represented the total number to be rescued, and then proceeded at 25 knots for Suda.

But as they passed the narrow outer entrance, the destroyers received a shock. Close under the cliffs there was a submarine entering. She was in an ideal position to deliver an attack but, in the somewhat confined waters, the destroyers could take no effective offensive action. The submarine dived immediately. Depth charges were dropped by both *Hotspur* and *Havock* as they made violent alterations of course and speed, but nothing more was seen of the enemy.

Thus ended a somewhat melancholy operation which might well have become a disaster. Without air support, the risks were tremendous, and had the enemy taken full advantage of his superiority in this connection, the story might have been different. The evacuation beaches could have been bombed by the light of flares, and it is surprising that the Germans did not do so. Another factor which could have influenced the outcome of the operation was the Italian Fleet. With their numerical superiority, they could have destroyed many of our ships had they displayed the slightest initiative.

For different reasons events ashore had moved with un-expected swiftness, communications had inevitably become chaotic and, in many cases, had broken down altogether. Intelligence, therefore, was only approximate. Hence, there is every reason to regard the evacuation of over 50,000 officers and men (out of a total of 55,000 whom it had been hoped to rescue) as a great achievement.

Chapter 8

SUBMARINE ACTIVITIES
JANUARY 1st — MAY 1st, 1941

DURING the opening months of 1941 ceaseless activity was main-tained by our submarine patrols operating between north Africa and Italy, in the Adriatic and Tyrrhenian Sea. Although the number of boats available had been increased with the arrival of some of the new, and particularly suitable, *Unity* class of submarines, it was a long way short of what was wanted. Nevertheless, there was seldom a patrol without, at least, one success to its credit. The toll on Italian shipping grew heavy; but not heavy enough to prevent substantial reinforcements reaching north Africa.

On passage from Alexandria to Gibraltar at the beginning of the year, *Pandora* (Lieut.-Commdr. J. W. Linton) had some exciting experiences. She was actually proceeding to the United Kingdom in a half crippled condition, so was not expected to carry out much in the way of a patrol. Off the island of Pantellaria Lieut.-Commdr. Linton was able to glean invaluable information about the routes used by Italian shipping to clear their own minefields. Though he did not find himself in a position to attack, he was able to make accurate observations of the courses taken by the enemy in this dangerous area.

In spite of engine defects which forced her to surface within fifteen miles of Pantellaria and remain stopped for five hours in bright moonlight, *Pandora* arrived safely on 8th January in the area east of Sardinia where it was intended she should maintain a short patrol. A few hours before dawn on the 9th, Lieut.-Commdr. Linton suddenly sighted a single dim light to the eastward, obviously emanating from an incompletely darkened ship which was approaching. Because of this fortunate lapse on the part of the enemy, he was able to reach an excellent position to attack as soon as it was light enough to see.

As dawn broke he was rewarded. Two heavily laden supply ships, each of 4000 - 5000 tons, three miles apart and unescorted, were closing his position. Pressing in to a range of 1400 yards, *Pandora* fired two torpedoes at the leading ship. One hit, causing a great portion of her hull to crumble away into the water as she rapidly settled down while the crew abandoned ship. The attack on the second ship was remarkable. Instead of taking immediate avoiding action when her consort was torpedoed, she came straight on, only starting to swing as *Pandora*, from a position fine on the bow, fired a torpedo. This missed, whereupon Lieut.-Commdr. Linton adopted a most unorthodox but successful ruse. Showing more periscope and thus making a big 'feather' in the water, he disclosed his position, prompting the merchant vessel to turn directly away from him. Thus, he could determine her exact course and no allowance had to be made for her speed—an ideal target in theory, especially at short range, but difficult in practice. The torpedo fired hit her right in the stern, and she started to sink rapidly.

Counter-attacks followed later in the day, but they were all singularly ineffective. Without further incident, *Pandora* reached Gibraltar on 14th January.

Among the more interesting patrols at the beginning of the year was that carried out between 14th January and 7th February by the minelaying submarine *Rorqual* (Commander R. H. Dewhurst) when she laid an effective minefield at the head of the Adriatic. She sailed from Alexandria on 14th January, embarked mines at Malta on the 21st and proceeded at noon next day towards the Straits of Otranto. Having encountered good weather, Commander Dewhurst found himself twenty-four hours ahead of schedule; but he pressed on, accepting the risk of numerous Greek submarines who had been ordered to retire eastwards so that there could be no question of mistaken identity when *Rorqual* was supposed to pass through the area next day.

The risk was justified, though it might have had fatal consequences. About six o'clock next morning a submarine was suddenly seen about 800 yards on the starboard beam. She had the advantage of light, had clearly sighted first and immediately turned to attack. As there was every chance of it being Greek, *Rorqual* altered course away just in time and dived.

Without further excitement and sighting smoke from time to time, *Rorqual* proceeded north until, three days later, she was near the Gulf of Fiume. Here she laid her first minefield. That it had, at least, some measure of success was proved by a subsequent broadcast from Rome reporting the "sinking by torpedo" of the Italian destroyer *Francesco Stocco* which "blew in half off Fiume at the end of January." As no British or Greek submarines were in this area at the time reported, obvious conclusions were drawn.

After laying a second minefield off Ancona during daylight on the 28th, *Rorqual* proceeded to patrol near the Dalmatian coast north of Kotor, where Commander Dewhurst was able to observe shipping creep close inshore along that coast. There were numerous opportunities for attack, but it was quite clear that none could be carried out in this area without violation of Yugo-Slav neutrality; so it was decided to search for a route outside territorial waters.

The afternoon of the 31st brought excitement. Shortly before 1.0 p.m. the masts of a ship were sighted through the periscope and, on closing, Commander Dewhurst discovered that they belonged to an armed tug towing something which looked like

H

a bombardment lighter. Anyhow, it had two guns of 4-inch - 5-inch calibre, a smaller H.A. gun, and was fitted with a kind of control top. These guns were covered. It was not considered worth while expending a torpedo on the tug, and the lighter was of such shallow draft that it was more than likely a torpedo would run underneath it. So, if reasonable surprise could be obtained, Commander Dewhurst decided to surface and attack with his gun.

About half-past one the opportunity occurred. Suddenly surfacing 500 yards abaft the beam of the lighter, *Rorqual* closed the tug at full speed, firing rapidly. After the fifth salvo, the men in the tug came to life and replied with both their guns just as *Rorqual* started to hit. The tug's after gun was quickly put out of action and the submarine then shifted target to the lighter, where a hit was scored amidships with the first round. But there was still life left in the tug who, after a short pause, re-opened fire with her foremost gun. Four or five more hits were obtained by *Rorqual*, and the tug was soon blazing furiously fore and aft.

Both guns on the lighter were now in action at a range of less than 500 yards, and the splashes of shells round the submarine were getting closer and closer. At that range, the Italians could not go on missing although the lighter was on fire amidships from the single round which had been fired at her. So *Rorqual* closed the gun action and dived, while those in the tug who were still alive frantically abandoned their flaming vessel.

From periscope depth, Commander Dewhurst decided to try and sink the lighter with a torpedo. As he manoeuvred into position several explosions were heard followed by splashes of water round *Rorqual*, and these were at first thought to be bombs from aircraft who had been summoned to the rescue. It was quickly established, however, that they were in reality bits of the tug being blown out in a series of explosions.

The burning tug kept drifting across the field of vision, and it was not until 2.30 that a chance occurred to fire the torpedo.

But at a shallow depth setting, the torpedo became temperamental. It broke surface and started to wander so erratically that it even endangered *Rorqual* by turning right round in its track. There was no alternative for the submarine but to go deep to escape its own torpedo.

On returning to periscope depth the tug was still burning furiously and the lighter, with a smaller fire, had a pronounced list to port. Men, however, were still manning the guns in the lighter ready for the submarine to re-appear, so Commander Dewhurst waited hopefully for another chance to surface and make a surprise attack.

At 3.45 p.m. aircraft arrived, forcing *Rorqual* to go deep. The last she saw was the tug almost completely gutted, but the condition of the lighter was unchanged, although a muffled explosion was heard as the submarine dived. When she returned to periscope depth two hours later, there was nothing in sight. Subsequent intelligence reports indicated that it was the Italian tug *Ursus* which had been sunk with considerable casualties, but that the floating battery had unfortunately been rescued by a Yugo-Slav merchant vessel who took it in tow. The Italian version of the action of course claimed that the submarine had been destroyed.

With no further incident *Rorqual* returned to Alexandria on 7th February.

About six weeks later *Rorqual* had another series of exciting and successful experiences during the patrol she carried out between 18th March and 12th April. Embarking mines at Malta on the 22nd, she left that same evening for a patrol area off Palermo on the north coast of Sicily. Having laid her mines, she proceeded to patrol the suspected route between Naples and the north-west corner of Sicily.

For the next three days she was unlucky. Frequent anti-submarine air patrols forced *Rorqual* to dive deep more often than she wanted, and ships sighted were, for the most part, well out of range. One which did actually present itself as a possible target was zig-zagging so violently that three torpedoes fired by *Rorqual* all missed. But on Sunday, 30th March, she was more fortunate.

In the early hours of the morning a fully laden tanker of just under 4000 tons was sighted at a range of about two miles and steering to the south-west on a steady course. Commander Dewhurst found himself in a good position to attack. After one abortive attempt he fired a second salvo of torpedoes from a distance of 1000 yards, scoring a hit underneath the funnel. The tanker settled down rapidly by the stern with a heavy list to starboard, but then hung in this position for some time. This was unsatisfactory, so *Rorqual*, not wishing to expend another torpedo, surfaced and fired five rounds of high explosive shell into her undamaged side. Three hits were scored and she began to settle more rapidly. As the submarine turned away to the north-west only the bow of the tanker was showing above water at a steep angle.

An hour later *Rorqual* received a signal from Captain 'S' One, ordering her to proceed towards the Straits of Messina with the object of intercepting any damaged Italian warships returning after the Battle of Matapan. In particular, it was hoped to intercept the crippled battleship *Vittorio Veneto* if she was making for Genoa or Spezia.

Soon after dawn on the 31st, when in her new patrol area, two destroyers were sighted proceeding to the north at high speed. Had there been any damaged ships in the vicinity, Commander Dewhurst argued, all available destroyers would be employed on escort duties. Thus, when he sighted a 'U' boat as a speck on the horizon in the early afternoon, he had no hesitation about using her as a target for his remaining torpedoes. Approaching undetected to a range of 1000 yards he fired a salvo of five torpedoes. Fifty seconds later he was rewarded by seeing a pillar of smoke and water rise abreast the 'U' boat's conning tower, followed an instant later by a double explosion as a second torpedo hit further aft. For a few seconds the bow of the 'U' boat remained showing at a steep angle, the rest of the submarine having disintegrated in a cloud of brown smoke. It is unlikely that there were any survivors.

Having expended all her torpedoes, *Rorqual* shaped course for her return journey.

The most fruitful area of operations during this period was, however, off the Tripoli coast, although two notable successes were scored off Calabria. Counter measures off Tripoli were generally more dangerous than elsewhere and, on 21st February, after sinking a heavily laden merchant ship in convoy, *Regent* (Lieut.-Commdr. H. C. Browne) was subject to persistent depth charging. Before she could fire any more torpedoes, escorting destroyers had made for her position and the first salvo of four depth charges was dropped unpleasantly close. In the submarine, glass was shattered, lights extinguished; many rivets were started causing leaks, while water gushed in through the stern glands into after machinery spaces. The boat took on a steep angle, and for some time was difficult to get under control.

One of the most successful patrols in this area was that carried out by *Upright* (Lieutenant E. D. Norman) towards the end of February. At 2.40 on the morning of the 23rd, Lieutenant Norman sighted a darkened vessel which was violently zig-zagging. In spite of this he manoeuvred into a position from which he could fire torpedoes. One hit, and the resulting explosion was so great that it was quite obvious that a valuable cargo had been sunk. This was in fact the case, the ship in question being the tanker *Meteor* with 1700 tons of petrol.

Forty-eight hours later three vessels were sighted in line ahead. The night was very dark, and *Upright* found herself almost in the track of the column. Running out, she attacked on an advancing turn and fired four torpedoes at the second ship. The last torpedo hit underneath the bridge and the ship sank almost immediately. It was the cruiser *Armando Diaz*. Counter-attacks from escorting destroyers followed quickly, but they did no damage.

A successful attack on a south-bound convoy in the same

neighbourhood was made by *Utmost* (Lieut.-Commdr. R. D. Cayley) during the forenoon of 9th March. The escort was allowed to slide by at a range of 200 yards and then *Utmost* turned to attack the largest ship in the convoy—an 8000 ton transport packed with troops. Two hits were scored, the first explosion being so heavy that *Utmost* was lifted bodily and shaken from stem to stern. The counter-attack consisted of depth charges inaccurately dropped, which probably killed most of the survivors swimming in the sea. Before leaving the scene, *Utmost* had a quick look round, saw the remaining merchantmen steaming away at full speed; but of her target there was no trace.

On 28th March—again in daylight—*Utmost* scored another success against an important convoy south-west of Lampedusa. There were six heavily-laden merchantmen, and Lieut.-Commdr. Cayley managed to avoid the escort, firing a salvo of four torpedoes. The first of these hit a 12,000-ton vessel— the largest in the convoy—and another found a smaller ship of 6000 tons. It was impossible to assess the damage as the submarine was forced to go deep, but it appeared that the escort were too busily engaged rescuing survivors than to spend time counter-attacking.

An attack which must have had a strong moral as well as material effect on the enemy occurred off Malito on the Calabrian coast during the forenoon of 5th March. *Triumph* (Lieut.-Commdr. W. J. W. Woods) was patrolling close in shore when two ships were suddenly sighted rounding Cape del Armi on the southernmost tip of Italy. They were of about 2500 tons each and both were fully laden. For a few minutes they were obscured in a rain squall. When it had cleared, *Triumph* was greeted by the truly remarkable sight of these two ships approaching the coast in her vicinity and coming to anchor. There was no escort. The submarine immediately closed and, with one torpedo, hit and sank the nearest vessel. It was then expected that the second would slip her cable and make away. Instead, the crew abandoned their ship, which was speedily despatched by *Triumph* to join her consort. The whole incident took place not more than half a mile from the shore and must have been watched by numbers of people.

In almost the same position, but further out to sea, *Parthian* (Commander M. G. Rimmington) achieved a success ten days later. On this occasion a convoy of three ships—two merchant vessels with a tanker in between—was sighted passing Cape del Armi on an E.S.E. course. It was strongly escorted, but *Parthian* managed to reach a suitable position about 2100 yards on the bow, from which she fired at and hit the leading merchant ship. Although one of the escorting vessels immediately turned towards the position of the submarine indicated by the track of her torpedoes, Commander Rimmington managed to fire a second salvo at the tanker. She also was hit, but *Parthian* could not wait to see the final result. Immediately after the last torpedo of the second salvo had gone, the first of a series of four or five depth charges exploded as the submarine went deep. These were disturbingly close shaking the boat severely but, in spite of subsequent depth charging, *Parthian* managed to steady on a retiring course and get away.

Towards the end of her patrol off the Tripoli coast in the middle of March, *Truant* (Lieut-Commdr. H. A. V. Haggard) was instructed to examine the harbour at Burat and, if possible, attack shipping lying there. A reconnaissance of the harbour was made on the morning of the 19th and the Commanding Officer decided to attack, that night, a small laden tanker which he had sighted inside. Lying submerged until dark off a buoy marking the entrance, *Truant* surfaced at a quarter to eight and, when just light enough to see, proceeded to the attack.

The enemy appeared as a dark shape, and buildings ashore could only be seen when lit up by lorry head-lights. Lieut.-Commdr. Haggard crept to within a range of 400 yards and then fired two torpedoes. But, instead of the tanker going up in a sheet of flame, there were two loud explosions ashore as the torpedoes hit near the pier. Unnoticed by *Truant*, the

tanker must have discharged her cargo during the day and
was now so light that the torpedoes must have run underneath
her. This was a bitter disappointment. It was necessary to
come to full buoyancy and turn on main motors in order to
clear the tanker's quarter as there was little room to manoeuvre.
As the conning tower slowly came abreast the after deck house
and only a few yards from it, a man came out, leant over the
guard rail and expressed evident annoyance. With a cry of
"Il Duce!" *Truant* passed from earshot and proceeded out of
harbour.

Besides those recorded, there were many other—though
perhaps less spectacular—successes during the period under
review, testifying to the resolution displayed by our submarines
at a time when their numbers were still too few to make any
really serious inroads into the flow of supplies from Italy to
North Africa. Their gallant efforts, however, must have convinced the enemy of the hazards facing them at sea which grew
more and more dangerous for them in the ensuing months.

Chapter 9

THE LAST THROUGH CONVOY

H.M.S. QUEEN ELIZABETH JOINS THE MEDITERRANEAN FLEET — MAY 1941

"*H.M.S. Queen Elizabeth* is to be attached temporarily to
Force H."

This signal was received when the ship was operating in
the Atlantic. It caused surprise. Force H was the official term
which included the ships under the command of Vice-Admiral
Sir James Somerville, based on Gibraltar. This command had
been much in the limelight operating either in the Atlantic
or Western Mediterranean, and everyone on board welcomed
the chance of belonging to it.

A few days later *Queen Elizabeth* reached Gibraltar. Dawn
was breaking as she passed Tarifa, the stone lighthouse marking

the southernmost point of Spain—an extended delicate finger
in the centre of the Straits. The Rock, with impressive majesty,
towered into a bank of cloud softly tinted by the rising sun,
and from Europa Point there flashed the challenge from the
signal station. Forty minutes later the battleship, having taken
a great sweep round the Bay, was passing through the northern
entrance to berth alongside the detached breakwater. The
Flagship of Force H, the veteran battle-cruiser, *Renown*, lay
alongside the southern mole, her fine lines proudly silhouetted:
astern lay the aircraft carrier *Ark Royal* who had already performed notable service in many parts of the world, and "sunk"
time after time by the wishful thinking of the enemy; two
or three cruisers were at buoys in the centre of the harbour,
and the penns were packed with destroyers.

Curious officers accompanied the Captain to a staff meeting
on board the flagship in response to an urgent signal. No one
in *Queen Elizabeth* had the remotest conception of the reason
for their sudden change of plans, but a general opinion inclined
to the bombardment of some Italian port. It was, therefore,
with immense interest that details of their proposed operation
came to light.

The army in the western desert were in vital need of urgent
military equipment, and the time factor was considered so
important that it had been decided to force a convoy of fast
merchant ships through the dangerous narrows separating
Sicily and Sardinia from North Africa. Considerable opposition
was naturally expected and, in the discussion, the hazards were
not minimised, but it had been agreed that risks were well
worth taking. Force H would cover the convoy to a position
close south of Sardinia; an escort of destroyers and two cruisers
from the United Kingdom would then carry on through the
narrows, meeting the eastern Mediterranean fleet the following
day. *Queen Elizabeth*, though forming part of Force H for the
first part of the operation, was herself to accompany the
convoy, and then join the Eastern Mediterranean Fleet.

As the convoy was not arriving until next day, shore leave

was given, and that afternoon, the narrow streets of Gibraltar—already overcrowded by the additional garrison quartered in the Rock—were thronged still further by six or seven hundred officers and men from *Queen Elizabeth*. It was fun to meet friends from other ships in the old haunts, to gamble on the *fruit* machines in the Bristol and Rock Hotels, or enjoy entertainment of a more stimulating nature at the *Universale*, and, as the evening progressed, sounds of music and revelry floating through the blacked-out café windows indicated that everyone was having a thoroughly cheerful time. Ignorant of their fate, large numbers of both officers and men thronged the shops to make purchases of material, silk stockings and souvenirs for their families before they spent money on their own enjoyment. It was safer that way because, once on the loose, a sailor seldom returns on board until all his money is spent.

Most exhaustive measures were adopted to preserve secrecy about the forthcoming operation, and only those officers who had to make the necessary preparations were allowed to know anything about it. Into the eyes of the remainder and the people ashore, dust was assiduously thrown. The impression given was that *Queen Elizabeth's* association with Force H was to be of a permanent character and, to mystify everyone still more, she was ordered next day to prepare for sea and sail at 4.0 p.m. into the Atlantic. So, when she slipped from the breakwater and, with a small screen of destroyers, sailed to the westward, knowledgeable people began to wag their heads. *Queen Elizabeth's* area of operations, it was felt, was obviously the eastern North Atlantic. But such an idea was quickly dispelled by the Captain when he spoke to the ship's company through the loud-speaker as soon as he could spare a few moments to leave the compass platform.

Queen Elizabeth's immediate role was to meet their convoy in the Atlantic and take over the escort. Later on, further units of Force H would sail from Gibraltar and rendezvous in a position north-west of Cape Spartel, subsequently passing through the Straits under cover of darkness. Thus, by dawn on the next day, they would be well to the eastward and out of sight of land.

With the first signs of daylight the following morning, those on the bridge of *Queen Elizabeth* stared eagerly to the westward, anxious to pick up the first indication of their convoy. As it grew light, a smudge was discerned on the horizon towards which all glasses were immediately focussed.

"That's *Repulse*, sir," the Chief Yeoman announced. It was known that this battle-cruiser was leading the merchant ships as far as the Straits where she would re-fuel and return to her place in the Home Fleet.

The Captain lowered his glasses. "Make the challenge," he ordered. The rapid chatter of the searchlight projector quickly produced answering flashes which spelt out the correct reply, and, as *Queen Elizabeth* closed, five large merchant ships of 12,000 to 15,000 tons apiece, disposed in two columns with destroyers on either bow, were revealed following in the battle-cruiser's wake. More signals were exchanged, followed by a long message from *Repulse* with technical and helpful details about manoeuvring the convoy. *Repulse*, with her destroyer screen, then increased speed, shaping course for Gibraltar, and *Queen Elizabeth* was left in charge. Though only five ships made up the convoy, their cargo was impressive. Decks were crammed with huge cases, tanks and vehicles. Altogether they carried about 300 tanks and over 100 aircraft, besides ammunition and miscellaneous stores most vital to the Libyan campaign. To see those sturdy ships proudly steaming in formation made a fine picture, and one of strength. The idea of a 'U' boat attack—a lucky shot and sudden disaster—seemed fantastic.

There was time to waste. Passage through the Straits was arranged to take place during the interval between moonset and sunrise, so the Navigator worked out a course to the southward as one promising most peace during the day.

"With any luck," he told the Captain, "we'll be able to spend a quiet afternoon, and snatch a bit of sleep."

"We'll need it," the Captain remarked. "There won't be any for either of us tonight."

But soon after 1.0 p.m., just as the Navigator had stretched himself on a camp bed in the chart house, there was a rude disturbance to the contemplation of calm seas and perfect weather conditions. Two corvettes sighted right ahead were frantically signalling.

"We are hunting an enemy submarine," they made.

The Navigator dashed up to the compass platform, as soon as the signal was reported to him down the voice pipe, arriving there an instant before the Captain. To be sighted and reported by a 'U' boat—even if the force was not actually attacked—at this early stage of the operation might prejudice its success.

"To port, I think," said the Captain, swiftly appreciating the situation.

The signal indicating an emergency turn in that direction was rapidly hoisted, answered just as quickly, and all ships heeled over together as they altered away from the threat. The Navigator cursed softly. It would take some little time to re-form the ships into their former cruising order, and then several more alterations would have to be made during the course of the afternoon in order to make the rendezvous with Force H. That rest to which he was looking forward would have to be dismissed.

At 6.0 p.m. the Admiral in *Renown*, with *Ark Royal*, the cruiser *Sheffield* and a number of destroyers were sighted to the eastward and, as they closed, a flag signal could be discerned flying from the yard-arm of *Renown* ordering *Queen Elizabeth* to take station astern of *Ark Royal*. Since it was intended that the convoy and the main body of warships should proceed through the Straits in two separate groups, the escort of the merchant vessels was turned over to destroyers, and *Renown* led Force H down to the southward.

Killing time by steering a variety of courses and thus puzzling any enemy reconnaissance which might be in the neighbourhood, the Straits were finally approached towards

3.0 a.m. It was quite dark, and keeping station on the totally darkened ships ahead, following in their wake when they altered course, and watching for any tendency to get too close or open out, required a high degree of concentration. By discovering the amount occupied by *Ark Royal* in the field of their binoculars when *Queen Elizabeth* was three cables (600 yards) astern in daylight, it was possible, by the same means, for those on the bridge to judge at night whether the ship was in station. There was no other way.

Hopes were high that this part of the passage would be undetected, since it was vitally important to deny the enemy information about their hazardous enterprise until the last possible moment. But suddenly there came across the water the sound of voices; men shouting in alarm and anger; the splash of oars. A signal from *Renown* ordered ships to turn together at once to port, then, to avoid running ashore near Tarifa, another to bring the squadron back on to the original course. Shapes of fishing boats, tossing wildly in the wakes thrown out by the warships moving with dangerous swiftness in the narrow waters, slithered past, their crews frantically gesticulating and shouting volumes of good Spanish curses. How any of them escaped destruction was a mystery, because they seemed to be spread right across the squadron's track.

"That chap's threatening us with the vengeance of all the Saints he knows," the Captain of *Queen Elizabeth* remarked as a chorus of expletives was even heard from the compass platform.

The Navigator grinned. "We don't mind them, sir, so long as they don't call upon the Hun."

"Unfortunate, but it can't be helped," the Captain muttered.

Dawn next day saw all the forces to the eastward of the Straits and out of sight of land. Ten miles to the north of the main body of warships, the convoy was steaming at a comfortable 12 knots escorted by the cruiser *Naiad* and a number of destroyers, while two other cruisers, racing from Gibraltar, were joining astern.

"*Queen Elizabeth* is to join the convoy," the Admiral signalled.

The Navigator had just started to attack a plate of eggs and bacon in the charthouse when the message was passed down to him.

"Damn!" he muttered. "Another ten minutes and, with that inside me, I'd feel a different man!" He dashed on to the compass platform, calculated the course to pass ahead of the convoy and, with the Captain's approval, hauled out of line increasing speed to 20 knots. The time taken to make the distance was, he estimated, a good twenty minutes, there was nothing in the way to cause any anxiety and he began to feel that those eggs and bacon had acquired a high degree of priority. He had been chewing a mouthful when he had appeared on the bridge, a fact which had not escaped the Captain's attention.

"Finished your breakfast, Pilot?" he enquired when the ship was steady on her new course.

"No, sir, I was just going to suggest if I could be spared ———"

"Go and finish it," the Captain ordered. "We'll let you know if we get into trouble."

Thankfully, the Navigator jumped down the ladder to the charthouse. It had several scuttles and two square ports, so he could keep an eye on what was happening. Ten minutes later he was back on the compass platform.

Turning round ahead of the convoy, *Queen Elizabeth* took station on the port quarter. There was an Admiral in *Naiad*, so the Captain was not in command of the escort.

Both forces now proceeded to the east on slightly diverging courses and, to confuse any enemy reconnaissance which might put in an appearance, the convoy made a feint to the north-east when past Cape de Gata, turning to the south-east and east next day. But nothing was sighted in the air or afloat to disturb the serenity of those two days. Towards evening of the second day, aircraft from *Ark Royal* were observed, indicating that the main body of Force H was not very far away.

At daylight the two forces made a rendezvous and, since they

were now approaching the most dangerous part of the whole
voyage, the next twenty-four hours promised to be full of
incident. The convoy continued to be led by *Naiad*, while
Renown, *Ark Royal* and *Queen Elizabeth* operated about two miles
astern. Other cruisers and destroyers were disposed to make
the screen as effective as possible, the whole arrangement
designed to give the maximum security while allowing for
freedom of manoeuvre.

"It is believed," signalled the Admiral towards the end of
the forenoon, "that the convoy was sighted and reported by
enemy reconnaissance at 0800 this morning."

When this message was relayed through the loud-speakers
of *Queen Elizabeth*, a distinct thrill pervaded the ship. Quite a
number of men had yet to experience a bombing attack at
sea, and those in upper deck positions by the A.A. guns began
to look furtively for their steel helmets. The weather was
perfect with the sea like the proverbial mill pond, and it
seemed impossible to believe that at any moment the sky might
be invaded by wings of death—the peaceful air shattered by
gunfire and explosions, and the placid sea itself torn into
mountains of spray by the bursting of bombs.

To allow more freedom of manoeuvre the larger warships
were spaced at a greater distance apart. This also permitted
Ark Royal to operate her aircraft with greater ease, and it was
fascinating to watch the way in which she hauled out of line
to fly on or fly off her machines constantly patrolling overhead,
and then resume her position.

Suddenly, about 2.0 p.m., there were indications that a large
number of enemy aircraft was approaching. The *Air Alarm*
was sounded and full of excitement, men rushed to their action
stations, manning guns, range-finders and other instruments,
clearing away anything that interfered with the supply of
ammunition and making the necessary arrangements for the
damage control organisation. Then, as clusters of black specks
in the almost cloudless sky indicated that attack was imminent,
the order was received to *snake the line*.

"Conform generally to *Renown's* movements," the Captain of *Queen Elizabeth* ordered his Navigator as he took over the conning of the ship from the Officer of the Watch.

Then things happened quickly.

The black specks resolved themselves into *Junkers* 88, *Heinkels* and Italian *Savoias* carrying torpedoes. Splitting up into small groups they swooped upon the ships from different directions, some coming low and others straightening out at a few thousand feet; twisting, turning and diving, at one moment catching the glint of the sun on their wings, at the next appearing black against the background of blue. *Renown* was the first ship to open fire, the flash and billowing smoke from the guns visible some moments before their report was heard. Every other ship, including the merchant vessels in convoy, immediately took up the challenge until the sky was full of bursting projectiles and the air around was stabbed by the tracers of short range weapons.

Then bombs fell, and the sea suddenly became a raging cauldron. Huge fountains of spray leapt high into the air, spreading as they rose and momentarily obliterating other ships from view. Each time a bomb fell, results were awaited with baited breath, and it seemed a miracle when ships were disclosed undamaged—steaming proudly on. A stick of bombs straddled *Ark Royal;* others fell close under the port bow of *Queen Elizabeth,* and a tremor ran through the great battleship. Sometimes the whine of bombs, as they fell could be heard above the noise of gunfire; at others the first indication was the splash. The volume of fire from the capital ships and cruisers was devastating and created curtains of bursting shells through which the enemy were forced to press their attacks. Before this hail of exploding metal, aircraft were seen to crumble and crash in flames, but there always seemed to be others to take their place.

There was much to distract the Navigator's attention from his duties on the bridge of *Queen Elizabeth*—the violence of the encounter—the noise—each helped to make the task of navigation more difficult. Once, he found himself sailing dangerously close to *Ark Royal*, who was combining efforts to avoid bombs with operating her own aircraft. There was only one thing for him to do—concentrate solely on handling the ship "snaking" first to one side and then to the other, and pay no attention to anything else going on. The Captain's chief concern was torpedo bombers, and occasionally he would direct the Navigator to alter more to the starboard or port, to throw them off their aim. But the T./B. aircraft did not press their attack: they dropped their torpedoes from a considerable range, as if in a hurry to be rid of them, and get away as quickly as possible from the devastating fire of the warships.

It was a grand sight to see the handful of Fulmars of the Fleet Air Arm, harassing the enemy though hopelessly outnumbered, diving through the bursting shells in pursuit of their quarry and paying no attention to the close range-fire from the ships which menaced them as well as their opponents. At least three or four enemy aircraft were destroyed by their efforts, others damaged and many more deflected from their targets.

As quickly as the attack developed it passed. At one moment there was a raging inferno, at the next everything was peace again. Apart from a few rapidly disintegrating smoke bursts in the sky from the final rounds of the A.A. guns and the wreckage in the water of several enemy planes, all was as it was before the attack developed, *for not one ship had been damaged*.

"Aircraft, apparently in distress, bearing Red eight-oh," a look-out suddenly reported.

"That's one of our own Fulmars doing a victory roll," the Pilot of *Queen Elizabeth's* Walrus announced, studying it through his glasses.

He was right. On came the plane, diving, twisting and turning like some fantastic wild bird, expressing in breathtaking flight the feeling of victory. *Ark Royal*, hauling out of line into the wind, hoisted a signal telling the machine to

I

land and then, before resuming her position between *Renown* and *Queen Elizabeth*, flew off another patrol.

"There's bound to be another attack soon," the Captain prophesied. "Pass the word for all hands to be prepared to close up at short notice, and keep the armament in the second degree of readiness."

There was not long to wait, and a few hours later, another group of aircraft was detected approaching at a great height. The alarm was sounded and all positions were scarcely manned before the bombs again began to fall and pandemonium raged. The attack on this occasion was carried out by both high and low level bombers, but no torpedo carrying aircraft put in an appearance. Once more the terrific barrage put up by the ships, and the stout-hearted efforts of *Ark Royal's* fighters confused the enemy and no ships were hit, although there were some dangerous near misses.

"That fighter of ours really is in distress," the Captain of *Queen Elizabeth* remarked, when the attack had passed, indicating an aircraft with smoke streaming from its tail, rapidly losing height.

As he spoke, the aeroplane fired the customary distress signal, and pan-caked into the sea. Fortunately, the crash was not far from one of the escorting destroyers, who immediately proceeded to the scene, where the crew were found only slightly injured on being rescued.

The convoy sailed on, and towards 7.0 p.m. the point was reached at which it had been arranged for Force H to part company. Turning 180 degrees to port, *Renown* led *Ark Royal* in a great curve, while *Queen Elizabeth* continued on her course to close the convoy which was now forming into single line ahead. Suddenly a few miles to the north, three large aircraft were sighted flying towards the east and only a few feet from the surface of the sea. The fact that they were so low, and proceeding in the same direction as the convoy, led people to suppose at first that they were friendly machines. Then a destroyer opened fire, and, as they turned making straight for

Ark Royal, it was suddenly realised that they were torpedo bombers.

The volume of fire then opened was terrific, but still they came on. *Renown* had just completed her turn, *Ark Royal* was following round, and *Queen Elizabeth* was altering course slightly to starboard to gain her new position astern of the merchant vessels. But, with the aircraft carrier as their objective, and showing the greatest resolution, the enemy pressed home his attack in the face of a barrage put up by every kind of weapon. It was the most spectacular incident yet experienced, and how the machines managed to continue on their course was a miracle. Shells burst all round them, tracer bullets were seen to enter their fuselage, but still they came on. At length, one was seen to crumble and crash, but not before it had dropped its torpedo at a range which must have been less than 200 yards. The other two released theirs at about the same distance; then, banking sharply to starboard, made straight towards *Queen Elizabeth*, passing so close to her port side, and only just above the level of the sea that hardly any guns could be depressed sufficiently to bear. Only from the bridges could any machine guns open fire and the Captain himself, seizing a twin-Lewis mounted on the compass platform, poured a stream of lead into one of the machines in whose cockpit could be clearly seen the faces of the crew. This aircraft wobbled, recovered slightly, then with its consort managed to escape and rapidly disappeared towards the south-west.

It was fortunate that *Ark Royal* was already under helm and turning rapidly when this unexpected attack developed. Thus she was able to comb the tracks of the torpedoes aimed at her and escape damage, but the incident doubtless provided the opportunity for the enemy to make another extravagant claim that this famous ship had been sunk.

In this dramatic manner, Force H parted company.

An hour later the sun set, and the full moon rose. All was apparently quiet. But the number of hazards which the convoy might now have to encounter were varied in the extreme—

attack by surface forces in the moonlight ranging from heavy ships down to fast 'E' boats, dive-bombing and torpedo bombers, the fire from the shore defences at Pantellaria, submarines and the continual danger from mines. Each, or all, might occur at any moment, but the principal menace was regarded as the heavily mined waters of the Sicilian channel.

Orders had been given to pass through certain positions which, it was believed, would provide a clear passage through the minefields. To ensure the greatest safety from mines, therefore, the merchant vessels had been placed in line ahead with destroyers—also in line ahead—disposed on either beam in order to give the convoy as much protection as possible. *Queen Elizabeth* brought up the rear, a cruiser led each of the destroyer lines and *Naiad* remained ahead of the convoy.

It was one of those perfect nights with the sea like a mirror in its smoothness, throwing up wakes of gleaming phosphorescence as the darkened ships moved on. By the light of the moon it was possible to see nearly every vessel from the bridge of *Queen Elizabeth* and, although their dull colour was designed to render them as inconspicuous as possible, their hulls were nevertheless reflected. But this romantic setting was not appreciated.

"About the worst possible conditions for a show like this," the Gunnery Officer muttered.

"I imagine that was all taken into account when the operation was planned," the Captain replied, "and they considered that the urgency for this convoy to arrive justified the additional risks caused by the moonlight. Besides," he added as an after-thought, "they'd have to do some of the passage with a moon, and it was probably considered preferable for the first part to be done during the dark period."

In view of the hazardous nature of this critical part of the voyage, all hands were kept closed up at action stations ready to react instantly to any threat. The compass platform of *Queen Elizabeth* was thronged with additional officers and men, but only a proportion were actually keeping watch, others being allowed to sleep in different corners. The Captain sat on a high stool in his special corner of the bridge, the Navigator had another in the opposite corner, and, between them the Gunnery Officer was huddled on the deck. Occasionally, the Navigator would slide down from his perch, take a bearing of Cape Bon lighthouse, flashing regularly from the tip of Tunisia, and check his position on the chart. Otherwise, there was little movement unless someone called for a cup of cocoa.

Shortly after midnight, course was altered more to the southward towards the island of Pantellaria, and all ships had barely followed round when, somewhere ahead of *Queen Elizabeth*, there was a sudden "woomph" which immediately galvanised everyone to a state of instant watchfulness. At first it was difficult to make out what had happened as there was no flash or any gunfire.

"Somebody's exploded a mine in their paravanes," the Captain decided.

Scarcely had he made this remark when there was another big explosion close ahead which made *Queen Elizabeth* shudder. A sheet of flame stabbed the night, seeming to split one of the merchant vessels in half and, when it died down, the air was heavy with a cloud of smoke. As the smoke cleared it was possible to deduce what had happened. The *Empire Song*, who was fourth ship in the convoy line, had actually struck a mine. For a few minutes it looked as if she had escaped serious harm for, to the amazement of those in *Queen Elizabeth*, the five merchant ships still appeared to be steaming unconcernedly in line ahead.

But gradually ships at the end of the line began to 'bunch' as the speed of *Empire Song* grew less and less, until *Queen Elizabeth* was forced to reduce to about six or seven knots to avoid collision. Then, under these awkward circumstances, a number of aircraft was suddenly detected approaching from the north-east and it was realised that a marvellous target, silhouetted against the moon was presented to them.

Naiad ahead opened fire: then some destroyers; and above

the gunfire could be heard the noise of aircraft, very close on the port side. It was hard for *Queen Elizabeth* to open fire unless she actually sighted the plane, as she was almost completely surrounded by ships and only able to steam at 7 knots. She offered a magnificent target against the moon. Suddenly the noise of aircraft rose to a crescendo, and a machine was sighted very close on the port quarter coming straight for the ship.

Immediately all the close range weapons opened fire, somewhat regardless of other ships, and above the din the Captain yelled the order—Hard-a-starboard—shouting in the Navigator's ear to put on revolutions for 22 knots, to which call the engine room staff nobly responded. Every form of noise was made on the siren, hoping that ships would clear out of the way, which they did, and *Queen Elizabeth* began to swing. Almost immediately after sighting, the aircraft was observed to drop her torpedo at not more than 300 yards range, and those on the bridge waited for the explosion. It did not come. The stern had swung clear in time. So low and so close was the aircraft that she hopped over the quarterdeck, finally disappearing in the darkness on the starboard side, apparently still intact.

The Captain dashed to the starboard side of the bridge and leaned over. Then, grabbing the Navigator, he pointed to the white phosphorescent wake of a torpedo passing only about 20 feet clear of the ship's side and parallel to it.

"That's a damn close one," he remarked as the din subsided. "Reduce speed now and straighten up."

At once *Queen Elizabeth* eased to slow as she was brought round to the course of the convoy. The firing had died away, and no further attacks appeared to be developing, but by now, ships appeared to be more bunched round *Empire Song* than ever. Then it could be seen that she had received a mortal blow, was slowly losing all her way and was on fire forward. Hauling out to starboard, the rear merchant ship overtook and passed her helpless consort, increasing speed to catch up with the remainder of the convoy. *Queen Elizabeth* and destroyers followed. As the battleship passed, it was possible to look down on the decks of *Empire Song*, to see them crammed with tanks and aircraft, all of which would probably be lost, and to observe the crew quietly making preparations to lower boats. Meanwhile a destroyer was moving alongside to embark survivors and see if there was any hope of saving the ship. But when the convoy had passed on, and all the crew of *Empire Song* had been taken off, there was a sudden terrific explosion. Flames had penetrated the magazine causing the whole ship to blow up in a sheet of flame, lifting tanks, guns, aircraft and motor vehicles high into the air where they seemed to hang grotesquely before they fell into the sea. To the destroyer lying only a few hundred yards away it was a terrifying spectacle, and one fraught with considerable danger to the crew, as the air was full of falling debris. A complete lorry did, in fact, crash on to her decks amidships. Casualties were, however, surprisingly few, most of them occurring in one of the destroyer's boats which was approaching *Empire Song* with the intention of putting a party on board to try and save the ship.

The course now led direct for Pantellaria, looming up distinctly in the moonlight. All was again quiet. Officers and men on duty swept the sea and sky with their glasses, and those standing-by dozed fitfully at their posts. At 2.30 in the morning an alteration of course was made more to the eastward, in order to leave the fortified island about four miles to starboard. Everything was still and very silent, but the atmosphere was charged with tense excitement. At any moment the shore batteries might open fire in conjunction with an attack by 'E' boats and more torpedo bombers for, in the conditions prevailing, it seemed incredible that the force could pass so close without being sighted. Besides, the Italian garrison must have had a report of its position, course and speed, a few hours earlier when the aircraft had attacked, and seen the gunfire. But nothing happened. Grim and foreboding as Pantellaria appeared, the island, to all intents and purposes, was fast asleep!

The moon sank lower and for a short space there was darkness. Gradually a pale dawn began to break, revealing grey, unshaven faces on the bridge of *Queen Elizabeth*, the litter of dirty cups, the remains of sandwiches, even pieces of orange peel and chocolate wrappings dropped by midshipmen. The Navigator looked at the mess and shuddered. He always loathed what daylight revealed on the compass platform, in whose cleanliness he took so much pride. Turning to his 'Tanky' he made a gesture of disgust, grumbling about the filthy habits of midshipmen. At the same time he looked in the direction of more senior officers whom he strongly suspected of causing much of the litter. Grinning wanly, the Midshipman summoned a messenger with a mop and bucket, an action not altogether appreciated by other officers who were expected to move from comparatively comfortable positions to allow the deck to be scrubbed. Smiling at the disturbance he had caused, the Navigator gathered up his charts and retired to the charthouse.

After the clear night and two days of uninterrupted fine weather, low clouds began to spread across the sky, wind tossed the sea into angry wavelets, and a light mist hampered visibility. Pantellaria was now well astern and soon units of the Mediterranean Fleet would be sighted. The Navigator of *Queen Elizabeth* was not surprised, therefore, when, looking through one of the chart-house scuttles, he suddenly saw the mist ahead broken by the light of a signalling projector. It was from the first of a flotilla of destroyers come to relieve those already on the screen who had to be diverted to Malta to fuel. As the relieving destroyers spread out to take up their positions, those that had accompanied the convoy from Gibraltar formed up in line ahead and were soon swallowed in the mist to the north.

More flashing from the east, and this time three specially fitted anti-aircraft cruisers were revealed, and they were followed by yet more destroyers. Then there were flashes overhead and identification signals fired from the sky, as

Beaufighters from Malta suddenly appeared and circled round.

The Navigator studied the weather, and looked at the fighters. "We ought to be pretty safe from attack now, sir," he remarked to the Captain.

The Captain grunted. "Don't talk too soon. If the blighters can find us, these weather conditions are to their advantage."

He had scarcely spoken when the *Air Alarm* was sounded, followed by the noise of men rushing to their stations and manning the guns from which they had been released at dawn. Enemy aircraft had been detected, and soon an escorting destroyer on the port wing opened fire as the planes were sighted.

"Bearing red nine-oh!" somebody shouted.

"Open fire!" yelled the Gunnery Officer.

A machine had swept through the clouds and was diving down towards *Queen Elizabeth* from the port beam. Pom-poms and four-point fives broke out into a roar, and machine guns chattered, giving the aircraft a severe welcome. It went on diving, tried to straighten out, then plunged wildly into the sea.

"Good shooting!" the Captain exclaimed as a cheer went up from those who had been watching.

Fortunately, the enemy was not attacking in force, or, if he was, only a few planes had been able to locate their target. Although further reports were received, attacks were intermittent and then carried out by only one or two machines. At least one more was destroyed by the fighter patrol, and no ships received hits.

Towards noon, through the haze to the northward, there loomed the shapes of three battleships, an aircraft carrier, cruisers and attendant destroyers. It was the main body of the Mediterranean Fleet and the sight was impressive. Signals were exchanged, then the great ships turned away and were lost in the mist. Presently they re-appeared on the same bearing and a signal was flashed from the Commander-in-Chief.

"*Queen Elizabeth* is to be in station astern of the battlefleet by 1900."

"Let's allow plenty of time and be there by 1800," the Captain told the Navigator. "When should we move off?"

It was decided to accept an hour for the manoeuvre.

When the time came to change station, the mist had thinned and a pale sun peered fitfully from behind low clouds. As *Queen Elizabeth* parted company with the convoy, it was apparent that she was not the only ship to take up a new position, for the whole fleet suddenly seemed to romp into activity. Destroyers and cruisers were altering their dispositions at high speed, some steaming north and others south; some closing in and others opening out, but all disposing themselves in accordance with a plan for the coming night. Only the battlefleet to the north and the merchant vessels to the south remained steady on their course. Thus, as *Queen Elizabeth* moved over to her new position, care had to be taken to avoid collision; and frequent alterations of course, which upset all previous calculations, had to be made. But the battlefleet was reached without mishap, signals of welcome were flashed, and the ship turned up into station at the end of the line. *Queen Elizabeth* had joined the Mediterranean Fleet.

Darkness fell, and, with the rising of the moon, the mist seemed to clear away. Though romantic, this was unfortunate, and it was, therefore, no surprise when the alarm was sounded, and the approach of aircraft detected. Deduction suggested that there were numerous machines approaching from each side and, as they closed, the order for rapid barrage fire was given. The result was the most terrific pyrotechnic spectacle anyone present had ever witnessed, for the danger was so acute that no attempt was made to conserve ammunition, and the rate of fire from the numerous combined high and low angle guns in each capital ship was enormous. It was as if sheets of darting flame enveloped each ship as broadside after broadside from both starboard and port batteries fired hundreds of projectiles at the approaching aircraft.

The noise was indescribable. Enemy machines appeared to be pressing in close on *Queen Elizabeth's* port side, and the

Captain ordered the Navigator to put the wheel to starboard. But this manoeuvre brought the ship almost within the arc of fire from her next ahead in the line, and it had to be abandoned. No one ever knew the result of this action, but the attacking aircraft met such heavy gunfire that they turned away without dropping their torpedoes—at least, no tracks were sighted—and some of them must have been damaged, if not utterly destroyed.

At length the firing subsided and it was possible to speak.

"I don't suppose you've ever had a party like that before, Guns," the Captain of *Queen Elizabeth* remarked.

The Gunnery Officer grinned. "Hope we don't have too many of them, sir, otherwise we'll run out of ammunition."

"Yes, I was thinking of that, but they'll attack again without doubt."

But the Captain was wrong. Gradually the moon became obscured, billows of white smoke rolled off the sea, and within a very short time, the ships were enveloped in a thick fog which was rare for the Mediterranean. An alteration of course to throw out the enemy's assessment of their future position was then made and one danger was removed. But there was a new anxiety, that of following darkened ships in thick fog—so thick that it was hardly possible to see the length of the foc's'le. Stern lights were, however, switched on, and by this means it was possible to distinguish the next ahead in sufficient time to avoid collision. This anxiety was, of course, only felt by those on the bridge; the remainder of the ship's company could sleep—if they could find a corner where the piercing note of the siren did not penetrate.

The fog persisted all night, clearing slightly shortly after dawn, and it was some hours before every unit, including the convoy to the south, could be sighted. During the next three days there was little excitement as ships gradually drew outside the range of enemy aircraft. But one or two attacks were attempted by small groups, which in each case were broken up by the Fleet Air Arm fighters from the aircraft carrier,

Formidable, before they could get near the fleet. One *Fulmar* failed to return—a grim reminder of the price paid for protection, and of the hazards faced by gallant airmen so that the ships should be unharmed.

On the fourth day the lighthouse of Ras-el-Tin topped the horizon, giving a first indication that harbour was almost reached. Minarets, towers, masts and spires quickly followed into view, and soon Alexandria was revealed, sparkling in the sunshine. The battlefleet forged ahead, turned into the Great Pass, round the sharp corners leading through the open boom between the breakwaters, and into the thronged and busy harbour. It was satisfying to navigate *Queen Elizabeth* to her berth in the outer harbour, drop both anchors, middle, and then secure the stern, but the evolution was completed as the four merchant vessels with their valuable cargo entered harbour to berth alongside the quays. With the loss of only one ship, a highly dangerous operation had been concluded.

Chapter 10

THE BATTLE OF CRETE

After Greece, Crete! To many, that was the most obvious threat; but the question was, how long would the Germans require to make their preparations? What length of time had we to organise resistance? Crete was no invulnerable fortress bristling with guns, provisioned and supplied for months and thus able to withstand prolonged assault. On the contrary, her defences were lamentably weak; the supplies available had been strained to the utmost by the sudden arrival of the evacuated army from Greece, 25,000 of whom had been retained on the island for its defence. The only port of any value—Suda—was quite unsuited to handle large cargoes at the best of times: how much more difficult it was with the harbour constantly being bombed. True, there were small landing places on the south coast where equipment could be got ashore, but then there was the trouble of transport. There was virtually none. A battalion could count itself lucky if it was the proud possessor of one motor truck, while mules were almost unobtainable. Many had been shipped to Greece during that campaign, and there they still were.

The troops themselves were of good heart, but in poor shape for a new campaign. Though they had their rifles, almost all their equipment had been left in Greece. There were no mess utensils, indifferent accommodation and, more serious, they had no wire or entrenching tools. Then, finally, there was the same terrible handicap we had experienced throughout the Greek campaign—lack of air support. On 19th May—the day before the Battle of Crete began—we had seven fighters on the island. As it was ludicrous to suppose that they could make any difference to the scale of attack which was to be expected before they were all destroyed, it was decided to withdraw them to Egypt.

Even the aircraft carrier, *Formidable*, was powerless to provide the fleet with air protection. The calls had lately been so heavy that she possessed only four serviceable aircraft and would be unable to provide any fighter protection before 25th May. Thus, it looked as if the British Navy, once again, would have to take on the German Air Force unsupported.

In the time available, between 29th April and 20th May, stores and guns were landed totalling 15,000 tons, but eight ships were sunk in Suda Bay. Day by day, the running of convoys from Alexandria grew more hazardous as the weight of air attack increased. It had been intended to transfer the whole of the Marine Naval Base Defence Organisation to Crete where already 2000 Royal Marines had established fortified positions, but the risk that this invaluable unit would be lost on the way was so great that the movement was not justified.

On 15th May, the cruisers *Glocuester* and *Fiji* embarked the 2nd Battalion Leicester Regiment at Alexandria and landed them at Heraklion, while the specially equipped fleet transport

Glengyle, took 700 Argyle and Sutherland Highlanders to Tymbaki.

It was not known when the attack on Crete would be launched, but intelligence indicated that the critical date would be about 17th May. The Navy's duty was crystal clear—to prevent any seaborne landing on the coast. The nearest base from which the fleet could operate was Alexandria—a distance of 420 miles from Suda—and this imposed immense difficulties. Ships had to be re-fuelled and their ammunition replenished, which meant the waste of two valuable days on passage.

In order that the fleet should be ready on the critical date, forces were sailed from Alexandria on 15th May. Vice-Admiral Sir H. D. Pridham-Wippell, wearing his flag in *Queen Elizabeth,* with the battleship *Barham* and a destroyer screen, operated to the west of Crete to provide general cover, while cruisers and other destroyers swept into the Ægean by night, making a rendezvous with the Vice-Admiral in the mornings. Owing to the nature of the whole operation, requiring the closest liason with military G.H.Q. in Cairo, the Commander-in-Chief directed movements from his offices at Alexandria.

The first two or three days at sea were remarkably peaceful. Occasionally a hostile aircraft would be detected some miles from the fleet, but none approached near enough to justify the hoisting of a 'yellow' warning. After each sweep into the Ægean the cruisers had nothing to report, and the optimists began to wonder if, after all, the threat to Crete was only a scare on the part of the Germans to hide either an undisclosed weakness or perhaps other sinister intentions.

On 18th May, Rear-Admiral H. B. Rawlings, commanding the 7th Cruiser Squadron, was ordered to hoist his flag in *Warspite* and, with the battleship *Valiant* accompanied by the light forces available, relieve *Queen Elizabeth* and the ships which had been patrolling off Crete. Next day the relieving force passed the Vice-Admiral at sea. Though the two battleships which had been recalled remained at Alexandria, the majority of the light forces proceeded to sea again as soon as they had re-fuelled.

That night was peaceful, but at 8.0 a.m. on 20th May, the Battle of Crete began. The Germans' first objective was the aerodrome at Maleme. From the window of his offices, Captain J. A. V. Morse, R.N., the Naval Officer in Charge at Suda, watched scores of enemy machines dive bomb the aerodrome, then swoop low and machine-gun defence positions. An hour later the sky was filled with different coloured parachutes floating down: then the heavy troop carriers landing on the beaches. By 11.30 a.m., 1500 enemy troops were reported to have landed from the air; others were still arriving. Bombing was continuous and, in the afternoon, several dive bombing attacks were delivered on the harbour. At 5.30 p.m. parachutists were reported descending on Heraclion where it was estimated that 400 planes were attacking over the town between 4.0 and 7.0 p.m. About 1000 parachutists had been dropped on that aerodrome, the majority of whom had been shot at once and the remainder mopped up later. By nightfall, the situation was everywhere in hand although 1200 of the 3000 who were supposed to have landed near Maleme were still unaccounted for. Enemy operational orders had been captured showing that Suda was to be the first day's objective after Maleme had fallen. The resistance must, therefore, have been unexpected.

Meanwhile, the ships at sea had still been left alone, although a few hostile aircraft had been sighted out of gun range. The light forces were to move in to the Ægean after dark, both from the east and west of Crete, but towards the end of the afternoon the Commander-in-Chief received reports concerning the movement of numerous caiques. At 6.0 p.m. the light forces were, therefore, ordered to move in at once. Each force was to patrol north of Crete, east and west of the meridian 25°E. and then retire to the south by daylight.

Only one of these forces encountered any excitement. Rear-Admiral E. L. S. King, commanding the 15th Cruiser Squadron with his flag in *Naiad*, the Australian cruiser *Perth* and four destroyers—*Kandahar, Nubian, Kingston, Juno*—entered by the Kaso Strait to the east of Crete. A few minutes before 11.0 p.m., while in the middle of the Straits, *Juno*, on the starboard wing, suddenly sighted three low shapes about 600 yards on her port bow. They were Italian 'E' boats: they appeared stopped, obviously keeping a very poor look-out. *Juno* immediately tried to ram, but they moved ahead just in time and the destroyer unfortunately missed. All *Juno's* close range weapons were now in action, and she was supported by *Kandahar* who was the adjacent destroyer. Events happened quickly, though in the darkness the time was so short and it was difficult to see what actually occurred. At least two of the enemy were badly damaged in this encounter. On turning back to regain her position on the screen, *Juno* sighted four more 'E' boats at ranges from 300 - 1500 yards. These were also heavily engaged before they retired, and at least two of them received serious damage. *Naiad* also fired at one. It was not known if the enemy discharged torpedoes—none were seen —but their desire to escape was obvious.

Captain D.14 in *Jervis*, with the destroyers *Nizam* and *Ilex*, had been ordered to bombard Scarpanto aerodrome to the east of Kaso. Here, it was reported, were numerous enemy aircraft in a most advantageous position to control the Straits. The destroyers arrived without incident, carried out a short bombardment at 2.40 a.m., and then retired to the southward. Although several fires were started, in the darkness it was impossible to see what damage had been done.

By daylight on 21st all forces were retiring from the neighbourhood of the Ægean, those who had entered from the Kithera Channel concentrating on the battleships to the west of Crete, while Admiral King's force moved clear to the southeast of Kaso. Now began the enemy's concentrated and vicious attacks upon our ships. None escaped this unwelcome attention. For a long period during the forenoon, and again for $2\frac{1}{2}$ hours after lunch, the battleships were subjected to a series of attacks. Machines, for the most part, came in singly or in pairs and, though they did no damage, the expenditure of ammunition was heavy. During the day at least five aircraft were brought down by ships' gunfire, and many others were severely damaged.

R.A. (D.)—Rear-Admiral I. G. Glennie—in the cruiser *Dido*, retiring to the westward on *Warspite* with *Orion*, *Ajax* and four destroyers, was bombed continuously for four hours from 9.50 a.m. during which time *Ajax* was damaged by a near miss. Most of this bombing was from a high level. Admiral King's force to the east was more unfortunate and, shortly after noon, a salvo of five bombs brought the first disaster. Three of these hit *Juno* abaft the funnel while the destroyer was going at speed. Men, pieces of ship and machinery were flung into the sea and, within 20 seconds of the Captain giving his last order, *Stop Both*, the destroyer had taken on a list of 70 degrees to starboard. One minute later, the stern broke away and sunk, while the bow rose vertically in the air and then began to disappear with alarming rapidity.

Two minutes after the bombs had crashed upon her, *Juno* was no longer visible. Instead, there was a large patch of steaming oil in which men were struggling for their lives. Petty Officer Edwin Lumley who had been thrown well clear by the first explosion saw a shipmate in difficulties. Swimming forty yards into the hot oil he gallantly managed to effect his rescue, but at the cost of severe burning about the face, hands and eyes. The destroyers *Nubian*, *Kandahar* and *Kingston* were ordered to pick up survivors, which they did most expeditiously. *Nubian*, being nearest to the scene collected the majority: *Kingston* picked up 8 survivors, of whom 5 died almost immediately. Altogether six officers (including the Captain) and 91 men were rescued.

Throughout the day—May 21st—air-borne attacks on Crete continued with increased severity. More ships were damaged in the harbour, and the effectiveness of the anti-aircraft defences at Suda was seriously reduced. During the afternoon, Maleme aerodrome was captured and our troops moved back

K

to new positions. To Captain Morse the army authorities expressed apprehension about a sea-borne invasion, but he assured them that the navy would deal with any such attempt. At Heraclion the enemy was still held. Using fifty Arab stevedores as body shields, they had advanced on the western mole, but this attack had been thrown back. Later, parties of parachutists had rushed into the town and occupied some houses but, during the night, fierce fighting took place in the streets and every German who had entered was either killed or captured.

Towards dusk, the light naval forces again moved in. From the eastward Admiral King re-entered the Kaso Strait with the intention next day of continuing to the westward and emerging by Kithera during the following afternoon. Admiral Glennie in *Dido*, with *Ajax*, *Orion* and his four destroyers— *Janus*, *Kimberley*, *Hasty* and *Hereward*—entered as before from the west, and two cruisers—*Gloucester* and *Fiji*, with the destroyer *Greyhound*—patrolled in the vicinity of Cape Matapan.

To the force of R.A. (D.) in *Dido* came unexpected success. Soon after being detached from the battleships they were attacked by a strong wave of *Junkers* 87. But no damage was caused; one machine broke in two from a direct hit as it dived and at least two more were brought down by gunfire— an encouraging start for what promised to be an eventful night.

At 11.30 p.m. they were about 18 miles north of Canea steering due east when *Janus*, on *Dido's* port bow, suddenly flashed an alarm. The flagship at once led round to the north and, on the turn, sighted a torpedo boat. In the beam of a searchlight, its ensign and immaculate coat of paint suggesting weeks in harbour, established its identity at once—Italian! Crossing ahead, it passed close down the starboard side of the cruisers. A splash, visible in the darkness, indicated that the enemy had fired torpedoes and the three cruisers immediately made a sharp turn to starboard to comb the tracks, close and engage the torpedo boat. An excellent burst was seen to rake the upper deck of the enemy who turned to starboard to pass in between *Orion* and *Ajax*. On fire and badly damaged, she received a full broadside up the stern from *Ajax* and disentegrated into small pieces.

Then things began to happen. Realising that the torpedo boat would not be alone, the cruisers swept the darkened sea with searchlights to reveal that target for which they had searched each night. With tense excitement each beam was followed by a thousand pairs of eyes. A Greek caique packed with about 300 German troops was caught in *Dido's* searchlight —five seconds later it was a blackened wreck with corpses lying on what remained of her decks and soldiers struggling in the water. Then another and another were illuminated; destroyers, risking collision with each other, dashed in to close range in order to ram and rake them fore and aft with pom-pom and machine-gun fire; and the cruisers, whenever they got the chance, opened with their larger guns. The searchlights continued to sweep and the destroyers, acting independently, played havoc with every caique discovered. Panic-stricken Germans leapt overboard and, weighted down by their equipment, rapidly sank with terrible cries which could be heard above the general pandemonium.

There were some small steamers, too, besides the caiques, and also a steam yacht. Into these crashed projectiles from the cruisers causing them to burst into flames and add to the general inferno. For two hours the holocaust continued, during which time it was estimated that at least 4000 of the enemy perished. When further search revealed that no enemy were left in the vicinity, Admiral Glennie carried out one more sweep and then turned to the west, making a rendezvous for 6.0 a.m. about 30 miles west of Crete.

Meanwhile, the ships under the command of Rear-Admiral King were sweeping north of Crete from the eastward. He had been joined by the A.A. Cruisers *Calcutta* and *Carlisle*, so the force now consisted of four cruisers and three destroyers. The night for them had been quiet, and at 6.0 a.m. ships reformed shaping course for the direction of Melos. Two hours later a look-out reported a single caique to port. Keen eyes soon observed that it was flying the German ensign and was packed with troops. *Naiad* opened fire with effect; then *Perth* was ordered to drop astern and finish it off, but she had scarcely moved off before heavy bombing attacks developed.

At first these were concentrated on *Naiad*, but, as *Perth* fell further astern, the planes mostly diverted their attention to her. A few well-placed rounds, and another 300 German troops had found that the invasion of Crete was not the pleasant, simple picnic they had been led to believe. But the bombing continued with unabated fury, and *Perth* appeared so hard pressed that *Naiad* turned round to support her. The planes now concentrated on *Naiad*, and *Perth* managed to draw ahead as the flagship turned round astern of the remainder of the force and resumed her course to the westward.

Suddenly *Calcutta*, who was a few miles to the north, started to flash. A merchant vessel had been sighted. She was making for Crete and was full of German troops! Swiftly a destroyer moved out and another German troopship tipped her load into the Ægean. A few minutes later an enemy destroyer was sighted in the same direction and all British ships automatically turned to close, both cruisers and destroyers opening fire. A hit was quickly scored, and the enemy turned away under one of those heavy smoke screens which the Italians are such adepts at creating. In pursuing her as she altered course, *Kingston* caught a glimpse of at least five caiques retiring behind the smoke screen. .

The first inclination of Admiral King was to pursue with all his ships, but a moment's reflection constrained him. All ships were now rapidly running out of anti-aircraft ammunition, the scale of air attack was increasing and, if they indulged in a pursuit to the north, the safety of his whole force might be jeopardised. The circumstances did not justify any course other than that of making for Kithera and getting clear of the Ægean as soon as possible. So, the destroyers were ordered to withdraw, and ships resumed their course to the westward. As it happened, the enemy were also keen to continue their retirement. Thus a second, and final, attempt at a sea-borne invasion of Crete had been foiled by the Navy.

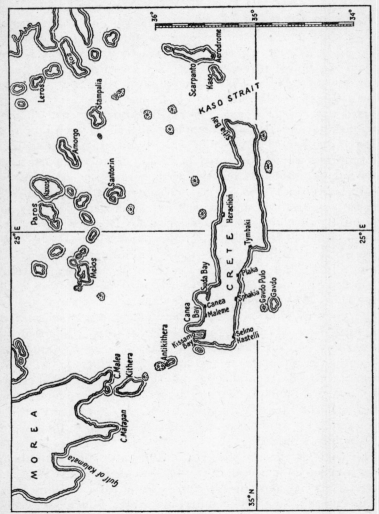

The force was now about 25 miles due south of the eastern end of Melos, *Naiad* was still astern and trying to catch up, bombing was continuous and she was herself in difficulties. The pumps controlling each of the after turrets had become overheated and the firing of these guns was only intermittent. As most of the dive-bombing attacks came out of the sun— that is, from right astern—*Naiad* had to turn each time an attack developed in order to get her forward guns to bear. This meant further delay, but Admiral King was loath to recall the rest of the force to his support.

At 11.25 a.m., however, ten *Junkers* 87 made a particularly vicious attack on *Naiad*, dropping in all some thirty-six bombs close round her. Though none actually hit, there were several near misses which punctured her hull; many compartments forward were flooded and her speed was reduced temporarily to 16 knots. Only two turrets were now in action and, unless the cruiser was to become a total loss, immediate support was essential. The other ships were accordingly ordered to close.

The situation regarding A.A. ammunition had now become critical, and Admiral King made an immediate signal to Admiral Rawlings in *Warspite* asking for his support. Careful records which had been kept showed that between 9.45 a.m. and 11.45 a.m. no fewer than 181 bombs had been aimed at *Naiad* and, in addition to this, many machines had attempted to rake her with cannon fire. With the support afforded by other ships in the force, attacks became less concentrated though equally persistent and at 12.35, *Carlisle* was hit by a small bomb. Fortunately, the damage caused was slight, she was able to maintain her speed and the fire produced was efficiently and rapidly extinguished. At 12.58 the enemy varied his tactics by sending in torpedo bombers, but they were successfully avoided.

Throughout the previous night, the battleships with their destroyer screen had been operating west of Crete. At 7.0 a.m. they had been joined by Admiral Glennie with his ships after their successful night encounter but, three hours later, this force was ordered to return to Alexandria, re-fuel and complete with ammunition.

At 8.30, *Gloucester* and *Fiji*, with their two destroyers, had re-joined. They had had a quiet night during their patrol off Matapan but, since daylight, had endured their full share of air attacks. Soon after dawn, sixteen *Junkers* 87 and 88 had dived on them, and some of their bombs had fallen unpleasantly close. One near miss actually punctured *Fiji's* hull under the starboard bow; another smothered her bridge in a deluge of black water. Half-an-hour later, a second wave of twelve attacked, again concentrating on *Fiji*, and a near miss close to the port side inflicted further slight damage. Ideas of a quiet breakfast were then dispelled by a further wave of high and low level bombing, followed by a single *Junkers* 87 who approached from astern and looked as if he was going to dive straight down the funnel. The bomb he dropped just missed the quarter-deck and put the after gun director out of action.

A reinforcement joined Admiral Rawlings about 10.0 a.m. Captain D.5 (Captain Lord Louis Mountbatten) in the destroyer *Kelly*, with *Kashmir*, *Kipling*, *Kelvin* and *Jackal*, had sailed from Malta on the previous day with instructions to rendezvous with *Warspite*.

When Admiral Rawlings knew that ships would be withdrawing through Kithera during the day, he patrolled with his force some 20 miles to the westward of the Straits, "serving" (to use his own words) "a useful purpose by attracting enemy aircraft." During this period, he ascertained the percentage of A.A. ammunition remaining in the ships of his force and was horrified to learn that *Gloucester* was down to 18 per cent and *Fiji* 30 per cent.

Then Admiral King's dramatic signal arrived. *Naiad* and *Carlisle* were both damaged, all ships were practically out of ammunition and he needed urgent support if his force was to survive. Ordering *Gloucester* and *Fiji* to prepare to take the damaged cruisers in tow—a precaution subsequently found unnecessary—he increased speed to 23 knots and decided to enter the Ægean. The time was now about half-past twelve.

Soon after one o'clock, the sight of A.A. shell bursts ahead indicated the position of the ships with *Naiad*. High level bombing attacks now became more persistent and, as the enemy's bases were approached, soon developed into the more deadly dive bombing variety. At 1.30 three *Junkers* 87 in line astern dived out of a cloud directly ahead of *Warspite* and, before the battleship had time to answer her wheel and swing away to port, the leader was over his target. It was impossible to miss and a heavy bomb wrecked the starboard 4-inch and 6-inch batteries, causing heavy casualties. By her prompt action, *Warspite* managed to avoid the other two.

From *Fiji* on her starboard beam, the determined manner in which the attack was carried out was most spectacular. Dense clouds of smoke caused by damage to boiler room intakes poured from *Warspite's* funnels as she altered violently to port, disappearing for a while in her own smoke. When she finally emerged, the signal for ships to alter course together to 260 degrees was flying from her yard-arm. The two forces were now about four miles apart.

Shortly before the attack had taken place on *Warspite* a caique had been sighted to the northward, and the destroyer *Greyhound* had been despatched to sink it. Having completed her task she was now returning to rejoin her position on the battleships' screen. When still a little distance from the fleet, a *Junkers* 87 made a sudden vicious dive. *Greyhound* fired steadily, but she was unsupported and the enemy was determined. Swooping down to a very low altitude, five bombs were dropped, three of which struck the unfortunate destroyer, who seemed to break up in a sheet of flame. Her stern sank rapidly, but to watchers in the fleet it was an inspiring sight to see her remaining guns still in action until she disappeared four minutes later.

Admiral King—he was the senior Admiral—immediately despatched the destroyers *Kandahar* and *Kingston* to rescue her survivors. As they approached the scene of the disaster, wave after wave of enemy aircraft concentrated on them with ruthless intensity, determined that the men in the water should be left to drown. Not only did they bomb the destroyers, obscuring them completely by great fountains of water which continually rose close on either side of them, but they swooped low and machine-gunned the men struggling in the water, causing many casualties. During a momentary lull each destroyer managed to drop a boat, but it was impossible for them to remain stopped themselves, so intense were the attacks from the air.

As the destroyers circled round, a particularly vicious machine-gun attack was made on *Kingston's* whaler whose crew had managed to haul about twenty survivors on board. Three officers were killed and several ratings, and only one man of *Kingston's* crew was left alive. Undaunted, the few survivors made room for more, and persevered in their attempts at rescue. So impossible had the situation become that Admiral King ordered *Gloucester* and *Fiji* to close and give support, not realising at the time that they, like ships in his own force, were practically out of A.A. ammunition.

Attacks persisted with unabated fury. Every attempt to close the survivors was the signal for concentrated dive bombing of the ships and machine-gunning of the men in the water. *Fiji* was hit and one of her turrets put out of action, killing several of the crew. At length there was a short lull; *Gloucester* ordered the destroyers to close, and a number of survivors were rapidly embarked, numbering altogether 63 officers and men (including the Captain) and 17 wounded.

By this time Admiral King had been made aware of the ammunition situation in the two cruisers and, as another air attack was obviously developing, he ordered the four ships employed on the work of rescue to withdraw and rejoin. They were now some distance to the eastward of the fleet which was retiring rapidly through the Kithera Straits. The 4-inch A.A. ammunition in *Fiji* was completely exhausted, but she could still keep her close range weapons in action.

Leaving a few rafts and lifebelts in the water for those men who had not been picked up, the two cruisers were seen moving up at high speed some distance astern of the battleships. The destroyers were proceeding independently, and *Fiji* was closing in on *Gloucester*, from whom she had become separated. Then suddenly everyone was horrified to see *Gloucester* become enveloped in smoke and flames as she was struck by a salvo of bombs. Brought to a standstill, she listed pathetically. As *Fiji* approached, *Gloucester* was hit again and again until she was blazing fore and aft, and it was obvious that her end could only be a matter of minutes.

Fiji steamed close under her stern and dropped as many carley floats as she was able to release. Many men were already in the water and, as the cruiser passed, they cheered. Most of those on *Gloucester's* bridge seemed uninjured and they signalled to *Fiji* for a destroyer to be ordered alongside. But attacks had by no means ceased; they had not even eased; bombs were still falling with alarming frequency and the air was still broken by the whine of the dive bomber. The Captain of *Fiji* knew that it would only invite further disaster both to ships and men, and he reluctantly decided to withdraw with the destroyers. It was a bitter decision to have to make, but there was no alternative. Even as he moved away, a signal was received from Admiral King ordering him not to stand by the sinking cruiser. A message was, however, sent to the Naval Officer in Charge at Suda asking him to despatch rescue craft. But there were none available.

As the main forces moved further to the westward, the scale of air attacks gradually decreased, but at 4.45 p.m. *Valiant* sustained a hit on her quarter deck. Fortunately, no serious damage resulted and her speed was unaffected.

Although the intensity of attack on the main body had become less, those on *Fiji*, *Kandahar* and *Kingston*—now some miles to the eastward—persisted in such regular succession that it was impossible to form any clear distinction between them. It was known that the battleships would be altering later to the south-eastward and, in order to rejoin at the earliest moment, *Fiji* decided to cut a corner and not proceed so far to the westward herself. Whatever she did, it was quite clear that the bulk of the German air force intended to concentrate on her, because she was unsupported save for the two destroyers both of whom were also short of ammunition and fuel.

Her pom-poms and 0.5-inch machine guns were now her first, and only, line of defence. By superhuman efforts these guns were kept in action during attack after attack, although they and their crews were continually being smothered in water and bomb splinters. With monotonous and consistent regularity the enemy showed his determination to destroy the cruiser. First, machines would be sighted moving forward on each beam and then circling ahead, while a formation would gather astern and try to deliver an unseen attack. Bombs would generally fall five at a time, sometimes exploding on the surface: sometimes exploding like depth charges. These were from a high level, but dive bombing attacks were delivered from the bow and quarter to synchronise with those dropped from a higher altitude.

Manœuvring at full speed, swinging violently first one way and then the other, the ship appeared to have a charmed existence as her track weaved its way through the columns of water thrown up on either side. Sometimes as many as five *Junkers* would dive at a time from different directions, and the bombs could be seen in the air hurtling down towards the unfortunate cruiser. A near miss on the port beam smothered the ship in water and severely wounded the gunnery officer on the bridge. He was carried down to the sick bay injured in the back and leg. Occasional *Messerschmidts* would swoop down and machine-gun the decks. Always *Fiji* answered back, but none of the enemy were seen to crash, though several must have been severely damaged as some jettisoned their bombs and ammunition at a distance.

At last there was a lull, during which *Fiji* formulated her night intentions which were to alter course to the eastward. Opportunity was also taken to repair some of the damage and make the wounded more comfortable.

All too soon the wailing of the destroyers' syrens indicated the approach of aircraft about 7.0 p.m. Clouds were now low, which made conditions more favourable than ever to the enemy and, without any warning, a bomb was suddenly seen to fall close ahead of the ship. A split second later, a *Messerschmidt* 109 emerged from the clouds on the port beam and dived straight at the ship. There was no time to take avoiding action, and *Fiji* had scarcely begun to swing in response to the frantic wheel order shouted down the voice pipe, when a bomb struck her on the port side amidships. She at once listed 20 degrees but maintained a speed of 18 knots, although one of her boiler rooms was flooded. Compasses were now out of action, the vessel was sluggish on the wheel and yawed wildly, but with the assistance of a destroyer stationed ahead to lead the way, it was hoped to save the situation.

But the list grew more pronounced; slowly but surely the ship lost all her way until finally she stopped. After all the miraculous escapes she had experienced since dawn, encouraging officers and men to believe she was unsinkable, this was a bitter disappointment. It was now just a question of sitting and waiting for the *coup de grâce* which was inevitable. There was still more than an hour of daylight, and in that hour the end had assuredly to come.

Then, from ahead above the clouds, the noise of aircraft was clearly heard approaching. It grew louder; the machine broke into view and came straight for the helpless ship. The starboard pom-pom, which was the only gun left in action, opened up with a steady fire, but all that the majority of the men could do was to watch, horribly fascinated. A heavy bomb was released. It came straight at them, passed over the foc's'le, missed the bridge and crashed with a terrific explosion between the funnels. Down came the mast; the deck was ripped open all along the port side, the cranes drooped drunkenly and the list on the ship grew ominously more pronounced.

The Captain gave the order to stand by to abandon ship, and the crew lined the starboard side calm and cheerful. A quick inspection showed that *Fiji* was a total loss and could remain afloat only a few more minutes.

"Abandon Ship!" The last order was given, many immediately taking to the water as a destroyer closed to pick up the majority of those who had jumped first. Within a few minutes there was no one left on board save for a forlorn figure sitting on the starboard propeller, who refused to leave his perch until the ship finally rolled over and disappeared from view.

Most of her life-saving gear had been dropped alongside *Greyhound* and *Gloucester*, so the three carley rafts available were all crowded beyond their capacity. With great efficiency the two destroyers began to rescue survivors, but the rapid approach of more aircraft made an immediate withdrawal essential. The day's experiences had been too bitter to justify their remaining. As they withdrew they seemed to take the aircraft with them. But hundreds of men still struggled in the water, enveloped now by a feeling of gloom, yet hopeful that the destroyers' promise to return after dark would materialise.

One of the last to leave the tragic cruiser was the Chaplain, the Revd. Christopher Tanner, who had stayed to save as many of the wounded as he could. In the water he exhausted himself—helping the men to rafts and floats and bringing to the rescuing ship those who were disabled or could not swim, until finally he collapsed and died. For this tireless devotion in saving life, he was posthumously awarded the Albert Medal.

Fighting off the aircraft with the few guns for which they now had ammunition, *Kandahar* and *Kingston* miraculously escaped damage, returning to the scene of *Fiji's* disaster after dark. By skilful handling, 523 officers and men were rescued, but a few solitary survivors had to be left as, because of their lack of fuel, it was essential that the destroyers should meet Admiral Rawlings at dawn. An added tragedy cast further gloom. The late Captain of *Greyhound*—Commander W. R.

Marshall-A'Deane—had been on board *Kandahar* helping in every way he could. Though he could not have recovered from the fierce ordeal to which he had been subjected a few hours before, he gallantly leapt over the side in the darkness to try and rescue a man from *Fiji* whom he saw to be in difficulties. Unhappily, the Captain of *Kandahar* was unaware at the time that this had happened. When he knew and returned to search, Commander Marshall-A'Deane could not be found. . . . A posthumous award of the Albert Medal was also made to this gallant officer.

At dusk, the main forces were some miles to the south-west of Crete when, on orders from the Commander-in-Chief, *Decoy* and *Hero* were despatched to embark the King of Greece, H.B.M. Minister and other important personages from the south coast of the besieged island.

In spite of grievous loss to themselves, the Navy had so far prevented a sea-borne attack against Crete where the situation round Maleme had steadily deteriorated. Troop-carrying aircraft had been arriving all day at the rate of twenty an hour; a plan to counter-attack had been abandoned, and our hard-pressed troops had withdrawn to a new line. At Heraclion, conditions were better and the enemy had inadvertently dropped stores from fourteen aircraft into our own lines.

Under the circumstances, Admiral Rawlings was determined to do his utmost to prevent the enemy repeating his attempt at sea-borne invasion. Most of his ships were short of fuel; many were without ammunition. Only the 5th Destroyer Flotilla which had joined that forenoon from Malta was in a fit state to take any offensive action. Accordingly *Kelly*, *Kashmir* and *Kipling*, who had first been directed to assist with the rescue of *Fiji's* survivors, were ordered to patrol inside Kissamo and Canea Bays, and *Jackal* and *Kelvin* were given another area. Meanwhile, the Commander-in-Chief had ordered *Jervis*, *Nizam* and *Ilex* to patrol off Heraclion. All forces were to be clear of the Ægean by daylight.

For the last two groups everything was peaceful and they withdrew in safety next day. As the three destroyers under the command of Captain Lord Louis Mountbatten approached the Kithera Strait, *Kipling* developed a defect in her steering which made it impossible for her to continue on an operation where violent alterations of course at high speed would be required. So she remained to the westward during the night to make good the defect.

Of the limited time at their disposal, *Kelly* and *Kashmir* made full use. Sweeping into Kissamo Bay, they set a caique on fire; then rounding Cape Spada they carried out a bombardment of Maleme, which appeared effective though it was impossible to see what damage had been done. On the way out, they encountered another caique full of troops which they quickly destroyed and, by dawn, were off the west coast of Crete. Again, no enemy troops had landed from the sea.

All forces which had been operating round Crete for the past few days had now been ordered to return to Alexandria with all despatch, in order to replenish their stocks of ammunition and re-fuel. Some miles to the south-east of *Kelly* were the battleships, later to be joined by *Decoy* and *Hero* with the Royal Party on board: further east, Admiral King was steaming with his cruisers and destroyers towards the base: *Kandahar* and *Kingston* were joining *Warspite*. *Glenroy* had sailed from Alexandria with 900 officers and men of the Queen's Royal Regiment to be landed at Tymbaki and two destroyers —*Jaguar* and *Defender*—loaded with urgently needed ammunition for the army were on their way to Suda.

At 8.0 a.m., *Kipling*, with her steering gear repaired, was some six miles to the south of *Kelly* when she suddenly saw twenty-four *Junkers* 87 swoop down upon her and *Kashmir* astern. In waves of three they dived with furious determination from either side. With the sixth or seventh bomb *Kashmir* was hit, and the result was disastrous. It must have penetrated the deck and finally exploded in the bowles of the ship, because her back immediately broke and her bow and stem were lifted high into the air. Her stern quickly submerged, and the destroyer rapidly began to roll right over.

The gunlayer of the port Oerlikon—Ord. Sea. I. D. Rhodes, R.A.N.V.R.—continued to fire his weapon until he and the gun were practically submerged. Then, with great difficulty, he scrambled up the deck which was now at a steep angle and got the starboard Oerlikon into action, actually hitting and destroying an aircraft which was attacking with cannon from astern. As the time which elapsed between the bomb exploding and the ship sinking was barely two minutes, this gallant act and devotion to duty was truly remarkable.

A few minutes after *Kashmir* had been hit, *Kelly*, heeling to port under full rudder at 30 knots in a vain attempt to avoid the rain of bombs, was struck on No. 3 gun deck by a thousand pounder. The effect was calamitous. Her list to port increased with alarming rapidity and, within a matter of seconds, she had turned turtle, her guns firing until the last. For half-an-hour *Kelly* floated upside down and then gently disappeared from view. Meanwhile, the enemy machine-gunned survivors in the water, causing many casualties.

Horrified at this sudden disaster, *Kipling* speeded to the rescue and was herself attacked. Heedless of the bombs falling all round her, she put up magnificent resistance and quickly reached the scene where the men were struggling in the water. During a short lull she lowered her boats and rescued seven officers (including Captain D.5) and 120 men who belonged to *Kelly*. So rapidly had the ship turned over that nine other officers and an equal number of men had had no chance to escape, although among the survivors there was a gratifying number of engine-room personnel.

Kipling then turned her attention to the survivors of *Kashmir* further astern, and started to lower her motor boat to assist. But, while the boat was in the water, another bombing attack developed. The attack passed and *Kipling* miraculously escaped. She then returned and managed to rescue eight officers (including the Captain) and 144 men of *Kashmir*. After three hours spent on rescue work it was imperative for her to move.

Without further incident, but with growing anxiety lest the fuel would give out, *Kipling* proceeded to Alexandria. Fifty miles from the base, they were met by the net-layer *Protector*, who provided sufficient oil to allow the ship to reach harbour.

Within a space of thirty-six hours, two cruisers and four destroyers had been lost, two battleships and two more cruisers had been damaged but—THE ENEMY HAD NOT LANDED IN CRETE FROM THE SEA. In view, however, of the ever increasing scale of air attack, *Glenroy* was recalled and the question of using faster ships to re-inforce the hard-pressed garrison was considered.

II

Although the enemy had been unable to make any headway at Heraclion, the situation in the Maleme area had become grave by the evening of 23rd May. A new line of defence had been formed, but the steady flow of re-inforcements by air had enabled the enemy's pressure to be correspondingly increased. Heavy attacks on the harbour at Suda had put out of action an entire group of M.T.B.'s besides causing considerable damage to the dockyard, and Captain Morse began to make plans to move his headquarters to Sphakia on the south coast of the island. That night *Jaguar* and *Defender* managed to land at Suda the ammunition they had brought from Alexandria, and they returned in safety; while the fast minelayer *Abdiel* left Egypt with stores and more ammunition for the same destination.

In spite of the deterioration of the position at Maleme, it was still hoped that the island would be able to hold out, and the Commander-in-Chief made an inspiring signal to the whole fleet.

"During the last few days," it read, "the Fleet has been having a hard battle against a high proportion of the

German Air Force and has kept its end up by dint of determination. We have sustained some hard knocks in the process of preventing any considerable sea-borne landing in Crete, but we have also given some. Some thousands of enemy sea-borne troops have been trapped and sunk at sea. The Battle for Crete is still in progress: to win is essential.

"The army is momentarily holding its own against constant re-inforcements of air-borne enemy troops. We must not let them down. At whatever cost to ourselves we must land reinforcements for them and keep the enemy from using the sea. There are indications that the enemy resources are stretched to the limit. We can and must outlast them. Stick it out!"

For ships to operate off the west of Crete and enter the Ægean *via* the Kithera Channel was too damaging to justify. The Kaso Strait promised less insecurity. News, therefore, of a possible attempt by the enemy to land at Sitia sent *Ajax*, *Dido*, *Kimberley* and *Hotspur* speeding from Alexandria towards the eastern end of Crete. They could patrol off the threatened coast during dark hours, possibly bombard Maleme and be clear of Kaso by daylight. The dark hours were short, the patrol was carried out without incident, but it was impossible for ships to reach Maleme without being caught during the day in the Ægean which had been made so deadly by the *Junkers* 87.

Three more destroyers—*Ilex*, *Hero* and *Nizam*—embarked two battalions of Special Service troops and sailed from Alexandria with the idea of landing them on the night of 24th/25th in the small open bay of Selinos Kastelli in the south-west of Crete. But, as dark approached, the wind freshened considerably, making such a landing quite impracticable. They returned to Egypt.

Throughout May 24th the enemy concentrated his attacks round Canea, seriously reducing all the A.A. defences in the neighbourhood. Heraclion still held out. Although Greek

THE BATTLE OF CRETE

troops there were getting short of ammunition, the Argyle and
Sutherland Highlanders who had been landed at Tymbaki,
had successfully fought their way through the enemy lines
and provided a welcome reinforcement.

It was appreciated that the great scale of air attack made
it no longer possible for the navy to operate off Crete in
daylight, and that no guarantee could any longer be given
to prevent sea-borne landings without seriously prejudicing
our command of the eastern Mediterranean. The determining
factor was not the fear of sustaining losses, but the need to
avoid crippling the fleet without commensurate advantage to
ourselves.

Information received showed that Scarpanto aerodrome east
of the Kaso Straits was being extensively used by the enemy.
A heavy blow here might seriously weaken their effort to
attack shipping passing through the Straits and thus render
the passage less hazardous. The aircraft carrier *Formidable* had
now built up her fighter strength to 12 Fulmars and it was
hoped that, in addition, she could operate as many as 8
Albacores. It was a poor enough striking force, but there
were no bombers available in Egypt for an attack on
Scarpanto, and it was considered that an operation of this
nature was essential.

On 25th May, therefore, Vice-Admiral Sir H. D. Pridham-
Wippell with his flag in *Queen Elizabeth*, proceeded to sea with
Formidable and *Barham*, escorted by eight destroyers. Course
was shaped towards the Kaso Straits. Other efforts were also
being made. *Glenroy*, having embarked 800 troops and 18
motor vehicles, sailed with a strong escort to Tymbaki, and
Abdiel, on her safe return from Suda, was immediately ordered
to embark the Special Service troops which had been unable
to land at Selinos Kastelli, and sail with them for Suda. She
was accompanied by *Hero* and *Nizam*. *Ajax*. *Dido* and the two
destroyers with them, were to carry out another sweep off the
north coast of Crete during dark hours.

About two hours before dawn next morning, when approximately 90 miles from Scarpanto, *Formidable* ranged her striking force of eight Albacores. A slight alteration of course was made into the wind and, one by one, the aircraft took off until six of them were in the air. Two, becoming temperamental, had to be struck down again. Quickly they formed up, then two were seen to break away from the formation and return to the carrier. The hurried efforts to make them serviceable had been unsatisfactory, and their pilots were reluctantly forced to withdraw from the operation. Thus, the striking force was reduced to the quite inadequate number of four.

Half-an-hour later, *Formidable* again turned into the wind and four fighters followed the Albacores to the target with the principle object of attacking grounded aircraft in the first light of dawn.

For an hour-and-a-half the squadron cruised in the vicinity and then the planes were heard returning. It was a satisfying sight to see the same number come back as had set out, and it was later learnt that the attack had been as successful as our meagre numbers had permitted. It had come as a complete surprise to the enemy, and the bombs dropped by the Albacores had destroyed two enemy aircraft, damaging several others. The fighters, when they arrived, found a most magnificent target—closely packed rows of *C.R.42's* and *Junkers* 87. Diving down, one after the other, they swept them with machine-gun and cannon fire, putting at least twelve out of action and damaging more.

Forces were now retiring through the Kaso Strait, and it was the Vice-Admiral's intention to give them general cover, but no material attack developed. Many reconnaissance aircraft were, however, detected throughout the forenoon, but *Formidable* was only able to maintain two fighters in the air at the same time. The feats they performed were, nevertheless, prodigous and three reconnaissance machines were shot down before noon. Later, one of our fighters was seen to be in difficulties as it approached the carrier for landing on. The engine spluttered; it dropped like a wounded bird, then landed in the sea. A destroyer rescued the crew, but a valuable machine had been lost.

The force—now joined by *Ajax* and *Dido*—moved down to the south and, as the distance to the enemy aerodromes in the Ægean increased, so did everyone's confidence. Shortly after one o'clock the tendency to over optimism was rudely challenged when a large group of aircraft was detected approaching from the direction of Derna on the African coast. Soon the 'red' warning flag was hoisted and controlled fire opened in the direction of approach, while ships turned to the most suitable course. Then they came—twenty *Junkers* 87 diving from different directions simultaneously and paying scant attention to the heavy barrage with which they were greeted. The majority concentrated on *Formidable*.

From the bridge of *Queen Elizabeth* it was an astonishing sight to see one aircraft dive straight on her from astern, to see the bomb released and watch it almost race the aircraft in its headlong dive. Then there was a flash under *Formidable's* starboard bow; an explosion followed by tongues of flame. The aircraft which had almost laid the bomb on the carrier's deck now wobbled drunkenly, made a half recovery about 20 feet from the surface of the sea then, as though falling over itself, plunged into the water. Almost immediately afterwards, another bomb hit *Formidable* further aft, but it passed through the overhanging deck and did not explode until it reached the water. Within ten minutes the flames were under control and the carrier resumed her position in the line, a gaping hole in her starboard side. But 11 of her ship's company had been killed and 8 more wounded.

Bombs had also fallen close round the battleships but no harm had been done. *Nubian*—one of the destroyers on the screen—was less fortunate. With larger 'game' to claim the attention of the enemy she had felt reasonably secure, and her guns fired in the umbrella barrage over the battleships. Suddenly, to her Captain's disgust, a *Junkers* 87 selected *Nubian* as a desirable target, screaming down on her at terrific speed.

Quick avoiding action made no difference, and a bomb struck aft fair and square on No. 4 gun deck, blowing off the destroyer's entire stern above the water line. It also exploded the container of the special smoke producing apparatus, and the result was spectacular. An enormous column of thick white smoke rose for hundreds of feet into the air which caused alarm to other ships for the safety of *Nubian*.

Her Captain could no longer see the stern but, to his great amazement, the ship still responded to the engines and he found himself able to maintain 21 knots. What had happened to the propellors he could not imagine, and why they were still there was a mystery. But the ship was sluggish on the wheel, tons of water had poured in board and she had begun to take on a dangerous list. So orders were given to jettison torpedoes, depth charges and any movable weight on the upper deck in order to lighten her. One enthusiast seized a bundle containing all the officers' washing and threw it overboard— much to the dismay of those affected. A high level bombing attack which followed drenched the decks but did no damage and, with another destroyer to stand by her in case of need, *Nubian* proceeded to Alexandria where she arrived safely that evening. Her casualties amounted to 15 killed or missing and 4 more seriously wounded.

When the attack took place, *Formidable* had just landed on two fighters, and the two reliefs she had flown off had not got sufficient height to give any protection. When the enemy began to retire it was a different story. Although the bombers were escorted by numerous *Messerschmidts*, the two *Fulmars* tore right into them, destroyed one each and then damaged two more before their ammunition gave out. When they returned, their own machines were undamaged, but the gunner of one had four bullet wounds in his leg.

In spite of her damage, *Formidable* continued to operate aircraft until dark, but she was no longer sea-worthy when steaming into the wind. So, at nightfall she was detached with a destroyer escort and proceeded to Alexandria. The battleships remained at sea to provide distant cover for light forces operating through Kaso that night.

Meanwhile, the desperate attempt by *Glenroy* to land reinforcements at Tymbaki had again been foiled. Throughout the day she and her escort had been subjected to one bombing attack after another. The nearer she got to her destination the more frequent they became and, at 6.20 p.m., dive bombing began. All ships were prepared, and two of the attacking aircraft were shot down into the sea. Though no direct hit was sustained by any vessel, near misses damaged *Glenroy* and caused 11 casualties. Her hull was punctured, three of the special landing craft were severely holed and—more serious— a large dump of cased petrol on the upper deck caught fire. In order to get the flames under control it was necessary to retire to the southward to bring the wind astern, and it was not until just on eight o'clock before the fire was extinguished. The force then turned round and, an hour later, a final attack developed. This was carried out by torpedo bombers, but all the torpedoes dropped were successfully avoided.

Three hours had now been wasted, landing craft had been damaged and the wind had freshened. With these difficulties it would have been quite impossible to land the troops during the few dark hours available: to do so would have invited disaster. The decision was then reluctantly taken to abandon the operation and the force, thereupon, reversed the course and steered back towards Alexandria.

By daylight on May 27th, the Vice-Admiral in *Queen Elizabeth* was about 200 miles south-east of Kaso; *Abdiel*, after landing at Suda the last reinforcements to reach Crete— 750 Special Service troops—was proceeding at high speed to the southward, and *Glenroy* was further to the west. As it grew light the presence of hostile reconnaissance aircraft was detected but there was no *Formidable* to provide fighters to shoot them down and they never approached within gun range. Then a large group was detected coming in from the westward shortly before nine o'clock and, as they circled round to make an attack out of the sun, the battleships turned to present the smallest target possible by steering a course at right angles to the enemy's approach.

Because of the conditions of light, nothing could be seen, but when it was known that they were within four miles of the squadron, controlled fire was opened towards the sun, and this probably upset the enemy. A few moments later they came—fifteen to twenty *Junkers* 88 and *Heinkels*—tumbling out of the sun and concentrating on the battleships which snaked independently, while their close range weapons augmented the heavy volume of fire already being put up by the secondary armament. *Queen Elizabeth* escaped damage, but a number of bombs fell close to *Barham* puncturing her under-water bulges. One actually struck the roof of her after-turret, penetrated into the gun-house, causing a fire and several casualties and putting the turret out of action. During the attack at least two aircraft were shot down and a third was badly damaged. For two hours the squadron steered down wind to allow *Barham* to get the fire under control, and, at 12.30, orders were received from the Commander-in-Chief to return to Alexandria.

The situation in Crete had now become most critical. The day before, troops had made a further withdrawal towards Suda and it was realised that the whole front might soon collapse, but hopes were expressed that the stiffening provided by the reinforcements landed from *Abdiel* might enable the position to be stabilised. Such hopes were groundless for, on the 27th, the line completely collapsed with great suddenness. A rearguard was, however, organised under the command of Major-General E. C. Weston, Royal Marines, and consisted of Royal Marines, detachments of Dominion troops and the Special Service battalions. But the possibility of being able to win the Battle of Crete no longer existed, and naval and military headquarters were transferred to Sphakia.

That afternoon, General Wavell informed the Prime Minister that, though troops at Heraklion still held out, we had to recognise that Crete was no longer tenable and that there was no alternative but to withdraw the troops.

In the battle which had raged, the Navy could claim to have prevented sea-borne invasion and kept the army supplied. They had inflicted considerable losses on troop convoys and destroyed numerous aircraft, but their own losses had been severe, and the prolonged strain on ships and men had been terrific. But there was no time for rest. A formidable task still lay before the fleet—the evacuation of 22,000 men in conditions both hazardous and difficult.

III. EVACUATION

The task facing the navy was not only one of embarking troops under conditions of great difficulty, but also of getting them safely back across the 360 miles of sea to Egypt. Even when the actual period of embarkation was limited to the hours between midnight and 3.0 a.m., ships loaded with troops would still have to steam for many miles in areas subjected to intense dive bombing. With Crete virtually in their hands, the enemy could concentrate almost their entire air arm on the destruction of our ships whose numbers had already been tragically reduced. To what extent could the R.A.F. possibly provide protection? The Air Officer Commanding-in-Chief assured Admiral Cunningham that he would do all that lay in his power but protection, he feared, could at the most only be meagre and spasmodic.

The first attempt at evacuation was planned to take place during the night of May 28th/29th, and it was decided to extricate that portion of the army who had resisted so gallantly at Heraclion. The troops retiring from the Suda area were reported as not yet being ready for a large scale evacuation from the south coast. At 6.0 a.m. on 28th May, Admiral Rawlings, now having returned to his own flagship, the cruiser *Orion*, left Alexandria with *Ajax*, *Dido* and six destroyers—*Decoy*, *Jackal*, *Imperial*, *Hotspur*, *Kimberley* and *Hereward*—to carry out the evacuation from Heraclion that night.

From 5.0 p.m. until dark the force was subjected to a series of air attacks during which *Imperial* and *Ajax* were near missed. At the time, *Imperial* appeared to be undamaged, but a fire had been started in *Ajax* where twenty men had been seriously wounded, and her hull had been punctured in several places. For the trials to which ships might be subjected during the night and would certainly have to face next day, Admiral Rawlings considered it essential that each of his ships should be 100 per cent efficient. A 'lame duck' might jeopardise the security of the whole force. *Ajax* was, therefore, ordered to return to Alexandria. As the force passed through the Kaso Strait and turned to the westward an attack was made by torpedo bombers, but all torpedoes were avoided and ships arrived off Heraclion in safety at 11.30 p.m.

Entering harbour two at a time, the destroyers embarked troops, ferried them to the cruisers outside and then returned to pick up their own complements. Everything proceeded smoothly. Although, for nights past, the enemy had been dropping flares over the harbour, on this particular night they refrained from doing so; neither did they launch an attack on the rearguard as the men steadily withdrew towards the jetties.

By 2.45 a.m. the evacuation was completed and, with 3486 troops on board, the force sailed at 29 knots. Except for a few wounded who had been cut off in a hospital at Knossos, the entire garrison had been embarked besides a few Greeks who had managed to get on board. *Orion*, for instance, had 90 officers, 1000 troops, 12 Greek military personnel, 6 male civilians, 2 women and 2 young girls. Unobserved, the latter must have crept on board one of the destroyers who passed them on to *Orion*, where they were stowed in an officer's cabin. The rearguard had been embarked in *Kimberley* and *Imperial*.

This promising start to the operation was soon followed by disappointment. At 3.45 a.m., *Imperial* suddenly found she could no longer steer. The near miss she had sustained the previous evening must have caused an undetected fracture, and she was now helpless. Yawing wildly, she narrowly escaped colliding with the cruisers and as she passed close under the stern of *Orion* just managed to flash the message: "My rudder . . ."

It could not have been more inopportune, and Admiral Rawlings was faced with a difficult problem. Should he wait on the off chance that repairs could be made good and thus run the risk of exposing the whole force in daylight in the most vulnerable area for bombing ? Or should he order another destroyer to embark all those in *Imperial* and then have her sunk ? The risk was too great and he was forced to accept the latter alternative. Speed was, therefore, reduced to 15 knots and *Hotspur* ordered to go alongside *Imperial*. By 4.45, *Hotspur* had embarked the crew and troops who were on board; then, with torpedoes, carried out the distasteful task of sinking one of our own destroyers (undamaged save for a defect which could probably have been rectified with proper facilities within the space of a few days). The force then proceeded, but ninety very precious minutes had been lost.

Because of the delay, it was sunrise before the ships passed through the Kaso Strait and, when it grew light, Scarpanto was actually in sight. Anxiously everyone scanned the skies for signs of R.A.F. fighters whom they hopefully expected. But none were seen. Instead, swarms of *Junkers*, *Heinkels* and *Messerschmidts* began to fill the sky and, from 6.0 a.m. onwards, one vicious attack was delivered after another.

Half-an-hour later the destroyer *Hereward* was seen to be hit. Dropping speed and listing badly, she soon fell out of her position on the screen and slowly passed astern. Admiral Rawlings was again faced with a difficult decision as to whether he should cover the damaged vessel and take her in tow, or, at least, rescue the crew and troops on board. But the scores of enemy aircraft in the air and the continuous attacks made only one course possible. She had to be left. It was hateful to have to abandon a ship like this, but land was close and there was a good chance that the majority of those on board would survive, even though they would probably be taken prisoner. When last seen, *Hereward* was making slowly for the eastern end of Crete, her guns gallantly engaging hostile aircraft until she faded out of sight in the Mediterranean haze.

Twenty minutes later *Decoy* reported a fractured turbine caused by a near miss, and the speed of the force had to be reduced to 22 knots.

The enemy now concentrated on the two cruisers *Orion* and *Dido*. At 7.0 a.m. a very near miss on *Orion* holed her forward, flooded some compartments and necessitated a further reduction in speed to 21 knots. Soon afterwards, Captain G. R. B. Back, R.N., the Flag Captain of *Orion*, was carried below mortally wounded by an explosive bullet from a *Junkers* 87. An attack at 9.30 which scored several near misses on *Orion* brought him back to semi-consciousness as he struggled to sit up, calling on everyone round him to "keep steady." In the momentary lull which followed, he cried: "It's all right, men —that one's over." Then he died.

At 8.15 a *Junkers* 87 broke through the barrage, dived low on *Dido* and dropped a bomb on one of her forward turrets putting all guns before the bridge out of action. The same thing happened to *Orion* causing many casualties both among the troops and crew, but the aircraft which had carried out this daring attack crashed into the sea. There was then a fortunate lull for 45 minutes which gave those on board a little time to clear away some of the debris and enabled medical parties to move the wounded further aft and attend to them.

Then they came again—the *Junkers* 87 making their final attacks before the ships passed out of their operational range. At first the cruisers escaped more serious harm although bombs fell close all round, but at 10.45 *Orion* received another damaging hit. A large bomb passed through the bridge and burst in the stokers' mess deck near the Lower Conning Tower, from which position the ship was being steered.

The havoc it created below decks was indescribable. All lights were extinguished; flames filled the boys' and stokers' mess decks which were crammed with troops; the forward sick bay was wrecked, both medical officers escaping miraculously with their lives; all normal communication between the bridge and engine room was destroyed; the steering gear was put out of action and the ship got quite out of control. Casualties were terrific both among passengers and crew, the death roll amounting to about 280 with an equal number wounded. Then began the struggle to extricate and tend the wounded, extinguish fires and restore lighting—a struggle in which all joined, including the soldiers, with a spirit of courage, initiative and determination. The soldiers were magnificent under these appalling circumstances and many high tributes were paid to their untiring and cheerful efforts by officers and men of the cruiser.

On deck another struggle was going on—to get the ship under control. After her first wild yaws, she had steadied herself somewhat inconsiderately on Scarpanto. But the hand steering wheel was rapidly connected and a human order chain, both of soldiers and sailors, was formed between the after-conning position and the engine room. Finally, the ship was more or less steadied on her proper course but, as her compasses were smashed, *Dido* took station ahead and led towards Alexandria.

After the great damage which had been sustained, there was natural anxiety as to whether main engines could be kept running and, when the ship took up a list of some 11 degrees to starboard, apprehension deepened. To those in the engine room it was more than unpleasant. They had suffered many casualties. The lack of light, the fact that the ship was not properly under control, the knowledge of fierce fires burning forward, the smoke filling the machinery spaces all produced uneasiness; but each man stuck to his post.

By jettisoning torpedoes and moving men over to the port side the list was eased, and magnificent efforts on the part of the engine room staff enabled the ship to proceed at an average speed of 21 knots, although sometimes it was necessary to come right down to 12. In the words of *Orion's* Commanding Officer: "Inspired by the good humour and encouragement of Admiral Rawlings, a strong spirit of determination ran through the ship, everyone feeling that all difficulties would be overcome."

Dive bombing had now ceased, but attacks continued from a high level until 3.0 p.m. No more damage occurred. About noon two *Fulmar* fighters of the Fleet Air Arm were sighted, giving great encouragement to the hard-pressed ships. R.A.F. fighters had been unable to make contact but, during the course of their sweeps, had shot down two *Junkers* 88 for the loss of one *Hurricane*, while the sight of bombs being jettisoned on the horizon showed that the enemy was not having everything his own way.

The force reached Alexandria at 8.0 p.m., *Orion* having only 10 tons of fuel left and two rounds of H.E. shell.

Two hours later there was a heavy air raid on the harbour.

Although the main evacuation for that first night had been from Heraclion, a force of four destroyers—*Napier*, *Kandahar*, *Kelvin* and *Nizam*—had embarked a smaller party of about 700, mostly wounded, from Sphakia. Local difficulties there were considerable. Sphakia itself is a small fishing village with a beach of shingle, only two hundred yards of which is suitable for boat work. The road from the interior over the mountains comes to an abrupt halt at the top of a 500-foot escarpment overlooking Sphakia. Thence, a precipitous goat track winds down to the village. Communication between the beach and the top of the escarpment had to be made on foot, the climb taking about two hours, and the troops remained hidden at the top until groups were summoned to the shore. In a cave near Sphakia village, the headquarters of the G.O.C. and Captain Morse were established, and a portable W./T. set was used to maintain communication with Alexandria.

Unmolested on the way, the destroyers arrived off Sphakia half-an-hour after midnight, but there were not many troops ready to be embarked. Indeed, the passengers taken on board were very mixed and *Napier* reported that her 'haul' consisted

of 36 officers, 260 other ranks, 3 women, 1 Greek, 1 Chinaman,
10 distressed merchant seamen, 2 children and 1 dog! They
sailed punctually at 3.0 a.m., were well clear by dawn and
only experienced one air attack at nine o'clock from four
Junkers 88. *Nizam* received minor damage, but the remainder
were untouched and reached Alexandria at 5.0 p.m.

It was now decided to use Sphakia as the only place for
further evacuation, but aircraft dropped a supply of rations
for troops believed to be near Plaka, which was further to the
eastward, together with orders to move towards Sphakia. On
the evening of the 29th a large force sailed from Alexandria
for this one embarkation beach. Led by Rear-Admiral King
in *Phoebe*, it comprised *Perth*, *Glengyle*, *Calcutta*, *Coventry* and
three destroyers. The inclusion of the *Glen* ship with her big
carrying capacity and special landing craft was a risk because
it reduced the speed of the force to 18 knots.

Three more destroyers were, however, sent to rendezvous
with the force next day—if *Glengyle* was damaged, they could
embark survivors.

As it happened, embarkation proceeded smoothly. The A.A.
cruisers *Calcutta* and *Coventry* and the destroyers patrolled to
seaward, the latter closing in one at a time to embark their
quota. The landing craft from *Glengyle*, assisted by two which
had been embarked in *Perth*, did the ferrying and, by 3.20 a.m.
over 6000 troops were safely on board. Leaving three of the
landing craft behind to assist with any subsequent evacuation,
the force then sailed. They were lucky; only three air attacks
developed during the following forenoon. In the first *Perth*
was hit and her foremost boiler room was put out of action,
but she could still maintain the speed required. In the other
two attacks no damage was sustained although more bombs
fell close to *Perth*. This relative immunity from serious air
attack was largely due to the presence of two or three R.A.F.
fighters which had made their appearance for the first time.
Once, indeed, they gallantly drove off a force of twenty
Junkers 87 and 88, shot down two *Heinkels* 111 and damaged

several others. More were damaged by gunfire from the ships.

Without further incident, the force with Admiral King reached Alexandria towards evening on May 30th, passing on the way more destroyers who were to continue the evacuation that night. Originally, there were four, but *Kelvin* had been damaged by a near miss about 3.30 p.m., when three *Junkers* 88 made an unseen dive from astern. As she was then unable to maintain high speed, she was ordered back to Alexandria. *Kandahar* had previously developed an engine defect and had also been forced to retire, so only two destroyers —*Napier* and *Nizam* actually reached Sphakia.

The landing craft which had been left behind by Admiral King drew alongside full of troops as the destroyers anchored. Embarkation was expeditious and at 3.0 a.m. on 31st, with 700 soldiers in each destroyer, they proceeded back to Alexandria. Friendly fighters were again sighted at daylight, and it was gratifying to see four enemy aircraft shot down and three more damaged. As a result only one air attack actually developed, in which *Napier* received minor damage from a near miss, while a *Junkers* 88 was brought down by ships' gunfire.

On the night of 30th/31st, the G.O.C., Major-General Freyberg, and Captain Morse were ordered to embark in a Sunderland flying boat which had been despatched for them, and the command was turned over to Major-General Weston, Royal Marines. Meanwhile, the enemy had been threatening to cut off the line of retreat to Sphakia, but the Royal Marine rearguard, assisted by the Special Service troops and some Colonial detachments repulsed every attempt. Headquarters at Sphakia now appealed for one more embarkation to be arranged which it was thought would amount to about 3000 men. Next day the numbers rose to 6500, but insufficient ships were available to embark that number. With orders to fill to capacity, Admiral King again sailed in *Phoebe* with the fast minelayer *Abdiel* and four destroyers.

That day it was decided to call a halt to further efforts at evacuation. Even if Admiral King's entire force returned without damage, the Mediterranean Fleet was now reduced to a pathetic number of ships to maintain command of a vital area.

Towards evening a signal was despatched from G.H.Q. Middle East stating that this was the last possible night for evacuation and authorised the capitulation of the remaining troops. Its despatch meant an irrevocable decision.

Meanwhile, Admiral King speeded towards Sphakia for the final trip. In the late afternoon three air attacks developed but no bombs fell close to any ship, and several large splashes on the horizon testified to the fact that R.A.F. fighters were in the vicinity and scoring successes.

At 11.20 p.m. the force arrived. As on the previous night the three special landing craft came alongside at once, loaded with troops, and the embarkation proceeded so rapidly that the beach was quickly cleared. Altogether about 4000 men were embarked. Landing medical stores and rations for the remainder, and destroying the landing craft which could not be hoisted, Admiral King proceeded at 3.0 a.m. and shaped course for Alexandria.

On orders from the Commander-in-Chief, General Weston had been instructed to embark in a Sunderland but, before leaving, he handed written orders to the senior army officer remaining to come to terms with the enemy. Among those unfortunately left behind were many who had taken part in a gallant rearguard action enabling others to get away, and these included the Special Service troops who had been landed at Suda and large numbers of Royal Marines. Of the 2000 Royal Marines who had originally helped to garrison Crete, only 1000 got back to Egypt.

In order to provide additional protection for Admiral King, the A.A. cruisers *Calcutta* and *Coventry* were sailed from Alexandria early on June 1st to make contact with the ships returning from Sphakia during the forenoon. This move was unfortunate. About nine o'clock hostile aircraft were detected; touch was then lost with them until suddenly two *Junkers* 88

M

dived out of the sun—one at each ship. A stick of bombs from one just missed *Coventry*, drenching her decks in water but doing no damage. The attack on *Calcutta* was mortifying. One bomb struck near the after funnel, another just before the bridge and, in a few moments, flames swept her fore and aft as she rapidly began to sink. Fortunately, there were no more enemy planes about and *Coventry* was able to rescue 23 officers and 232 men, but casualties were naturally heavy. In the meantime, the ships with Admiral King had a remarkably peaceful passage and reached Alexandria in safety at 5.0 p.m.

So ended the Battle of Crete, in which the Mediterranean Fleet could claim to have played a worthy part. While fighting ashore had been in progress, the navy had landed reinforcements and supplies, and prevented sea-borne invasion. When orders were given for the withdrawal, some 17,000 soldiers were brought safely back to Egypt, while provisions and stores were landed for the remainder. But the fleet had suffered badly, and the losses and damage sustained were such as would normally only occur during a major fleet action, in which the enemy might be expected to incur even greater losses. In this case the enemy fleet did not appear—though it had many opportunities—and the battle merely raged between ships and the German Air Force.

For those soldiers who had fought so heroically there was nothing but admiration and sympathy throughout the fleet. Had they been supplied with anything like the equipment to which they were entitled—so much of it had been lost in Greece—the story might well have been different.

IV. AFTERMATH

The sun shone over Alexandria, but in the harbour there was sorrow and disappointment. A violent battle had been lost, the blue waters of the Mediterranean had closed over gallant comrades, and familiar, friendly ships had taken the final plunge.

In one of the battleships the ship's company was addressed in the following terms:

"It is only natural that we should feel very disappointed with the German successes in Crete, especially after the valiant and determined efforts of the Fleet to help our comrades in the army there, and the heavy losses we have thereby sustained.

"Under these circumstances it is inevitable that the picture of the war as a whole should be obscured by the cloud which temporarily hangs over our own theatre of operations. At the moment we cannot disperse that cloud, but we can get behind it, see its silver lining and the blue sky beyond. To begin with, it is quite obvious that in their attack on Crete the Germans put in all their resources, called up their reserves of aircraft from all over Europe and threw them, regardless of cost, into the battle in order to secure victory in this one small area. That at once proves that there is a limit to German resources and the number of aircraft they possess, and, in the course of the battle, we have undoubtedly eaten into those reserves to an enormous extent. If we knew the number of aircraft we have brought down and damaged during the past ten days we would be encouraged, for it must amount to several hundreds.

"With the successful invasion of Crete by German air-borne troops, it is only natural that we should consider the threatened invasion of Great Britain. In this connection, I feel that the results of the Battle of Crete should give us the greatest encouragement. With virtually no air opposition and inadequate A.A. defence, we have managed to destroy hundreds of German aircraft and exterminate thousands of Germans. Though they had complete mastery of the air from the very beginning, they have only conquered after twelve days of the fiercest fighting they have probably ever faced. It is, I feel sure, no exaggeration to say that had we been able to put into the air over Crete a tenth of the aircraft used by the Germans the story would have been very different. We know that at home we have a very large air force capable of operating from a number of widely separated bases. Therefore, for an invasion of England to stand the slightest chance of success, the Germans would have to launch an attack on a scale at least twenty times heavier than they delivered in Crete. Are they capable of it ? It is reasonable to suppose that they are not.

"I do appreciate that in moments of defeat and humiliating reverse—and I do not intend to deny that the loss of Crete is such a defeat—however great our spirit—unwelcome and demoralising thoughts creep into our minds, especially when they are tired.

"I am going to make a bold statement, that the Battle of Crete, though a temporary defeat for us, marks the final defeat of Germany as nothing has marked it before. I have already explained that it must have shaken their confidence in an ability to invade Great Britain, but I am prepared to say more. I believe that the opposition the Germans have encountered both in Greece and Crete has possibly called a stop to their eastward advance in the Mediterranean and most certainly has upset their programme. This will undoubtedly have a most important effect on the whole course of the war and thoroughly justifies the strategic policy in this theatre of war. Naturally, I cannot enlarge on this point without giving away secrets, but it is no secret to say that we'd be happier if we were stronger, especially in the air, and that we know—in time—we'll have sufficient men and material to throw the Germans back to where they belong."

Chapter 11

THE SUDA BAY LOCAL PATROL
MAY 1941

VARIOUS small craft—A./S. vessels, motor launches, lighters, etc.—operated from Suda Bay prior to and during the early stages of the Battle of Crete. Their duties were many— patrolling, escorting lighters, ferrying, supplying water and steam, and even fighting fires in ships damaged by enemy action. When the army was forced to withdraw and Suda became directly threatened by the enemy, Captain Morse, the Naval Officer in Charge, gave them orders to try and find their way back to Alexandria, keeping hidden by day when in the vicinity of the coast. Several were bombed and wrecked in harbour; nine set out on the journey; only three reached their destination, but all had startling adventures.

On the second day of the German attack—21st May—*Syvern* was on patrol near the entrance of Suda Bay. Although German troop planes, dive bombers and fighters seemed to pass overhead in an endless stream, it was thought likely that they would all be too occupied with the fighting ashore at that stage to pay much attention to an isolated small patrol vessel. Nevertheless, so far as her duties allowed, *Syvern* tried to remain reasonably inconspicuous near the land.

It made no difference. At 1.45 p.m., above the steady drone of aircraft which had been going on all day was suddenly heard the more ominous sound of an engine rising to crescendo. A *Junkers* 88 had spotted *Syvern* and, instead of 'ground straffing' positions ashore, was diving to attack the patrol vessel. With all her small automatic guns *Syvern* retaliated, but the enemy closed and, from a range of a few hundred yards, raked the ship's decks with machine-gun and cannon fire. Every gunner in *Syvern* fell wounded—one mortally—and her rate of fire was thereby reduced. The enemy, growing bolder now that the scale of opposition had decreased, turned and came in closer. Six runs did the *Junkers* carry out: each one nearer to the target where injured men were doing their utmost to repel this murderous assault which they had begun to feel could only have one ending.

During the last attack bullets entered the starboard ready use ammunition locker which was on deck. Ammunition caught fire and shells started to explode in every direction; but so close was the aircraft that it was actually hit in the port engine by a piece of the ammunition locker which had been thrown in the air by the series of explosions. The pilot immediately lost control of his machine which side slipped across *Syvern*, carried away her mast and plunged into the sea on the other side.

Small fires now raged on deck, but two young Ordinary Seamen—Gutteridge and Egan—who were practically the only unwounded members of the ship's company, coolly threw the remaining hot live ammunition overboard and then successfully attacked the fires. The ship was saved.

On the evening of the 26th Captain Morse gave orders for all small craft to make their way to Alexandria, but *Syvern* did not actually receive the message until it was too late for her to take advantage of the darkness that night to slip away unobserved. So, in company with *Kos* 22, she tried to remain hidden in a small cove near the outer boom during daylight hours on the 27th.

The time passed and both crews began to hope that they would be undetected when, towards evening, they were spotted. At 8.0 p.m. two aircraft swooped low and, dropping bombs on each of the unfortunate vessels, left them both in flames. After destroying all confidential books, the crews scrambled ashore—some of them not required for the guns had already taken refuge in a cave—and after a series of incredible experiences worked their way through the German lines, received food and hospitality from Cretan villagers, and finally reached Sphakia. Here they were evacuated in one of the naval ships.

Kos 21 was more fortunate. She received the order to sail in good time and by 6.0 a.m. on 27th May was off the south-west coast of Crete—but not far enough away to escape the vigilance of the German Air Force. Shortly afterwards, three *Junkers* 87 made a concentrated machine-gun attack, but *Kos* 21 replied, Able-Seaman Dent, though seriously wounded manning one gun most heroically until the enemy had been beaten off. There were two casualties—one killed and one wounded.

Everyone was badly shaken, but half an hour later the attack was repeated—this time with bombs as well as machine-gun fire. Again the vessel's sustained fire drove the enemy off, but a near miss brought the engines to a standstill and caused the steering gear to jam. Great efforts on the part of the engine room staff repaired the defect, and *Kos* 21 was again under way by the time the next attack developed at 8.30. Four *Heinkels* 111, either having no bombs to drop or considering it not worth while to expend one on a small vessel of this type, swooped down and again machine-gunned her decks. Two men were killed but the damage sustained was negligible. One of the *Heinkels*, however, was badly hit and appeared to crash near the horizon.

For the next four hours they were left in peace, but a final attack took place at 12.20. Two more *Heinkels* dived, one from either side, and the bombs released caused more damage from near misses, though there were no serious casualties. The engines again broke down and the starboard oil fuel tanks were cracked, giving the ship a heavy list to port which was assisted by the volume of water thrown on board by the splashes in the sea alongside. The list increased, and serious consideration was being given to abandon ship, when the engine room again reported that they had the situation under control. By constant baling the ship was more evenly trimmed, and *Kos* 21 proceeded towards the south-east.

But when the African coast was reached two days later, the Commanding Officer only had the remotest idea as to where he was. He was in an uncomfortable position. The compass was smashed, the wireless was out of action and he was running very short of fuel, almost all that from the starboard tanks having disappeared. The weather was hazy and, as he approached the shore to try and discover where he was, the vessel suddenly stopped. She had grounded on an outlying shoal.

Efforts made to get the ship off finally succeeded, but—she left her propellor behind. This was awkward, and *Kos* 21 was now helpless. An anchor was accordingly let go, and three men were sent ashore on a raft to try and establish communication with somewhere. All boats had been damaged by the machine-gunning and the raft was found to be very cumbersome, but they eventually landed and, after walking some distance, got in touch with Alexandria. Later in the day, the escort vessel *Flamingo* appeared, but the water was too shallow to allow her to approach, and all she could do was to send a motor boat to embark the wounded. The situation was signalled to the base and, on 31st May, a small craft arrived to tow *Kos* 21 to *Flamingo*, who finally brought her into harbour.

Motor launches were for the most part unfortunate. M.L.'s 1030 and 1032 left Suda Bay in company after dark on the 27th, but got separated during the night. When dawn broke next day, M.L. 1032 saw no sign of her consort and it was pointless to try and search for her as she might be anywhere. So she continued on her journey to Alexandria experiencing during the early part of the afternoon only one air attack, which she was able to beat off without sustaining casualties or damage. The rest of the journey was made without incident.

But M.L. 1030 fared differently. She had presumably taken a more northerly course, and dawn of the 28th found her within a few miles of Gavdo Pulo. She was immediately spotted and, almost before the sun had risen, a *Junkers* 88 came diving on her, spitting out machine-gun bullets. It also dropped a bomb which fell close alongside causing serious damage. The M.L. immediately began to sink, and the crew had scarcely abandoned her, crowding into a damaged dinghy or hanging on to a raft, when she completely disappeared from view.

Then began an arduous pull. The sea was rough and a fresh breeze was blowing from the north-east in which direction they had to drive the crazy overcrowded boat. There were nine of them altogether, but it was impossible for more than six at a time to be in the dinghy, and those who were not actually on the oars had to spend every moment baling. Taking it in turns, three men would climb out on to the raft which was in tow and cling madly to it until they were too exhausted to hold on any longer. Frequently, seas would wash one of them off, but whoever it was always managed to get back again. For over twenty-one hours this laborious process continued, but dogged determination eventually enabled them to reach Gavdo Pulo in the early hours of the following morning. There they rested.

By 11.0 a.m. they had somewhat recovered, the boat had been patched up and, as the sea was calmer, they all embarked in the dinghy to reach the mainland of Crete some fourteen miles away. Happily undetected by aircraft, they struck the coast 15 miles west of Sphakia at 5.30 next morning after a gruelling pull. Here they fell in with some Australian soldiers, who provided them with water, and they eventually reached the embarkation beach. . . .

When Captain Morse decided that the time was coming when he would have to move his headquarters to Sphakia, he loaded his confidential books and cyphers, together with a portable naval W./T. set, into M.L. 1011. His Secretary and the Warrant Telegraphist embarked with them, and orders were given to proceed under cover of darkness on the night of May 23rd. On rounding the south-west corner of Crete, the M.L. encountered such heavy weather that the Commanding Officer was forced to take shelter off Selinos Kastelli, where he anchored about 50 yards from the shore in what he considered the most inconspicuous position.

But the eagle eye of inquisitive *Junkers* was not to be fooled. At 6.30 next morning the drone of aircraft was heard approaching and, looking out through the hatchway, the Commanding Officer saw seven *Messerschmidts* and two *Junkers* 88 pass overhead. At first he thought that he had not been spotted but, much to his dismay, the two *Junkers* suddenly broke formation, circled back, and began to dive on the M.L. The *Messerschmidts* followed.

Opening fire with their one Lewis gun, the little boat fought back gallantly as a hail of bullets riddled her side and great spouts of water from falling bombs rose up close by. Although one aircraft was seen to crash—it had come so close that the Lewis gun was able to empty itself into the machine—the gun was put out of action in the first attack, and damage from a near miss caused the boat to heel over alarmingly.

There was nothing for it but to take to the sea and swim ashore. As they swam for their lives, the enemy continued to machine-gun the men in the water, but without harm. Only one casualty had been sustained, but that was bad enough. The Warrant Telegraphist was sleeping on a settee when the attack began and must have been killed as soon as the aircraft started to machine gun the boat.

M.L. 1011 had listed and settled down on her starboard side in shallow water by the time the enemy had gone, and strenuous efforts were then made to try and recover the confidential books which were in a steel safe under water. Time and again officers and men dived, but the task was impossible without some sort of salvage equipment.

They were now some 30 miles from Sphakia, and the crew were in an unenviable position. They were unarmed, inadequately booted for a long walk across the mountains, and German parachutists were known to have descended in the vicinity. Fortunately, they encountered a mixed party with a Fleet Air Arm officer who had made a miraculous escape from Maleme, and together they attempted the journey. After proceeding some distance with considerable difficulty, they managed to embark in a caique which took them the rest of the way under cover of darkness.

The story of the Suda Bay Local Patrol cannot be concluded without reference to the 'A' lighters which performed much useful and continuous service. They were always doing something: carrying troops, discharging cargo, ammunition, and even Bren guns; embarking clothing, food and stores, and delivering them at various points. 'A' 16 was the last of these lighters left at Suda and, during the attack on Crete, was dive-bombed no fewer than thirty-seven times. Though she was never actually hit, she experienced numerous near misses, all of which must have imposed a severe strain on the crew. Her final task was to disembark the Special Service troops from *Abdiel* when she brought the last reinforcements to Crete. 'A' 16 was then sunk and the crew embarked in *Abdiel* for passage to Alexandria.

Chapter 12

FLEET AIR ARM ADVENTURES IN THE BATTLE OF CRETE

Up to May 1st, 1941, Maleme aerodrome had been under the command of the Fleet Air Arm, but on that date it was officially turned over to the R.A.F. Some Fleet Air Arm personnel, nevertheless, stayed, largely in an advisory capacity —even when the aircraft had all been withdrawn—and the station itself, for various reasons, remained under the direction of Commander G. H. Beale, R.N. During the period between the evacuation from Greece and the Battle of Crete, every effort was made to improve the defences; but difficulties were immense, lack of tools and material, together with inadequate labour, being the chief handicaps. On 12th May the aerodrome experienced its first really serious attack, when swarms of enemy machines bombed and 'ground straffed' the defences. These attacks, increasing in intensity from day to day, interrupted the work more than ever.

As twilight began on 20th May all the troops 'stood-to.' It was a routine which had been carried out for the past few days in order to make men familiar with the various defence positions to which they had been assigned; for attack, when it came, was expected to materialise at dawn. The sun rose, and everyone was dispersed to wash and breakfast. Then suddenly, while the troops were scattered and in different stages of undress, the air raid warning sounded and they all took cover in the nearest shelters. Almost immediately wave after wave of enemy fighters and bombers streaked round the aerodrome, shooting up the camp and paying particular attention to defence positions all round. The actual landing ground they left alone.

For two hours they continued to circle round at heights from 100 - 500 feet gunning and bombing; creating dust, smoke and noise, which was frightening in its intensity, keeping everyone under cover. There was a pause; men began to emerge, and what they saw galvanised them into instant action. Overhead were swarms of troop carrying aircraft, from whose interiors hundreds of parachutists were dropping. Some had already landed, and the air was full of reinforcements as an endless stream of aircraft came and went. The invasion of Crete had begun.

Officers and men rushed to their posts, and Commander Beale moved rapidly towards the 22nd Battalion (N.Z.) headquarters, which was his action station. Shortly afterwards, he was badly wounded from a hand grenade and subsequently became a prisoner of war. Lieutenant A. W. F. Sutton, R.N., who had been his principal assistant, dashed into his own tent, grabbed his rifle and bandolier and, passing through the north camp which he found deserted, took up a position on the hill just below some 4-inch guns, from which he could command a clear field of view. For yards all round him the area was deserted and blasted by bombs.

Presently a Lieutenant R.M. shouted at him. The guns under which he thought he was sheltering had apparently been put out of action and their crews had retired to some positions further back. Parachutists were dropping all round and, where he was, Lieutenant Sutton ran every chance of being rapidly surrounded by the enemy. So he decided to retire also, in company with the Royal Marine Lieutenant, his Sergeant and two R.A.F. ranks. Aircraft skimmed overhead, bombing and machine-gunning any movement of our own troops, so progress had to be made with the greatest caution. Finally, they reached the barbed wire defences round two 3-inch H.A. guns at the top of the hill which were manned by Royal Marines. Here he felt less insecure.

For the greater part of the day, Sutton sat in a position below the summit of the hill where he dug himself a hole in the ground with his bayonet, because he frequently came under fire from snipers. All the time he fired at parachutists who continued to drop round him in every direction, as troop carrier followed troop carrier, and strings of gliders, together with numerous dive bombers and fighters, seemed to fill the entire space overhead.

L.A.C. Denton, of 815 Squadron, could be seen manning an air Lewis gun in a pit at the bottom of the hill near the aerodrome. For the past fortnight he had manned this position at the morning 'stand-to' and had been subjected to many attacks from bombing and 'ground-straffing,' but his orders were not to open fire until the invasion actually started. Now he was fighting, but he was alone. Parachutists appeared to be falling all round him, but he kept his gun in action, inflicting a considerable number of casualties, until at length it burnt out and he could fire no more. Then, picking it up, he scrambled to the defended position at the top of the hill.

Of what was happening Lieutenant Sutton had not the remotest idea. Nor had anyone else round him, apparently. But it was quite obvious that the situation had rapidly become most involved and, in many cases, approached chaos. Pockets of men had swiftly been surrounded and forced to surrender, communications had been thrown into the utmost confusion, the enemy had been dropped everywhere, and it was impossible to tell if that party moving round the corner or over that hill was friend or foe. Many of the Germans spoke reasonable English and, when shouted at, would respond as though they were friends until close enough to disclose their identity with a hand grenade. There was only one sure password—the ubiquitous naval adjective!

Sutton learned that the R.A.F. camp, where the men were virtually unarmed, had been one of the first positions which fell to the enemy, and the prisoners captured had been driven ahead of the Germans as body shields. Pilot Officer Crowther had gallantly led a mixed party of men against one of these groups of Germans advancing behind their prisoners. Some of these unfortunate men were unhappily killed in the ensuing fray; many were released and—the Germans were driven back with considerable loss.

From his position on the hill, Lieutenant Sutton marvelled at the enemy's magnificent air co-operation. In some camouflaged position a gun would fire; perhaps at troops, perhaps at aircraft; but the result was always the same. Within a few minutes a dive bomber would come screaming down on the hidden gun and often put it out of action. This had happened to the 3-inch H.A. manned by the Royal Marines, but heroic efforts brought one of them into action again. Not for long was it allowed to fire, its accuracy bringing down the enemy's special hate. The whole hill rocked with falling bombs, the ammunition dump exploded, stores and undergrowth were set on fire.

That particular hill, Lieutenant Sutton reflected, was not a healthy place, but he stuck it out and fought back hard all day. In fact, it was almost impossible to move because the whole ridge was commanded by snipers, enemy machine guns and a heavy mortar. Once during the day, a Royal Marine crept round on his stomach with a few welcome rations, but towards evening the men began to get depressed. There was no water, very little food and scarcely any ammunition left.

Darkness fell at last, and those who had been manning positions on this particular hill were ordered back to the top —a motley collection from miscellaneous units. Here a Royal Marine Lieutenant had organised rations and water, after which guides were provided and they moved to new positions east of Maleme village. Lieutenant Sutton then found himself in command of a miscellaneous crowd of 'homeless' men who had no officers and had lost their units—R.M.'s, R.A.'s, Bofors' gunners, Tank details, as well as R.A.F. and F.A.A. personnel. Altogether they were about 150 strong, and Sutton led them to the headquarters of the 21st Battalion near which they settled down in an olive grove for the night.

Next day, Pilot Officer Crowther joined Sutton with a party of about forty R.A.F. ranks, while most of the military details found their way back to their own units. As the majority of the R.A.F. were unarmed, or at least without ammunition, they lay hidden in the gullies for most of the day; those who had rifles mounting guard round the group. Aircraft circled overhead at low altitudes but they remained undetected and during the afternoon, received another reinforcement in the shape of men from 805 Squadron under the leadership of Lieutenant (A) A. R. Ramsay, R.N.V.R.

805 Squadron had had their share of excitement. Three officers and forty men had been left behind as a retard party when their machines had flown back to Egypt, and, as soon as the attack began, they managed to muster on high ground overlooking their camp into which parachutists were falling. They were quite inadequately armed but, in spite of being bombed and machine-gunned, attacked by infantry and bombarded by a trench mortar, they managed to hold on to their position for the greater part of the day, inflicting a considerable number of casualties on the enemy.

During the forenoon, Chief Petty Officer Hall gallantly made his way back to the camp through the enemy lines, bringing back rum and provisions.

Later in the day, these men of 805 Squadron were joined by Petty Officer Wheaton and a few more R.A.F. ranks. This Petty Officer did not belong to the Fleet Air Arm but was an L.T.O. who, with two Able-Seamen (S.T.), had been loaned for electrical work on the aerodrome. His experiences were amazing. When the attack began, he made for the nearest slit trench in company with one Able-Seaman and five R.A.F. ranks, but this position was an early target for the parachutists. A hand grenade thrown into the trench, killed two of the R.A.F. and severely wounded the other three. But, though shaken, Wheaton and the Able-Seaman were unhurt. At that time it was impossible to evacuate this poor shelter, so they tended the wounded with field dressings, making them as comfortable as possible.

When things began to calm down in this sector, the two seamen decided to work their way to a trench further up the hill. They broke cover and ran, being joined by an R.A.F. rating from an adjacent position. But Germans were scattered in the trees all round them and opened fire with Tommy guns, killing the R.A.F. man. Unscathed, Wheaton and the A.B. reached the comparative security of the other trench, where they found ten R.A.F. ratings and one soldier.

For an hour-and-a-half they fought back with rifles and then retired to another position already occupied by a further twenty R.A.F. But two grenades thrown by the enemy forced them out; they found themselves surrounded and were compelled to surrender. After being disarmed and searched, they were led away to a group of Germans and told to sit down. A few questions were asked and an officer then gave Wheaton a red flag emblazoned with a black swastika, ordering him and an R.A.F. rating to march ahead of a group of Germans armed with Tommy guns. He was further told to shout at any British troops they encountered, calling on them to surrender.

Petty Officer Wheaton saw that he might be given a chance to escape. It was desperate, but worth while trying. Whisper-pering to the R.A.F. man that he intended to make a break at the first opportunity—a course with which the airman associated himself—they approached the first post which was a machine gun manned by some New Zealand soldiers.

"I'm ordered to tell you to surrender," shouted Wheaton, "but I'm going to run for it."

At once he dashed forward with the airman beside him as streams of bullets flew past in each direction. The airman fell, shot in the back, but Wheaton reached the trench unhurt, while the Germans were driven back, leaving some of their number still and silent on the ground. The New Zealanders dashed out and rescued the R.A.F. man, but he was badly injured.

Reporting to the officer in charge of the section, Petty Officer Wheaton eventually found himself in the main New Zealand camp where he met Commander Beale, who was wounded and on his way to the hospital. Later, he encountered the men of 805 Squadron holding a front line position under Lieutenant (A.) Ramsay.

Towards evening they were all ordered to another position lower down the slope and nearer to the aerodrome but, at 5.0 a.m. next morning, they heard that the army had been forced to make a retirement during the night and were now established two ridges behind them. Fighting their way back and suffering a few casualties themselves, they finally made contact with Lieutenant Sutton's party in the olive grove.

What could now be the objective of this miscellaneous party of R.A.F. and F.A.A. officers and men who numbered about 160 ? The majority of them were unarmed, and the ammunition for those who had rifles was almost expended. To the army they could only become an embarrassment, and it was therefore decided that they should try and make their way to Canea, the Colonel commanding the 21st Battalion agreeing to them, as a first step, contacting the 23rd Battalion further to the eastward. To this position they marched after dark but their reception, though friendly, was not encouraging. German advanced posts were reported 300 yards down the Canea road, much fighting was expected in that sector during the night, and a body of unarmed men would most definitely be in the way. If they wanted to reach Canea, they would have to make a wide detour, but it would be better if they returned to 21st Battalion headquarters. Drawing rations, the party marched back to the olive grove they had left where they settled down for the second night.

A short time later the Maoris launched their counter-attack, and it was magnificent. Sweeping into the enemy lines they overcame all opposition, wiping out one group of Germans after the other until, supported by the remaining New Zealanders, they reached as far as Maleme village. But when

N

daylight broke they could go no further. Strong posts of enemy machine guns blocked the way, inflicting severe losses; the attack slowed down and presently came to a halt. Against this opposition, rifles and bayonets were useless and, when the dive bombers began to plaster the gallant New Zealanders while the enemy received a continual stream of reinforcements from the air, further offensive action became impossible.

Long before morning twilight the airmen were mustered and formed into two groups—the armed and the unarmed. Between them they mustered sixty rifles and a few revolvers. While the unarmed party took cover, the remainder established defensive positions round the camp which had largely been deserted by troops engaged in the counter-attack.

Towards noon, news came through that the attack had been held up. Presently the wounded came streaming back with tales of fierce fighting and how hopeless it was to try and silence the enemy machine guns when they had so few of their own. Then the retreat began. Especially anxious that the skilled air mechanics who composed the majority of his party should not be sacrificed unnecessarily, Lieutenant Sutton asked permission to withdraw. On his way to battalion head-quarters—a distance of about a mile-and-a-half, much of which was covered by enemy rifles—he met Lieutenant (A.) Keith, R.N., stalking a sniper with a pistol! On the day before, this officer had been down with dysentery, but his determination to do something had forced his strength back and he had spent most of his time indulging in this somewhat fantastic pastime.

On arrival at headquarters it was first agreed that the airmen should withdraw but, when details of the casualties the soldiers had sustained began to be considered, the Major in command decided that Sutton's men must hold positions on each flank during the night. Considering it best for his whole party to be kept together, Sutton arranged the defence positions required, ordering the unarmed group to remain under cover as before. Lieutenant Ramsay with the F.A.A. established himself on the right flank, while Lieutenant Sutton with R.A.F. details organised the defence on the hill to the left. It was now quite dark.

Seeing the majority of them settled with their rations, Lieutenant Sutton and three R.A.F. men moved off to his own position—a trench supposed to lie a short distance to the right. They never found it. After blundering about for some time in the darkness, they stumbled into a machine gun post which opened fire with startling suddenness. Obviously they had reached the enemy lines. Falling flat on their faces, they crawled away in a south-easterly direction and settled down in some cover for the night. One of them was always awake.

At first light they moved, with the object of regaining touch with their outposts. But, having only the vaguest idea of their own position, they were soon quite lost. Suddenly files of men were sighted silhouetted against the sky line. They approached and, to Sutton's great relief, he recognised the steel helmets of British troops. They were the 23rd Battalion of New Zealanders who reported that a general withdrawal was taking place. They had no idea of the whereabouts of 21st Battalion headquarters, but were able to give Sutton the general lie of the land, from which he gathered that the rest of his men must be in one valley to the eastward. As there was some doubt as to whether he would succeed in finding them, he left the three R.A.F. ratings with the 23rd and struck off due east by himself.

His direction was correct and he soon found himself back with the 21st where everyone was getting ready to move off. Lieutenant (A) Ramsay had the Fleet Air Arm mustered, the unarmed group were getting themselves together, but where was the party who had been sent to man the positions on the left flank on the hill? It was thought that they had been ordered to withdraw, but no one could be quite certain. That was not good enough for Sutton, who decided that he must verify it himself.

"If you find them," said the Major, "it would be best for you to proceed due east across the Platanias River about four miles inland. You ought to have plenty of time, as there's still a screen of New Zealand troops between here and Maleme."

That was the last Sutton saw of his men. Under the command of Lieutenant Ramsay they managed to reach Canea and thence, Suda, where they embarked in *H.M.S. Hero* on the night of 26th May when a battalion of Special Service troops had been landed by her, *Abdiel* and *Nizam*.

With all haste Lieutenant Sutton proceeded to the outpost which had been held by the R.A.F., arriving there about 6.30 a.m., two hours after he had encountered the 23rd Battalion. All the positions were empty. Save for some figures on the sky line to the westward there was no one in sight, so he made his way due east at the double, while a few bullets whistled overhead. Though he took no steps to verify it, he imagined that the figures he had seen were the New Zealand rear guard. In point of fact, they were Germans, our own troops having withdrawn about an hour before. Thus, Sutton was in the rear of a retreating army and close ahead of the Germans.

For two-and-a-half hours he tramped up and down over the hills, avoiding the sound of machine gun fire when he heard it right ahead. At length, about nine o'clock, he reached a small village where the Cretans crowded round him with cries of sympathy, patting him on the back and producing for him milk and bread and cheese. Advising him to keep inland and avoid recognised tracks, they sped him on his way.

Shortly afterwards Sutton found company. Four New Zealanders of the 22nd Battalion, who had been cut off by the Germans while on a watering party early that morning, had also taken to the hills; and they met just outside the village. Together they proceeded towards the Platanias River. Progress was slow. The going was not only rough, but they frequently had to take cover from low flying aircraft which were scouring the countryside; and the river plain was reached towards noon.

Firing in the vicinity decided them to move further inland,

towards a village at the bottom of some foot hills. Suddenly, they found the tracks of a German parachutist but, agreeing that five rifles were a match for one Tommy gun, they did

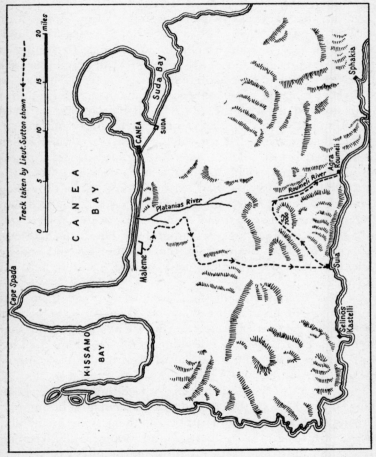

not allow this to deflect them from their course, and even trailed him. Presently, on turning a corner they abruptly met their quarry. He was in the midst of a band of Cretans, all of whom threw their hands up in the air when surprised by the unexpected arrival of a naval officer and four soldiers. The German, suffering from two sprained ankles, had already been taken prisoner, so he was left alone.

At the village they were again hospitably received, but were warned that there were parties of German troops all round. One Greek took it upon himself to advise their remaining in the village until dark, when he could provide a guide to take the party through the German lines to Canea. Sutton did not believe him and suspected the man of being a fifth columnist trying to hold them in the village until the Germans arrived and occupied it. So, after a short rest, the party pushed on.

They had scarcely left the village a bare 100 yards when an unarmed British soldier came dashing after them. Breathlessly he reported that a Greek guide, provided from the village they had just left, had led him into a trap. Promising to take him through to Suda, the guide, instead, had led him straight towards twenty-five Germans who were under cover only a short distance away. Half-an-hour later, machine-gun and rifle fire was heard from the direction of this village indicating that the Germans had arrived. Sutton had left only just in time.

A Greek encountered in the hills now informed them that the entire right bank of the Platanias River was occupied by Germans, a fact corroborated by the sound of firing in that direction. There was only one thing to do—abandon the idea of trying to make for Suda Bay and strike across country towards the south coast.

Then began a gruelling march over the mountains. Each village through which they passed treated them most hospitably, showing real affection and supplying them with bread and honey, wild cherries, mulberries and oranges. By keeping strict march discipline with a halt of ten minutes every hour, they made excellent progress and, towards evening, caught up with an Australian Lieutenant of Artillery and a mixed group of men who had been cut off from their different units—Royal

Marines, Gunners, New Zealanders, Australians, and even one or two R.A.F. ranks. Altogether, the party now numbered about twenty and they had an excellent guide. That night they slept high up in the mountains.

Long before dawn on May 24th, they were astir, determined to try and get over the mountain top before it grew light. It was rough going and they did not succeed, but in the low clouds which covered them they were safe from the eyes of hunting aircraft. By 8.0 a.m. they were over the pass where they rested for breakfast. Then, on again for what seemed miles and miles until, at length, at 1.0 p.m., they reached the little village of Suia, nestling in a bay on the south coast.

Here they found a large body of men belonging to practically every unit, including Australians from a rest camp which had been cut off. These latter had moved over in a body with their Bren gun and rifles, and all were living in caves on a plateau above the village. A Pilot Officer R.A.F. had gone off in a boat to the eastward to try and get help in the shape of sea transport from a larger village, in order that the party could join up with the main forces.

As the men seemed disorganised, Lieutenant Sutton appointed a quartermaster to control money and arrange for the collection and equitable distribution of food. Look-outs were posted to seaward, the armed men were organised in defensive positions and the remainder ordered to sleep together on the beach in case a ship arrived during the night.

On the following day (25th May), the officers and crew of M.L. 1011 which had been bombed and sunk at Selinos Kastelli, a few miles to the westward, joined the group at Suia, and the officer in command told Sutton that there was certainly a W./T. station at Sphakia to which place, he said, naval and military headquarters were moving. As the Pilot Officer who had gone for help had obviously been unsuccessful, Lieutenant Sutton resolved to organise a party himself and make an effort to reach Sphakia.

With the crew of the M.L. and some Australian and New

Zealand troops they set out at 5.0 p.m. that evening. To move east along the coast was impossible, and it was necessary to strike inland and proceed along the backbone of the island. Leaving all signs of cultivation behind them, they climbed a track leading over the 7000-foot mountain pass. There was no moon; it was very cold and progress was rough and cruel. By 2.0 a.m. men began to get exhausted, necessitating three hours' rest in a shepherd's hut from whom they bought cheese as they thawed round his fire. Dawn found them at the top of the pass, which was unfortunate, as it exposed them to aircraft. But, by walking hard when they could and freezing into immobility as an *Messerschmidt* 110 or a *Junkers* 88 skimmed low over their heads, they managed to get across in safety.

Descent to the coast was slow and painful. Sharp rocks had played havoc with their footwear and Sutton, himself, finished the journey in shoes which were completely soleless. Making their way down an old glacier bed they leapt from rock to rock, then followed a small rivulet which gushed down through a great chasm. Gradually it grew wider, becoming a swift stream, finally flowing as a river into the sea at Agia Rumeli, where they all arrived exhausted about 1.0 p.m. on 26th May.

There they met the Pilot Officer who had set out from Suia three days before, and he told them that a caique would pick them up that night. When it arrived there was only time to reach Sphakia by dawn—to be caught at sea in the daytime would be certain to invite the attention of patrolling Junkers. On the following night the caique would make the trip to Suia.

On arrival at Sphakia, the party were dispersed with other troops among rocks and caves above the town, while Lieutenant Sutton, at the request of a Lieut.-Colonel who was the senior army officer present, surveyed the beaches from the point of view of evacuation, and arranged small navigational lights for ships approaching. Troops continued to arrive.

During the afternoon, Sutton learned that the skipper of the caique refused to take his boat to collect the party from Suia. He was frightened. So Sutton decided to commandeer the boat and, manned by the crew of M.L. 1011, with a few Australians as an armed guard, take her to Suia himself. This scheme was unfortunately upset when it was discovered that the caique only had six gallons of deisel oil on board, and that no more was obtainable. There was nothing more that could be done, except report the situation to the officers in charge of the evacuation who promised to do their best to rescue the party at Suia.

No ships arrived that night. On 28th May more troops assembled above Sphakia until, by evening, it was estimated that there were at least 3000. Though they were bombed and machine-gunned during the afternoon, no attack was actually made on Sphakia where General Freyberg and Captain Morse had established their headquarters.

At 10.30 p.m. ships were observed closing the shore and shortly afterwards, four destroyers—*Napier*, *Nizam*, *Kelvin* and *Kandahar*—anchored within a few yards of the beach. Stores were landed, walking wounded were embarked and as many others as time permitted. With the naval staff ashore there was nothing further for Lieutenant Sutton to do, and he was ordered to take passage in *Napier*, where it was most gratifying to hear remarks of appreciation made by all the soldiers on the high standard of organisation for accommodating the troops and tending the wounded in the destroyers.

With the sailing of the ships at 3.0 a.m. for Alexandria, the remarkable adventures of the Fleet Air Arm in Crete came to an end.

Chapter 13

H.M.S. MARIA GIOVANNA

It was during the early stages of the first advance in the Western Desert when *H.M.S. Dainty* captured her. On the morning of 1st January, 1941, after a night patrol in the vicinity of Tobruk, the destroyer began to close the land in order to ascertain her position. Suddenly, a look-out reported a mast on the starboard beam towards which *Dainty* immediately turned. The object was soon identified as an auxiliary schooner—*the Maria Giovanna*—flying the Italian naval ensign.

She at once hove-to and, in a state of panic, the crew—consisting of twelve men—frantically lowered a boat and began to abandon ship. A burst of 0.5-inch machine-gun fire ahead of the schooner in order to make them desist, only increased the panic; the entire crew throwing themselves flat on their faces. As soon as the firing stopped they leapt, yelling, to their feet and, with hands raised up in surrender, jumped overboard —some into the lifeboat, others into the sea. Finally, with the aid of a rating in *Dainty* who could speak fluent Italian, they were prevailed upon to return on board, preceeding the British boarding party in case any booby trap had been laid. The white ensign was hoisted superior to the Italian and, with a Lieutenant from *Dainty* in charge, she was ordered to proceed to Sollum. During this period, a Savoia 79 made a mild protest, but the destroyer's guns quickly drove the aircraft away.

Almost immediately afterwards, and before her aircraft had returned, *Dainty* sighted another mast which turned out to belong to the Italian motor vessel *Tiberio*—slightly smaller than *Maria Giovanna*—who was captured under similar circumstances and also ordered to Sollum. Both vessels were in ballast at the time and proceeding to Tobruk in order to embark supplies for Bardia.

An auxiliary, 255-ton, three-masted schooner, 180 feet long; capable of carrying over 200 tons of cargo and having a speed of six knots, could be most useful at a time when all the small craft possible were needed for a variety of jobs connected with the support of the army. To Lieutenant A. B. Palmer, R.N.R. —a seasoned seaman in command of the lighter X39—the sight of *Maria Giovanna* arriving in Sollum Bay awakened an instant desire to lay the first claim to her. X39 was all very well in her way, but her maximum speed was 3 knots. Up to date she had been the only craft of any size available to go alongside the jetty at Sollum and, for the past ten days, had been transferring all the stores, troops, wounded and ammunition to and fro, from ship to shore. She was, however, well manned, and Lieutenant Palmer maintained that he could run the two vessels—temporarily at least—with the men he had available. Thus, he obtained command of the *Maria Giovanna*.

As the advance continued and tens of thousands of Italians threw down their arms at the slightest provocation until the whole foreshore was thick with them, the transport of these prisoners to ships lying off the coast became one of *Maria Giovanna's* principle duties. Seven hundred and fifty would be carried on each trip and, on one day alone, more than 14,800 were transported by this schooner. The return trip to the beach would not be wasted and troops, mail and other stores would be loaded into her. The Italians, Lieutenant Palmer found, were not over particular on the question of cleanliness, so he 'tamed' ten of them (as he expressed it), who lived on board during this period and cleaned off the visible signs of their dirty compatriots.

Few of these prisoners seemed to have any heart in the war, and sometimes they were difficult to control. On one occasion, instructions were given for a whole load of 750 to be embarked in the *Knight of Malta*. For some reason or another this ship failed to appear, and *Maria Giovanna* was left with these Italians on board for a period of six hours. Eventually, orders were received to transfer 250 of them to a small Egyptian pacquet—*Farouk*—but when *Maria Giovanna* drew alongside there was a blackguardly rush to the guard rail as they all tried to swarm on board. In vain Palmer shouted and the Egyptian Captain gesticulated, but the situation was beyond control. When *Maria Giovanna* finally cast off and returned to shore where it was possible to make a count, it was discovered that over 580 had embarked in *Farouk*. The Egyptian Captain was not pleased!

Of course *Maria Giovanna* was bombed off the Libyan coast. It was a regular feature for the so-called Italian circus, comprising fifty bombers with strong fighter escort, to pay frequent visits, and at this period the schooner's armament consisted of only two rifles. As time wore on, however, a 3-pounder was fitted in the stern and, by devious methods, Lieutenant Palmer managed to obtain a 12-mm. Breda mounted in the bow, a 20-mm. Izzoti amidships and two Lewis guns.

While the advance continued, *Maria Giovanna* made a few trips to Mersa Matruh for stores, and the times spent there were regarded as red letter days. The men got rest which they had been forced to do without, and there was relief from the constant bombing.

On 24th Febraury, by a strange coincidence, *Maria Giovanna* happened to be off Tobruk when the destroyer, to whom she owed her existence under the white ensign, met her end. It was towards evening when *Dainty*, followed by *Hasty*, steamed out of Tobruk. Sudden flashes, explosions and gunfire astern indicated that an air raid had developed. Darkness, however, was falling and this gave rise to the very reasonable hope that the destroyers would be able to get away unobserved. But there was no such luck; the noise of aircraft was heard overhead, followed by the whine of a falling bomb which struck *Dainty* aft, penetrating into the Captain's cabin where it exploded.

The oil fuel in the tank immediately below caught fire, which spread so rapidly that the most strenuous efforts could not bring it under control; ready use ammunition on 'X' gun deck started to burst and the after magazine was threatened. The situation was hopeless, and the Captain ordered every man on to the foc's'le, while the destroyer continued ahead leaving a path of flames from burning fuel pouring into the sea. Then the torpedoes exploded, shaking the ship with a terrific concussion and sending up a great shower of torn metal and other debris to cause some casualties in *Hasty's* whalers which were rescuing men who had been blown into the sea.

For a few moments *Hasty* swung her stern in under *Dainty's* starboard bow. Some men jumped to safety but, as there were now several in the water, she could not use her screws to keep herself in position. The bow of the stricken vessel rose higher and higher as her stern settled in the water, and the remainder of the ship's company lowered themselves into the sea and got away before she made her final plunge.

By this time other small craft, including *Maria Giovanna*, were on the scene to help pick up those men who had not been rescued by *Hasty*.

At the end of February, *Maria Giovanna* was ordered to Alexandria where she was given her first thorough overhaul since her capture, refitted in some respects and accommodation improved. This took a fortnight, at the end of which she sailed for Tobruk and thence to other places along the coast, landing stores, embarking prisoners and doing a hundred other odd and useful jobs.

When the swift German advance took place and pushed back our forces, sadly depleted by the responsibilities we had assumed in Greece, *Maria Giovanna* performed many useful services. One of the last craft to remain at Derna while the enemy were hammering at the port with their artillery, she loaded stores until the wharf itself actually came under the fire of hostile tanks which appeared over the hill. Then, embarking an Indian regiment with their British officers, she proceeded to sea with shells falling round her, and formed the escort for the *s.s. Hanne* also loaded with troops. Together they proceeded to Mersa Matruh, but the Captain of the *Hanne* was somewhat concerned at having an inadequately armed schooner as his sole protection during this dangerous passage.

Then back to Tobruk where, in Palmer's own words, they embarked their best-looking cargo. Sixty-four Australian nursing sisters had to be evacuated and *Maria Giovanna* was the only vessel available. This presented a big problem with her very limited accommodation, but difficulties were overcome with good humour, and the 'cargo' was landed safely at Mersa Matruh.

From then onwards this indefatigable schooner was employed in carrying stores to the besieged garrison at Tobruk, during the course of which she experienced many adventures. With the establishment of an enemy battery along the coast, able to command by accurate shooting the entrance to the harbour, the port could only be approached after dark. This was by no means easy and numerous wrecks, some showing above water but more just submerged, provided navigational hazards. Apart from this, when approaching from seaward, especially in a slow vessel which might have been set a considerable distance off her course by the uncertain current, an accurate landfall was generally problematical.

Taking advantage of these difficulties, the Germans placed lights further down the coast similar to those used to mark Tobruk, with the object of luring ships on to the shore. On one occasion *Maria Giovanna* was actually led astray by these lights, but Palmer fortunately discovered the mistake in time. Infuriated by the deception which had nearly proved disastrous to him, he swung his stern on to the offending lights and opened fire on them at almost point blank range with his 3-pounder. After the fourth round, the Germans replied with 6-inch shells, and matters began to look unhealthy for the little schooner; but she escaped damage and withdrew into the darkness quite assured that the offending lights had been demolished. Anyhow, Palmer never saw them again.

On 12th May, *Maria Giovanna* happened to be in Tobruk during one of the times when a cloud of *Junkers* 87 dive-bombed the harbour. On this occasion they concentrated on the gunboat *Ladybird* who, with her light draft, had been performing invaluable service. Almost immediately her stern received a direct hit which wrecked the after pom-pom killing the crew. A second bomb burst in the boiler room, blowing out the sides of the ship. In spite of her damage and casualties, and the fact that an oil fuel fire was raging from the foremast to the stern, her remaining guns continued to fire even when the vessel had settled on the bottom of the harbour. Not until the fire got so fierce that the magazine (the flooding valves were now inaccessible) threatened to blow up and the guns had been put out of action, was the ship abandoned; but her shooting had destroyed at least one of her attackers. *Maria Giovanna* helped to rescue the gallant survivors.

More than once the schooner was, herself, the chief object of attack by hostlie aircraft, and she could even claim to have brought down at least three by her own fire. Two *Heinkels* thought they had an easy target, and approached close to rake her with machine-gun and cannon fire. Her own fire was held until the enemy got near—then she opened up. Black smoke immediately began to pour from the engine of one machine who turned away, tried to recover from a steep bank and then side-slipped into the sea. The other aircraft kept its distance and, after a few more bursts of ineffective fire, made off. Another time a *Savoia* 79 tried conclusions with *Maria Giovanna*, and the effect of the withering fire encountered caused the aircraft to turn upside down, in which undignified position it plunged into the sea.

On the third occasion the schooner had held off to the north-west of Tobruk during daylight, so as to enter after dark. To the annoyance of the crew, an Italian *Macchi* suddenly appeared and cautiously approached in gradually decreasing circles. But *Maria Giovanna* held her fire until the enemy had plucked up sufficient courage to attack. Then the aircraft was met by a hail of bullets from the schooner's four guns. It crashed.

But there were many occasions when she was not so successful, and once the little schooner received a severe hammering without doing any apparent damage herself. During a deter- mined attack by two *Heinkels*, *Maria Giovanna* sustained 79 holes from near bomb misses and cannon-fire: 26 of these were below the water line. Three men were killed and five others wounded—a big proportion out of a total ship's company of twelve (including the Captain). With six feet of water in the hold and another eight feet in the engine room, the schooner managed to struggle in to Mersa Matruh, and thence to Alexandria where five plates were needed to replace those damaged.

Some of these attacks were not without their humour. The cockney cook manned the Italian Izzoti gun and, during one attack, he ran out of ammunition. Infuriated at being unable to reply to the enemy's fire, he took off his steel helmet and flung it at the *Heinkel* as it passed spitting out machine-gun bullets!

This cook was very fond of dressing up in gay Italian uniforms whenever he got ashore along the coast and one day, to his great indignation, he was captured by some Australians. When asked at the point of the bayonet if he could speak English, his feelings were positively outraged.

"Wot me—a bleedin' cockney?" he screamed!

He was a great character, and it was a sad day for his shipmates when he left the ship to go into submarines, where he considered he would be safer!

Another time, a plane was approaching from astern, and Lieutenant Palmer saw four bombs released. The ship seemed sluggish on the wheel, and two of these looked as though they were going to hit.

"Duck!" yelled Palmer to a stoker of the fire party who was standing in rather a conspicuous position. Having mislaid his steel helmet, the stoker merely covered his head with an ordinary tin wash-basin.

"That's about as much use as a pocket handkerchief," laughed Palmer when the attack had passed, the bombs having missed.

The stoker's expression was a study. "Do you really think so, sir?" he said, and then automatically threw the precious basin overboard!

Between April and October 1941, *Maria Giovanna* made twenty-three journeys to Tobruk, the round trip taking about six days if calling at Mersa Matruh. The following extracts from Lieutenant Palmer's reports will indicate with what they had to contend.

August 13th: After having sailed from Alexandria, he states:
    2020. Sighted submarine on starboard bow. Challenged
with trigger lamp. Received no reply. Challenged again
with Aldis lamp—no reply. Proceeded to ram submarine.
Called a *Southern* class patrol vessel and requested assistance. Submarine dived and later surfaced on port bow,
when she revealed herself as friendly.

Next afternoon, *Maria Giovanna* arrived at Mersa Matruh,
whence she sailed for Tobruk at 3.0 p.m. on the 15th. The
weather made it uncomfortable.
    1900. Vessel rolling heavily. Main fuel tank sheered
its moorings and banging ship's side badly. All hands
employed securing and moving cargo.
    Midn't. Sea angry. Shipped several good ones into
engine room. All cabins flooded.

A few hours before dawn two days later, they reached the
entrance to the Tobruk Swept Channel, where a pilot boarded
them so as to guide the vessel clear of the latest danger areas
due to enemy mines. By 6.0 a.m. they were secured. The
report continues:
    0700. Air raids. These kept on all day, and so hampered
the discharging. The total number of raids for the day
was 19, the smallest formation being two planes and the
largest 18 *Stukas* supported by 10 fighters. This raid was
intended for *Maria Giovanna*. One lighter was sunk alongside, the pier badly damaged and several killed. Damage
to this ship slight. Port shrouds carried away; several
holes in the ship's side and deck houses. Blast from 1000
pounder carried away after part of wheel house which
contains lavatory and wireless room.
    2100. Slipped and proceeded for Alexandria.
    2340. Had to alter course to avoid a running sea fight.
Not being a vessel of the line and not being able to run
fast, this was considered to be the most prudent move.

On the 18th they had a short action with hostile aircraft:
    1300. Aircraft sighted. Enemy. Proved to be *Savoia* 79.

We exchanged a few shots. Consider we handed out more than we received. Action only lasted ten minutes. One window smashed and Pluto, our dog, sprained his ankle getting out of the way.

This report ended like practically every other with the statement:

No Complaints.
No Requestmen.
No Defaulters.

In spite of all the discomforts and dangers, it would have been difficult to find a happier vessel in the fleet. By October 1941 two of the crew had won the D.S.M. and Lieutenant Palmer had been decorated with the D.S.C. There was only one punishment—being discharged and sent to another ship. Though the discipline was high, there was naturally not the spit and polish, nor that attention to etiquette expected in larger ships.

In the middle of the summer at Alexandria, the Commander-in-Chief decided to pay *Maria Giovanna* a visit, and the barge drew alongside the Arsenal Quay, at one of whose wharves the schooner was lying. A stoker in a dirty pair of shorts, with his cap on the back of his head, was the only man on deck.

"Is the Captain on board ?" asked the Commander-in-Chief.

The stoker scratched his head, not knowing who was addressing him. "Yus, sir, I thinks so. Comin' aboard ?"

Admiral Cunningham climbed over the side.

"D'yer want me ter fetch the Old Man ?" enquired the stoker.

"No; not yet, I want to talk to you."

For a few minutes the Commander-in-Chief chatted with members of the crew, and then told the stoker to fetch his Captain. On poking his head into Lieutenant Palmer's cabin, the stoker announced:

"There's an important sort of looking bloke on deck. From the way 'e's togged up, I think it's an Admiral. You'd better come and 'ave a look!"

When the second battle of the Libyan Desert began in November 1941, *Maria Giovanna* was on the job, carrying important stores to Tobruk. Four days later there was a distressing message from one of our reconnaissance aircraft: "Schooner, believed to be *Maria Giovanna* ashore on enemy territory."

Further investigation proved this indeed to be the case—she was wrecked and abandoned. We can only hope and believe that Lieutenant Palmer and his gallant crew were made prisoners of war.

Chapter 14

SUPPLIES TO TOBRUK

WHEN the German drive through Cyrenaica in the late spring of 1941 was finally halted on the frontier of Egypt, there remained a threat in their flank which they were unable to eradicate—TOBRUK. With the utmost gallantry the garrison of this port, so strong in its natural fortifications, held out. It was quite obvious that its retention would be of inestimable value in subsequent operations against the enemy, besides providing, in the meantime, a veritable thorn in their flank. Day after day it was bombed and bombarded, but surprisingly little damage was done and our own patrols ceaselessly attacked, inflicting continual casualties on the foe and capturing many prisoners. For month after month during the summer and autumn of 1941, Tobruk held out.

Cut off in three directions by hostile forces, occupying positions in the desert, the only way in which Tobruk could be supplied and maintained was by sea. By this route alone, troops, ammunition and stores of all kinds continually flowed. Within a few miles of this besieged and stubbornly defended port were several air fields, from which numerous aircraft—for a long time far superior in numbers to those we possessed in the entire western desert—tried time and time again, with concentrated and vicious attacks upon our shipping, to strangle this life line upon which the garrison entirely depended.

Pressed home with bravery and ruthless determination, it was inevitable that enemy bombs should sometimes find a target and cause us serious loss, but the supply line was maintained, thanks in great measure to the courage of the small escorting craft, and the stolid resolution of the Masters commanding the merchant vessels used to transport all kinds of stores. Though Tobruk was rationed in certain respects, the flow of essential commodities continued.

Among the smaller vessels which distinguished themselves in these hazardous escorting duties were the South African whalers *Southern Maid*, *Southern Isles* and *Southern Sea*, while the escort vessels *Flamingo*, *Grimsby* and *Auckland* performed special stirring actions. There were others, too—destroyers, schooners, lighters and tugs—who played equally gallant parts in this dangerous undertaking.

With the establishment on the coast of enemy batteries, which commanded the entrance to the harbour with disturbing accuracy, ships could, as a rule, only arrive under cover of darkness, discharge during the night and sail again before dawn. But they still had many dangerous miles to traverse in daylight, both when proceeding to Tobruk and on the return journey to Alexandria. It was after passing the longitude of Ras Azzaz, that promontory terminating the northern sweep of the western coastline round Sollum Bay, when the real excitement generally started.

On Saturday, 24th May, a small convoy consisting of *s.s. Hecla*, a 3000-ton water, benzine and store carrier, escorted by *Grimsby* (Commdr. J. K. D'Arcy) and *Southern Maid* (Lieut. Hall, S.D.F.) was approaching Tobruk. Conditions were most unpleasant because a sand storm was raging over the coast, and the hot grit-laden air filled every corner of the ships. But it had one great advantage—it reduced the visibility to an extent which made a visit from *Junkers* most unlikely.

The convoy was due at Tobruk at 10.0 p.m., but the persistence of the sand storm, though it hid the ships from the

Junkers, also hid the land from the ships and made an accurate landfall extremely difficult. In fact, it was found impossible to enter harbour until so long after the time arranged that *Hecla* could not be unloaded before dawn. Ships were, there-

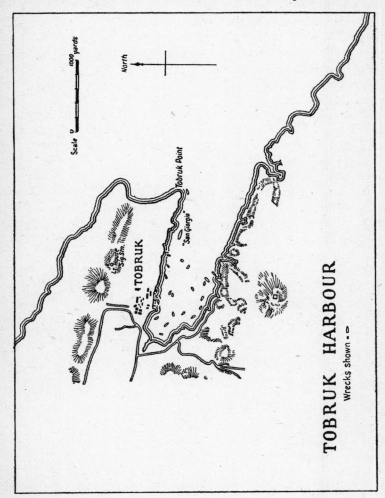

TOBRUK HARBOUR
Wrecks shown ▫

fore, ordered to remain at sea another day and enter Tobruk the following evening.

Throughout Sunday forenoon they steamed away: then turned again towards Tobruk. Proceeding at six knots with *Southern Maid* zig-zagging seven cables ahead of *Hecla*, and *Grimsby* performing similar manœuvres in her wake and four cables astern, hostile aircraft—subsequently identified as *Junkers* 88—were suddenly observed approaching from the north-west about 1.40 p.m.

Grimsby immediately opened fire with a medium level barrage, but the planes came on until, from a height of 5000 feet, they broke up and began to dive singly from different directions. *Southern Maid* held her fire until the planes had dropped to 3000 feet and then opened up with her fore and after Breda guns. Projectiles were seen to hit at least two machines, though neither of them crashed.

Hecla was the principle target but, though several bombs exploded within 25 yards of her and others fell close to *Grimsby*, ships suffered neither damage nor casualties. From a height of 500 feet *Southern Maid* was machine-gunned, but, here again, no casualties were incurred.

This attack ceased at 2.0 p.m. but, now that the visibility was good and the convoy had been discovered, everyone realised that the afternoon's questionable entertainment had only just begun.

Two hours later a large number of planes approached from such a height that they were neither seen nor heard until they started to dive. It was estimated that at least twenty-seven *Junkers* 87, accompanied by a strong fighter escort, took part in this attack. They began by concentrated dive-bombing on *Grimsby* and *Hecla* from different directions at the same time.

Zig-zagging at full speed across the bow of the convoy, *Southern Maid* kept up continuous fire with every gun she possessed, and several planes were observed to be hit, one of which crashed. With the first attack, *Hecla* was struck by two bombs forward of the bridge—fortunately on the water tank and not on the benzine—and was seen to break in two. *Grimsby* sustained two direct hits aft. This resulted in the stern compartments being flooded, causing the ship to take a dangerous list to port. She managed, however, to shoot down at least two of the enemy. The fact that for the twenty minutes during which the raid lasted, *Southern Maid* expended 1750 rounds of 20 mm. Breda ammunition, besides a quantity of smaller calibre, testifies to the stout defence she put up against this powerful raiding force.

As soon as the attack had passed, she closed the two damaged vessels and, lowering a boat, rescued those of *Hecla's* crew who were clinging to the forward part of their ship which was rapidly submerging. The Master and remainder of the crew in the after part managed to get clear in their own boats.

Grimsby had lowered all her available boats and thrown carley rafts into the water, as it was obvious that she could not remain afloat much longer. But, not until she had assumed a list so alarming as to place her in imminent danger of foundering, could the Commanding Officer be prevailed upon to leave.

By 5.10 p.m. *Southern Maid* had embarked 160 survivors, including a number of wounded and, because of the likelihood of another raid, decided to steam at full speed away from the scene of disaster on a north-easterly course.

Although they had fought the enemy magnificently, standing up to their guns in the face of furious onslaught, it was only natural that everyone should feel severely shaken. In fact, their present situation was far from pleasant. Now quite alone and some distance from the land, loaded to six times the ship's normal complement and expecting a third raid at any moment, no one pretended to be happy. Lieutenant Hall accordingly gave orders for a tot of rum to be issued both to his own crew and to the survivors. Able-Seaman 'X' of the South African whaler had always been a staunch teetotaller but, on this occasion, he broke the pledge and, in addition to his own tot, accepted a further nip from a generous messmate.

Suddenly there was a cry from the look-out: "Aircraft right ahead!"

With the efficiency and alacrity which had always been a marked feature of this South African flotilla, all guns were manned and pointing at the approaching aircraft within an instant of the alarm being given. Able-Seaman 'X' felt strangely elated. He scrambled swiftly to his gun above the bridge, feeling as if he had been endowed with a pair of wings and, full of enthusiasm, levelled his Lewis gun. But, to everyone's relief, the planes proved to be friendly fighters.

The incident had been a shock to jaded nerves, but Able-Seaman 'X' felt so sure of himself, so full of confidence and of the spirit animating his ship, that he had to express it. Standing up, he shouted to the men below with an impressive gesture:

"It's all right. *Southern Maid* will bring you home. So don't you worry!"

This speech, greeted with cheers and laughter, had a tonic effect on all the men.

Casualties had been remarkably light, only one reported killed and one missing from *Hecla*, while the corresponding figures for *Grimsby* were four and four. There were, however, several wounded—some seriously—and, under conditions of extreme difficulty, the Medical Officer of *Grimsby* worked continuously throughout the night, even carrying out an amputation in a vain attempt to save the life of a P.O. Cook. But the unfortunate man died before *Southern Maid* reached Mersa Matruh the following morning.

Less than a week later, *Southern Maid* was again detailed for similar escort duties and, in company with *Auckland*, left Alexandria on Sunday, 1st June, to convoy the petrol carrier, *Pass of Balmaha*, to Tobruk. Monday was quiet, but on the next day it was the turn of *Southern Maid* to receive the full attention of several hostile aircraft of different types.

At 12.20 those in the whaler were suddenly startled to hear the angry whine of aircraft diving at them out of the sun.

But every gun was instantly alert and the enemy, consisting of two *Junkers* 87, though not observed until they had dropped to 700 feet, were met by such withering fire that no bomb was dropped within 40 yards of *Southern Maid*.

Immediately afterwards, four more planes—identified as *Messerschmidts* 109—dived straight on her at tremendous speed from the starboard beam. Pressing home their attack, they opened fire with machine guns and cannon: then, swooping down to a height of 50 feet, each one in turn raked the decks of *Southern Maid* fore and aft. Under this unnerving hail of fire, the men manning the guns showed the most commendable steadiness, their own fire being so well sustained and accurate that Breda shells were observed to burst directly on one of the leading planes. Subsequently, the floating body of a dead German airman was sighted near a patch of oil, which indicated that this machine had been brought down.

At the starboard Fiat gun, a young Telegraphist who was manning it, refused to take cover and kept his gun in action until at length he fell mortally wounded. The after Breda gun sustained a direct hit by cannon which put it out of action and wounded two members of the crew, while the gunlayer of the forward Breda was wounded in the wrist. Having caused these casualties and superficial damage to the superstructure, the planes beat a hasty retreat; nor did they attempt to renew the attack after the fierce battering they had received.

The convoy steamed on and arrived at Tobruk according to schedule, where the subsequent delivery of 750 tons of bulk petrol by *Pass of Balmaha* was chronicled as the most satisfactory event of the week.

The death of the Telegraphist and his burial at Tobruk cast a gloom over the whole ship's company of *Southern Maid*. It was the first fatal casualty which had been sustained by any of the three ships comprising the South African flotilla and they all felt it keenly. But the gloom had to be dispelled if they were to carry on with their usual efficiency. So, that very evening, they all gathered in an 8-inch turret on board the wrecked Italian cruiser *San Giorgio*, where they held a rousing concert, and thus restored their jaded spirits.

II

This trip with *Southern Maid* was not the first to Tobruk for the gallant little petrol carrier, *Pass of Balmaha.* Neither was it the last. Situated on top of a highly inflammable and explosive cargo, and subjected to persistent attacks from the air to which, for many weeks, they had no direct means of replying, these experiences must have imposed a severe strain on the Master and crew. But she cheerfully carried on until one unfortunate night in mid-October. In the early hours of the morning, when about 50 miles from Alexandria and loaded with her usual precious cargo for Tobruk, a 'U' boat caught her. There was a terrific explosion seen by all ships in harbour at the base. Flames leapt to a great height and the shattered hull burnt so fiercely that it was impossible for a small escorting craft to approach. The entire crew unhappily perished in this disaster.

On June 22nd, however, she left Alexandria, protected by the New Zealand escort vessel *Auckland* (Commdr. M. S. Thomas) and the Australian vessel of similar type *Parramatta* (Lieut.-Commdr. J. H. Walker). The first day at sea was peaceful. But at 8.40 a.m. on the 24th, when approaching the longitude of Ras Azzaz, a hostile reconnaissance aircraft was sighted. Though *Auckland* opened fire and drove her away, the convoy had obviously been reported and, since the weather was clear, they could now look forward to considerable attention from a persistent enemy.

For some hours, however, raids were only made by a series of single aircraft—*Savoias* 79—the first taking place half-an-hour after the original reconnaissance machine had been sighted.

Attacks on this small scale were encouraging to the ships and, when the afternoon passed peacefully, it was hoped that the enemy had found an occupation more profitable than to assault the convoy. But at 5.30 p.m. such hopes were rudely disturbed. First one large formation, then another, and yet a third, were detected approaching, and when a few minutes later they were observed, at least sixteen machines appeared to be in each of the three formations. They were all of the same type—the deadly *Junker* 87.

As they worked round in order to dive from the direction of the sun, both *Auckland* and *Parramatta* opened with the heaviest barrage the guns could give, but the enemy were so numerous that the fire from the two ships was insufficient to deter them.

Pandemonium was terrific. Added to the bark of gunfire and the continuous staccato of machine guns, was the angry hornet noise of dive bombers swooping down from every direction; then the hiss of falling bombs, followed in some cases by the roar of an explosion. Like swarms of flies darting on their prey, the enemy machines concentrated two-thirds of their first attack on *Auckland*, and the remainder on *Parramatta* and *Pass of Balmaha*.

Auckland, snaking ahead between huge columns of water rising up one after another, close on either side; ahead and astern; was suddenly obscured from *Parramatta* by thick brown smoke. She had been hit, the whole of the stern section above the water having been blown to pieces. With her foremost guns still firing, *Auckland* managed to continue at about 10 knots with the wheel jammed hard-a-port; yet, for some unaccountable reason, she turned rapidly to starboard.

To the amazement, therefore, of *Parramatta*, *Auckland* was seen to emerge from the smoke and head straight for her. Just in time, Lieut.-Commdr. Walker managed to put the wheel over to avoid collision. *Auckland* presented a pathetic sight with no stern visible, heeling heavily to port, and her available guns still firing at the diving aircraft.

Almost immediately, she was hit again by three bombs simultaneously. One passed through the sick bay skylight and seemed to be fitted with delay action; another passed right through the bridge and exploded as it emerged through the ship's side abreast the compass platform. The third struck and exploded somewhere amidships. Yet *Auckland* continued to fire until the enemy had dropped all their bombs and flown away about fifteen minutes later.

Both *Parramatta* and *Pass of Balmaha* had miraculously escaped damage and casualties, although bombs had fallen all round them. When the enemy drew off, *Auckland* lay stopped, flames and smoke pouring from her decks and the ship listing more and more heavily to port. As her end was obviously near, orders had been given to abandon ship. Boats and rafts were already in the water.

Parramatta closed and stopped to windward of the sinking vessel where, regardless of what might subsequently happen to her, she dropped both whalers, skiffs, lifebelts and more floats. The majority of the men could still be seen on the upper deck working about boats and tending the wounded, while officers were disposing of confidential books: the port gunwhale was almost awash, and the brown smoke from the fires raging below decks streamed to leeward.

Suddenly there was a terrific explosion, caused presumably by the bomb which had failed to go off on impact. This lifted *Auckland* slowly and steadily about six feet into the air. Her back broke with a pronounced fold down the starboard side. Then she settled down with an increased list to port and a few minutes later—at 6.29 p.m.—finally rolled over and sank. The explosion had thrown many men into the sea and, it is feared, caused casualties among those already in the water. The behaviour of everyone had been magnificent, and the great unselfishness everywhere displayed contributed largely to a reduction in the casualties which might, otherwise, have been exceedingly heavy.

Another attack was obviously developing and it was, therefore, quite impossible for *Parramatta* to stop and pick up survivors from the disaster. As she was actually gathering way, the raid began and consisted of deliberate low level bombing by six *Savoias* 79 with fighter escort above. But the steady fire with which they were met enabled *Parramatta* to escape with nothing more than several near misses, which seemed to lift the ship two or three feet out of the water.

The enemy then turned for a second attack, which was concentrated on *Pass of Balmaha*, who zig-zagged frantically to throw off the bombers' aim. She was successful, although a near miss damaged the bunkers and brought her to a stand still. Furious at their lack of success, the bombers swooped low and machine-gunned the survivors from *Auckland* as they struggled in the water; but, here again, they happily did little harm.

It was now quite clear to Lieut.-Commdr. Walker that attacks would be continued until dark and it would, therefore, be impossible for *Parramatta* to pick up survivors before nightfall. The Commanding Officer of *Auckland*—Commander Thomas—hailed *Parramatta* from the water and told Walker to remain at a distance, while the boatloads of survivors were instructed to spread well out.

Pass of Balmaha now lowered her boats, and all her crew abandoned ship. It was the wisest thing they could do. The ship could not steam, although she was otherwise intact; they had no guns and did not relish the idea of being blown sky high by their dangerous cargo. If she was still afloat by nightfall they could always return on board.

As the sun began to sink towards the horizon (and how anxiously everyone watched it!), the sky became alive with aircraft. At first it was hoped that British fighters were among them and attacking bomber formations, but it was soon realised that all in sight were hostile.

At 7.55 p.m. the attack developed and, from that moment, the air seemed so full of shrieking and diving planes that it was impossible to count them. There was always one formation overhead falling about like leaves and diving in succession, another formation moving forward into position, and a third splitting up and approaching at an angle of 45 degrees.

Snaking at high speed, *Parramatta* tried to turn beam on to each successive attack, firing continuously with all her guns and causing considerable damage to the enemy. At least two machines received direct hits from 4-inch shell and disentegrated; others were obviously damaged. Each dive bomber appeared to release one large bomb and four smaller ones in a pattern, and they fell, for the most part, in the water close to *Parramatta* shaking the ship violently. But, though struck by many splinters, she escaped damage and suffered no casualties.

For the best part of an hour-and-a-half attacks continued until, at length, as the sun touched the horizon at 8.25, the enemy drew off. From the direction of the darkening sky, Lieut.-Commdr. Walker now expected torpedo bombers to approach, but none appeared, and *Parramatta* steamed towards the open boats in which survivors from *Auckland* were cheerfully keeping up each others spirits.

To the great relief of everyone on board, they suddenly sighted the destroyers *Waterhen* and *Vendetta*, both manned— like *Parramatta*—by Australian crews. They had begun to feel lonely, and the timely arrival of these two destroyers was much appreciated.

The task of picking up survivors was quickly carried out and, with 162 on board, *Parramatta* proceeded towards Alexandria, while *Waterhen* took *Pass of Balmaha* (now re-manned) in tow and delivered her safely at Tobruk. Thus, another 750 tons of petrol reached its destination.

The scale of attack had been one of the heaviest experienced and, though the loss of *Auckland* was a serious blow, the fact that the whole convoy was not wiped out testifies to the stout defence maintained by the escort vessels during the long period in which they were heavily assaulted. In the circumstances it was almost impossible to know with any exactness how many aircraft were brought down, but it appears that there were at least three certainties, and many others must have been seriously damaged.

Towards the end of June, a larger convoy was more successful in the face of continuous and heavy air raids, all supplies arriving intact and H.M. Ships only incurring minor damage with few casualties, none of which were fatal. The convoy, on this occasion, consisted of two Greek merchant ships— *Miranda* and *Antiklia*—escorted from Mersa Matruh to Tobruk by the escort vessel *Flamingo* (Commander R. J. O. Otway-Ruthven) in station astern, the South African whaler *Southern Isles* (Lieut. A. C. Matson, S.D.F.) as anti-submarine screen ahead, and the gunboat *Cricket* leading the two ships in convoy.

As usual all was peace until west of Ras Azzaz. Then, at about 1.45 p.m., ten *Junkers* 87 suddenly dived on *Flamingo* and the merchant vessels, released their bombs at 1000 feet and flew ahead at 50 feet above the water. Bombs fell close to all three ships but, beyond shaking them, caused no damage. *Flamingo*, on the other hand, destroyed at least two machines and damaged another, while *Southern Isles* most effectively deterred two aircraft which turned to attack her with cannon, by firing her 4-inch low-angle Q.F. with fuzes set to burst as short as possible.

An hour later, a very sudden attack was launched on the entire convoy by about twenty aircraft, consisting of *Junkers* 87 and 88, and *Heinkels* 111. Near misses were scored on *Flamingo*, bomb fragments spattering her decks, but no serious damage resulted and her sustained fire caused more than one plane to limp crazily away. Two bombs fell even closer to *Southern Isles*, deluging the whole ship with water, but that made no difference to her standard of defence. As one *Junkers* 87 passed astern of her, after carrying out an abortive attack on *Cricket*, the after Breda opened up hitting the plane with at least fifteen shells. Suddenly developing a steep vertical dive, the *Junkers* plunged straight into the sea, one of the crew baling out on a parachute which failed to open.

At 5.30 p.m. a third, and fiercer, attack developed carried out by forty or fifty aircraft—all *Junkers* 87. The whole sky appeared to be full of diving planes, pulling out at different levels and approaching, two or three at a time, from more than one direction. Eight planes seemed to concentrate on each ship and, for the next fifteen minutes, the sky rained bombs. They were of a lighlter calibre than those previously used, and some bounced a few times as they hit the water.

Having dropped their bombs, none of which had scored a direct hit, the enemy flew ahead to machine-gun *Southern Isles*, who had also endured her full share of bombing. The forward Breda, unfortunately jammed, but the after one and the Lewis guns fired whenever they had a target. For some minutes after the attack had passed over the other vessels, the unfortunate *Southern Isles* was subjected to wave after wave of machine-gunning during which she suffered four casualties.

One *Junkers* in particular was most aggressive, and the Sub-Lieutenant in charge of the 4-inch Q.F., the fuze setting of whose shell was at 900 feet, waited coolly despite the rain of bullets, until the machine had closed to that range. Then he opened fire. The result repaid him for his pluck, because the shell burst on the tail of the aircraft, setting the engines on fire and compelling the pilot to sheer off. About 400 yards away, the plane got completely out of control and plunged into the sea.

By 6.10 attacks were over; all ships were still afloat and scarcely damaged. Only *Cricket* found herself in difficulties, her boiler room being flooded aft, which reduced her maximum speed to five knots. The damage to *Flamingo* was merely superficial.

After dark *Southern Isles* transferred her wounded to *Flamingo*, then led *Miranda* and *Antiklia* to Tobruk. Both these vessels had evoked the highest praise by the great steadiness they had shown during a trying period. *Flamingo*, meanwhile, took the damaged *Cricket* in tow and shaped course for Alexandria.

Once again the enemy had failed completely in his objective —the throttling of the life line to Tobruk.

Chapter 15

THE PART PLAYED BY THE NAVY DURING THE SYRIAN CAMPAIGN

WITH the German occupation of Crete, there was a real danger that they would continue their drive to the East. Cyprus was then undefended; Germans had already begun to infiltrate into Syria whose aerodromes they were using, and Iraq was just recovering from the Nazi inspired revolt of Rashad Ali. Turkey was sitting very shakily on the fence, and there were indications that she might succumb to strong German pressure. Our air strength was still pitifully weak, and the enormous amount of material we had lost in the Greek and Crete campaigns made our whole position extremely vulnerable. We were undoubtedly faced with a grave situation.

There was, however, one step we could take, and that was into Syria.

About 8.0 p.m. on 7th June, 1941, a Naval force, consisting of the cruisers *Phoebe* (wearing the Flag of Vice-Admiral E. L. S. King) and Ajax, together with the destroyers *Kandahar*, *Kimberley*, *Janus* and *Jackal*, was in a position some sixty miles south of Cyprus and steering east. At dawn next day Syria was to be invaded by Imperial and Free French troops, and this force was to play an important part in the whole operation, harassing the enemy by fire from seaward and preventing reinforcements from reaching the country.

Steaming up from the south was the anti-aircraft cruiser *Coventry* with the destroyers *Isis* and *Hotspur*, and as daylight broke on the 8th they met *Phoebe* off the Syrian coast which they all closed in the gathering light.

It had been hoped to find suitable targets to bombard immediately, but considerable difficulty was experienced in making contact with the head of our advancing columns. Numerous troops and lorries were observed moving in each direction on the coastal road, but it was impossible to distinguish whether they were friend or foe; and, at length,

Kimberley was sent close inshore to discover particulars about the army's progress. Eventually, it was ascertained that Tyre had been occupied without difficulty, and the only bombardment required by the army was a few bursts at some French positions near the Khan Bridge—a well fortified post and a tiresome obstacle three miles north of Tyre.

The first day's advance had been in the region of ten miles, which was quite a satisfactory achievement, but the River Leontes, spanned near the coast by the Khan Bridge, now provided the first serious resistance. To overcome this, it was decided to land Special Service troops at the mouth of the river before dawn the following day from *H.M.S. Glengyle*—one of the specially fitted transports for operations of this kind. The weather was suitable, and it was hoped that a combined attack from sea and land would enable the army to consolidate themselves on the north bank of the river.

During that night the squadron steamed out to sea, but at 3.0 a.m. *Phoebe* suddenly saw the tracks of two torpedoes pass ahead. This proved the existence of French submarines, and made it essential for the cruisers to be screened as much as possible by destroyers.

An hour later landing craft from *Glengyle*, covered by the naval force, crept towards the coast, landed a strong contingent of the Special Service men and then retired in the direction of Haifa, escorted by *Ilex* and *Hero*.

As the situation inshore was too confused to permit of supporting fire, Admiral King stood off with his cruisers to the westward, while *Isis* patrolled close inshore and *Janus*, with *Jackal* and *Hotspur*, carried out an anti-submarine sweep about four miles from the coast. Suddenly, at 1.35 p.m., *Janus* sighted two destroyers on the horizon bearing north-east and steering straight in her direction. They were French destroyers of the latest type—*Guepard* and *Valmy*—outranging our own over which they had 10 knots margin in speed. Having seen our cruisers make off to the west, enemy air reconnaissance had undoubtedly reported that this was the moment for French surface forces to make an attack.

Realising the superiority of the French destroyers in the matter of speed, the Commanding Officer of *Janus* decided to sacrifice the tactical advantage of concentrating his small force which would have involved delay, and, instead, increased to

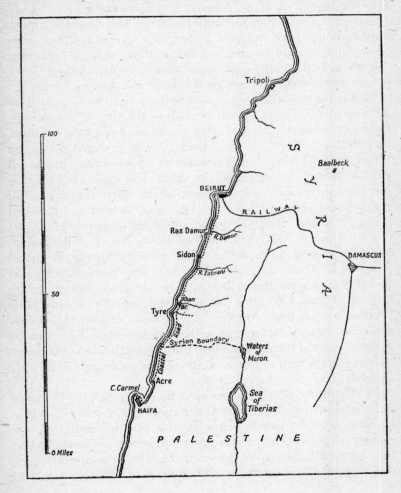

full speed altering course towards the enemy. *Jackal*, from eight cables astern on his starboard quarter, endeavoured to form astern, but *Hotspur* soon dropped to at least a mile.

Four minutes later, from a range of 17,000 yards, the enemy opened fire and, to distinguish their salvos, the splashes from one was red and those from the other were green. *Janus*, however, did not open fire until the range had closed to 15,000 yards about three minutes later. The green splashes were remarkably accurate—the first salvos falling only 50 yards over —and, as both enemy destroyers were concentrating on *Janus*, it was inevitable that sooner or later she would be hit.

Eight minutes after the action had started three shells from a salvo struck *Janus* simultaneously, one hitting the bridge, killing or wounding all the bridge personnel except the Captain, and cutting all fire control leads; another burst in No. 1 boiler room, killing the entire boiler room crew, cutting off electric power and stopping the ship. The third shell entered the Captain's cabin aft and burst in the spirit room, but did not affect fighting efficiency. Fire was, however, continued in local control until the guns would no longer bear.

Twice more *Janus* was hit—again in No. 1 boiler room, while a second unexploded shell penetrated the seamen's bathroom. The situation of *Janus* was now most critical, and had it not been for the gallant way in which the Commanding Officer of *Jackal* handled his ship, she would probably have become a total loss. Manœuvring *Jackal* between the enemy and *Janus*, whom he covered with a smoke screen, he managed to draw most of the enemy's fire, but was fortunate in receiving only one hit which did comparatively little damage. The only casualty was a wounded seaman.

By this time *Isis* and *Hotspur* were in action, helping to screen *Janus* and hitting back hard at the enemy, whose fire had now become erratic. Down below in the British destroyers, engineers were working feverishly to produce a speed beyond that for which they were designed, but the French destroyers, deciding that the party was no longer healthy, had turned round and were fast increasing the range. *Isis* had hoisted the famous signal—*Engage the enemy more closely*—but, in spite of every effort on the part of our ships, the French destroyers, by their superior speed, were unfortunately able to make good their escape—but, it is believed, not without some nasty scars.

As soon as the first enemy report from *Janus* had been received by Admiral King, he turned his cruisers and raced back at full speed; but, by the time he arrived on the scene, there was no sign of the action beyond the disabled *Janus* drifting helplessly to leeward. Leaving *Ajax* and two destroyers to stand by the damaged vessel, Admiral King pressed ahead in the vain hope of catching up with the retreating enemy, but he soon encountered *Isis*, *Jackal* and *Hotspur* returning from the chase which they had been forced to abandon.

The next consideration was to get *Janus* back to Haifa, and *Kimberley* was detailed to take her in tow. This was done without much difficulty and she was soon towing at 12 knots, but the enemy was not going to leave the ships alone. Two air attacks took place, but each was successfully frustrated by protecting *Hurricanes*, who caused casualties to the enemy without much harm to themselves. Our only casualty occurred during the second raid, when a French and British machine were seen to collide in mid-air, but both pilots were picked up by *Kandahar*.

The troubles of the unfortunate *Janus* were by no means over, for an oil fuel fire suddenly broke out in the damaged boiler room. By 7.30 this fire was almost smothered when a second one burst forth and was still burning fiercely when they entered harbour. But in the local auxiliary fire service, which rendered yeoman work with a foam making apparatus, there was some compensation, for it was manned by attractive little Jewesses! The flames, nevertheless, took a long time to extinguish, and just when they were finally smothered an air attack took place on the harbour. Unexploded bombs fell near the Seamen's Home where many of *Janus*' ship's company had gone to rest and recover from their experiences. The Royal

Marines, however, in a camp near by, put themselves to great inconvenience and discomfort to offer hospitality to the wretched sailors who had thus been ejected from the Seamen's Home.

Meanwhile, *Phoebe* and a few destroyers were sweeping north towards Beirut in order to cut off any more French destroyers if they dared to make another attempt to bombard our lines ashore. Nothing was sighted beyond a reconnaissance aircraft and, at dawn, they turned south to close *Kandahar* and *Kimberley* who had been detailed to shell positions north of the Khan Bridge where our troops were still encountering difficulties. On this occasion the two destroyers spent a most successful forenoon, getting close inshore, creating havoc among enemy motor transport, blowing up ammunition dumps and doing great execution with numbers of tanks. One tank had the impertinence to drive to the edge of the cliff and direct all its fire at one of the destroyers—but not for long!

This bombardment was of the very greatest assistance to our troops and enabled them to make a progress which, at this time, would otherwise have been impossible.

Six more destroyers had now augmented Admiral King's force, and the cruiser *Leander* had relieved *Ajax*. During the next two or three days, an inshore division carried out an almost continuous bombardment of targets north of a line indicated by the army, and assisted a military advance to a position on the Zahrani River about $3\frac{1}{2}$ miles south of Sidon. Here a number of unlocated batteries of 75 mm. guns held the advance for three days, and even tried to hit the destroyers at sea. It was an aggravating check, but air reconnaissance eventually established their position on which *Ilex*, *Hero* and *Jackal* opened deliberate fire, thus removing all opposition to the north of Sidon which our troops entered on 15th June.

The effectiveness of the bombardments had been materially assisted by the establishment of a naval liaison officer in the front line of the army. He was able to find out the particular objectives which the military required to be demolished, and it was a simple matter to signal this information to the ships concerned.

That the bombardment had been appreciated by the army is shown by the following signal made by the naval liaison officer: "Brigadier Stevens has asked me to convey his warmest thanks for the fine job of work carried out by the destroyers this morning. The results obtained were the means of saving many lives and greatly hastened the achievement of the objective."

While these operations were in progress, other units were taking effective steps to see that there was no further interference by the French destroyers, who could have delayed our advance had they been permitted to get within range of the coast. It was on the afternoon of the 14th June when they made another attempt to break out.

At 4.20, *Griffin*, who was bombarding positions north of Sidon, suddenly reported two destroyers some fifteen miles to the north and steering south, parallel to the coast. At this time *Leander*, with a screen, was about ten miles to the south-west of *Griffin* and immediately increased to full speed in order to close the enemy. But, at 4.45, when the range had been reduced to 20,000 yards, the Vichy destroyers decided that discretion was indicated, and turned back to the northward. The chase was continued until well to the north of Beirut, but it was found impossible to close the range, and our forces were reluctantly compelled to return to their patrol off Sidon.

II

For the first six days of the campaign, naval forces had only to contend with a few attacks by French aircraft, but information was received which led Admiral King to expect attacks on a considerable scale by *Junkers* 87 and 88. The first of these occurred on the afternoon of 13th June when eight

Junkers 88 endeavoured to bomb the cruiser force operating off the coast. No damage was caused to any ship, and three of the enemy were shot down by fighters, two more being severely damaged.

Two days later a further eight *Junkers*, followed by twice that number of French aircraft, made a determined assault on the squadron. *Isis*, who happened to be with two other destroyers screening *Phoebe* and *Leander*, received the full attention of one particularly aggressive *Junker*. Leaping ahead at full speed and under starboard wheel to avoid the bombs which she could see the aircraft about to release, *Isis* was suddenly lifted about six feet three times in rapid succession. A particularly heavy bomb had exploded close to her starboard side.

Watchkeepers were thrown off their feet by the violence of the explosion, torrents of sea water poured on board and down through the engine room hatches, and steam pressure began to fall an at alarming rate. The extent and locality of the damage was unknown. Unable to get into communication with No. 1 boiler room, the Engineer Officer dashed along to investigate. Fighting the oil fumes which assailed him, he succeeded in making an entry after two attempts and discovered that oil fuel was two feet above the gratings. All conditions were present for a serious fire which threatened to break out at any moment, and the Engineer Officer, therefore, decided to isolate the boiler room, evacuating those who, with great devotion to duty, were calmly shutting off valves.

Meanwhile, the ship had settled down about seven feet by the head and taken a severe list to starboard: oil fuel had begun to pour into the forward magazine which was then abandoned by its crew—and another danger from fire immediately appeared. Appreciating the position, an E.R.A. in charge of the forward flooding keys—he had, at first, been knocked almost senseless by the explosion—with great presence of mind flooded the magazine.

The coolness and efficiency of the engine room staff undoubtedly saved the ship from disaster.

Isis eventually settled down thirteen feet by the head, investigation showing that her sides and deck had been badly buckled. In order to reduce this heavy trim, all men not required for duty were mustered aft, where the ship's band— having rescued the remains of a piano and their musical instruments from the wrecked mess decks—gave a concert on 'X' gun deck as the ship proceeded at slow speed, but under her own steam, towards Haifa.

In the second attack, *Ilex* was the ship singled out by the only *Junkers* which caused any damage, a 500-lb. bomb falling close alongside abreast No. 3 boiler room. But, though badly shaken, she was able to steam at 15 knots until water was found to have penetrated into the oil fuel tanks. *Hasty* then towed her to Haifa.

It had been learnt that a third French destroyer of the Cassard class was proceeding north of Cyprus to reinforce the Vichy vessels in Syrian waters so, during the night of 15th June, Admiral King patrolled to the north of Beirut with the object of intercepting her, and engaging *Guepard* and *Valmy* if they came out of harbour.

Creeping in close to the shore off Beirut in the early hours of the morning, and long before dawn, *Jervis* and *Kimberley* suddenly sighted the two destroyers which had been such an irritation since the start of the campaign. Opening fire before they themselves were sighted, both our ships claimed hits on one of the enemy, who retired rapidly under a smoke screen to the protection of the shore defences.

As dawn broke on the 16th June, there was no sign of the *Cassard* destroyer, but at 8.0 a.m. encouraging news was received from 815 Squadron. Swordfish of the Fleet Air Arm had intercepted and torpedoed her forty miles north-west of Beirut. From the S.O.S. sent out, she proved to be the flotilla leader *Cheavlier Paul*.

The advance ashore had now reached the Damur River where the troops were encountering the fiercest resistance they had met, and it was decided to call a temporary halt until further progress had been made inland. Beyond, therefore, short bombardments at dawn in the Damur area, the army did not require naval support, nor were they able to provide fighter protection for much daylight activity at sea until the advance was resumed on 6th July.

During this period, Admiral King's principle objective was to prevent destroyers based at Beirut from harassing our own forces ashore, and to stop further reinforcements in the way of ships and material from reaching the enemy. On the 17th June the Flag was transferred to *Naiad* who had arrived from Alexandria, to which port *Phoebe* sailed next day.

The tactics adopted by the French destroyers were on the tip and run principle and, though generally ineffective, were distinctly annoying. It would have been easy to shell them in harbour at Beirut, but the risk of damage to the town could not be accepted. Admiral King accordingly asked for, and obtained, the services of a submarine to patrol where she might have an excellent chance of delivering an attack. On the 23rd, therefore, *Parthian* arrived off Beirut, in which area she remained for over a week. Though she was unfortunate as far as French destroyers were concerned, she did achieve one notable success. Sighting a submarine of the *Requin* class, exercising between Beirut and Damur in the middle of the day, she closed unobserved and sank it.

For several nights, our surface forces swept to the north of Beirut to catch additional *Cassard* class destroyers which were known to be arriving, but the one that did arrive made the coast in daylight and was heavily escorted by about twenty aircraft.

Returning from one of these sweeps in the very early hours of the morning of June 23rd, *Naiad* sighted first one, and then another, French destroyer on the port bow creeping north near the coast and at a range of about 5000 yards. Cruisers and destroyers opened fire immediately and, during the subsequent action, which lasted for eleven minutes, hits were registered on each of the enemy, who then retired under smoke. From this date, no further attempt was made by enemy destroyers to interfere with any of our forces—ashore or afloat.

So the days passed during which the situation ashore seemed to stagnate. At dawn each day—with one or two exceptions—a force of cruisers and destroyers, or destroyers alone, appeared off the coast and bombarded enemy positions at Damur, and on one occasion *Naiad* illuminated targets with star shell in the middle of the night while *Kandahar* carried out a short bombardment. On 28th June, however, the army called for an intensive bombardment which was carried out by the Australian cruiser *Perth*, *Carlisle* and four destroyers, who arrived off Damur at 3.30 in the afternoon and did not withdraw until four hours later. *Perth's* fire was particularly effective, silencing the Khalde battery, which had been a great obstacle to the soldiers.

Throughout this period there was remarkably little interference from the air—due principally to intensive attacks carried out by the R.A.F. on enemy aerodromes—and it looked very much as if the Germans had deserted their Vichy confederates to transfer their aircraft to another theatre of operations.

On 2nd July, while returning from a forenoon bombardment of Damur, *Naiad*, *Perth* and four destroyers became involved in one of those incidents of mistaken identity from the air which are from time to time inevitable; especially when the airman has had little experience of working with naval forces. On this occasion it was amusing, though it could well have ended in tragedy.

Suddenly, when everything seemed to be at peace, a report was received from a reconnaissance aircraft to say that three merchant vessels escorted by three destroyers were in a certain spot steaming north. Frantically the position given was plotted on the chart and, to everyone's surprise, found to be in the neighbourhood of *Naiad*. Why hadn't the look-outs reported them? Was everyone asleep?

The answer came from an unexpected quarter. Swooping down on *Perth* was one of our own *Blenheims*—the originator of the report—who let go a stick of bombs which fell unpleasantly close but happily caused no damage. But the incident was not over, and everyone gazed with apprehension at twelve more *Blenheims* which had answered the report and were now on their way to attack what they imagined to be a force which was going to attempt a landing in the rear of the army. Signals flashed from every ship and identification was, at last, established.

On 3rd July, *Ajax* (now wearing the Flag of Rear-Admiral H. B. T. Rawlings) returned to Syrian waters together with *Phoebe* and two more destroyers. Thus, a considerably strengthened naval force was available for the resumption of the military advance timed to begin at dawn on the 6th. For two days previous, naval vessels plastered targets in the Damur area for long periods at a time, breaking up enemy concentrations, smashing guns and armoured vehicles and inflicting heavy casualties on the enemy.

At 5.0 a.m. on the 6th, Rear-Admiral Rawlings in *Ajax*, with *Perth*, *Carlisle* and six destroyers, arrived off Damur and, as the army swept forward in a determined and gallant assault of the heights above the river, opened up a terrific bombardment on targets which had been arranged with the military.

Against the strong defensive positions, and in most difficult country, the progress of the army was necessarily slow but, by the end of the day, they were established on the north bank of the river and the capture of Damur became only a matter of time.

From 5.30 a.m. to 4.0 p.m. the shelling continued from seaward with practically no opposition. Emboldened by their immunity, ships closed to almost point blank range until a shore battery suddenly turned its attention to *Perth* and straddled her with two shells. A withdrawal to a position six miles from the shore prevented a repetition of this impertinent action. Fighter protection arranged for the bombarding squadron on both 6th and 7th July was so efficient that no enemy aircraft came near the ships. In fact, Vichy French bombers sent to attack were heard reporting their inability to do so; presumably, because of the fighters.

Meanwhile, Admiral King in *Naiad* with *Phoebe* and four more destroyers, carried out a sweep to the north as a result of reconnaissance reports about the approach of three French destroyers, while four Motor Torpedo Boats, which had arrived from Famagusta, were ordered to establish a patrol close north of Beirut during the night.

As the hours passed and nothing happened to relieve the monotony of the M.T.B. patrol, Lieutenant R. R. Smith, R.N.V.R., of M.T.B.68, decided to investigate three small lights which had appeared near the coast about three miles to the north of Beirut. Having established the fact that they came from the shore, and finding himself close to the coast, he was unable to resist the temptation to investigate Beirut harbour itself.

Sharp flashes, explosions, fires and the reports of gun fire suddenly broke out over the city and indicated that an air raid was in progress. To Lieutenant Smith in the M.T.B. this was most opportune for, by the light of a large fire in the vicinity of the gas works, he was able to distinguish clearly the details of the harbour, where he observed a large number of ships.

The opportunity was too good to miss, and he decided to explore further and discover the best method of entering through the boom defences. Creeping up to the northern breakwater, he found a boom laid in an easterly direction, but between the end of the boom and the extremity of the break-water there was a most inviting gap, marked by buoys. Temptation was now irresistible. Starting main engines he leapt ahead, determined to torpedo the largest merchant vessel, berthed on the eastern side of the coaling wharf.

The noise of his engines caused the gunners ashore to believe that a further air attack was about to develop, and that a particularly pugnacious machine was pressing home a close attack on the harbour. Hence, to Lieutenant Smith's amusement, the gun fire which he expected to be directed at him was aimed into the air, and his approach was completely unobserved.

Firing one torpedo at his objective, he turned back towards the entrance, but, to the disappointment of his whole crew, no explosion followed to indicate that he had achieved any success. To Lieutenant Smith there was only one alternative— to turn round and try again with his second torpedo.

This time he proceeded further in to the harbour and nearer to his target which he found, to his disgust, was closely protected by a net defence in which his first torpedo had probably been caught. Rapidly selecting another target, he turned towards two vessels of about 3000 tons each alongside the northern breakwater but, as space was insufficient for a torpedo attack, he decided to use depth charges.

Dropping one alongside each of the ships and abreast their engine rooms, he increased speed and made for the entrance through which he had first penetrated into the harbour. The result of the attack had apparently been most successful, but Lieutenant Smith had no opportunity to observe what had happened with any accuracy. He was now under fire from both a machine gun and one of about 4-inch calibre situated on the breakwater. But the surprise caused by his unexpected visit rendered the fire inaccurate, and M.T.B.68 was able to escape unscathed.

The capture of Damur and the irresistible advance of the army had crumbled the last serious resistance offered by the Vichy forces, who were unable to obtain reinforcements. Thus, on July 9th, they had no alternative but to ask for an armistice, which was finally signed five days later.

Without doubt, naval support of the coastal column, and the effective shelling of enemy positions, made a material contribution to the successful conclusion of the campaign, which might otherwise have become dangerously prolonged.

The fact, also, that strong naval forces were operating off the coast not only prevented the enemy from using his destroyers to arrest our advance, but also made it impossible for him to receive the supplies and reinforcements necessary to maintain an adequate defence.

Chapter 16

SOME SPIRITED ACTIONS

DURING the night of 13th June, 1941, the trawler *Jade*, commanded by a Boatswain R.N., Mr. J. Hughes, was carrying out an anti-submarine sweep to the north of Malta when, about 4·15 a.m., her Asdic set suddenly picked up the beat of fast propellors. The Executive Officer—a Midshipman R.N.R.—was on watch and immediately sounded the 'alarm.' Thus, as *Jade* turned to investigate, every man was at his action station.

The night was not dark, and *Jade* was unfortunately silhouetted against a reasonably full but waning moon. Suddenly about 300 yards on the port bow, two low shapes were observed, one larger than the other. They were enemy 'E' boats. Sighting must have been simultaneous, because challenges were made at the same time.

But *Jade* opened fire first, both with her 4-inch Q.F. and the two forward twin Lewis guns. The enemy's reply was immediate, and their machine guns raked the bridge and upper deck of the trawler with an accurate fire. The R.N.R. Midshipman, while taking up his action station in charge of the Lewis gun, fell mortally wounded, but he was the only casualty. Two torpedoes narrowly missed *Jade*, one passing down on either side.

Jade first headed towards the larger boat and, with the third round from her 4-inch Q.F. hit the enemy in the stern, lifting the boat right out of the water. Then, her machine guns poured such a deadly and accurate fire into the damaged boat that she stopped and took no further part in the action.

The smaller boat now continued to attack, first from one beam and then from the other but, by rapidly altering course to present as small a target as possible, *Jade* managed to avoid two more torpedoes, one of which missed ahead and the other astern. With the 'E' boat's superior speed and manœuvrability, *Jade* found it difficult to hold her, but the Boatswain in command pressed his attack home until, at length, two shells from the 4-inch fell very close to the enemy. At the same time, one of her machine guns was silenced by Lewis gun fire from the trawler.

Once *Jade's* shooting began to take effect, that of the enemy grew wild and inaccurate and, a few minutes later, the 'E' boat decided on discretion, broke off the action and retired. As her maximum speed was only 9½ knots, it was quite impossible for *Jade* to pursue, but when dawn began to break at 5.30 the two boats were sighted about eight miles away. They were stopped, and the smaller one was taking the larger in tow.

The Sicilian coast was close; it was more than probable that the enemy had signalled for assistance which would take the form of aerial escort, and *Jade's* speed was unlikely to bring her within range before that assistance arrived. She, therefore, regretfully retired towards Malta, hoping that the help she had requested from the R.A.F. would complete the destruction of the enemy. It did.

Apart from the accuracy of her fire at fast moving targets, the success of the action was due largely to the promptness of the R.N.R. Midshipman in sounding the alarm and having every man at his action station before the enemy was actually sighted.

This action is comparable to that which occurred between a *Hurricane* and an 'E' boat in the same neighbourhood a few weeks later. Diving down on the enemy, the plane raked her with accurate fire, killing or wounding practically all the crew. But the *Hurricane* itself had been hit, and was in difficulties. Finding it impossible to climb, the pilot pancaked into the

sea and, though slightly wounded himself, swam to the 'E'
boat. After hauling himself on board, he took command and
successfully brought his prize into Malta.

Another spirited action by a small craft, quite inadequately
armed for the purpose, is worthy of record. Tug *C* 307, also
commanded by a Boatswain, left Alexandria for Tobruk early
in May 1941, armed only with four light machine guns. On
May 17th she was lying alongside one of the many wrecks
in Tobruk harbour when, suddenly, the 'Red' air raid warning
flag was hoisted at Admiralty House. *C* 307 immediately got
under way and manned her machine guns. As she cast off
and passed round the bows of the wreck, a *Junkers* 87 was
observed dive-bombing the distillery store, after which the
aircraft circled round the wreck just ahead of the one *C* 307
had left.

The Commanding Officer of the tug immediately engaged it,
and bullets found their mark at once. The enemy lost height
until the markings on the fuselage were clearly distinguished:
it then banked in an effort to recover, but failed to do so.
A stream of smoke began to issue from its tail as it caught
fire and crashed in the direction of the aerodrome.

The South African whalers *Southern Maid*, *Southern Isles* and
Southern Sea took part in several spirited exploits. Manned
by volunteer officers and men, quite a number of whom had
never been to sea before, they not only carried out anti-
submarine patrols but were used on escort duties, towing
disabled ships, ferrying prisoners and stores and doing a variety
of other tasks. On numerous occasions they repelled enemy
aircraft, and often a *Southern*, as sole escort, fought off dive-
bombing attacks on her convoy.

On the 14th April, 1941, *Southern Isles* (Lieut. Netterburg,
S.D.F.) was at Tobruk and ordered to lead the hospital ship
Vita out of harbour and escort her to Alexandria. *Vita* had a
large number of wounded on board, many of whom were laid
out on the upper deck, and she was, of course, entirely unarmed. About half-an-hour after they had passed the boom,

Q

there was the sudden scream of diving aircraft as eight *Junkers* 87 swooped down on the inoffensive *Vita*. Without a second's hesitation *Southern Isles*, who was leading, turned right round, placed herself virtually alongside the hospital ship and, with her determined and concentrated fire, undoubtedly kept the enemy at a height which prevented accurate bombing and so saved the hospital ship.

Unfortunately, a small bomb had struck *Vita* in the vicinity of the engine room before *Southern Isles* had reached her side, but once there, the hospital ship sustained no further damage. Shortly afterwards, R.A.F. fighters appeared on the scene, and it was a heartening sight for everyone to see four of the enemy shot down in flames.

Only two days earlier, *Southern Isles* had been detailed to escort the troopship *Barmora* to Sollum but, on arrival off that port, the Commanding Officer's suspicions were aroused. Strange columns of smoke were seen rising from the town, and a strong smell of cordite gave the impression that matters inshore were, at least, confused. Ordering *Barmora* to wait outside, *Southern Isles* decided to investigate. Proceeding cautiously towards the shore, Lieutenant Netterburg discovered that the quay was ruined and in flames and, as the water front appeared deserted, he approached to within two cables of the beach.

His suspicions were suddenly confirmed as a volley of machine gun fire rang out and bullets fell all round the ship. The enemy was in possession. It was fortunate that a sandstorm and consequent poor visibility prevailed: otherwise *Southern Isles* might have suffered very severely. She turned round, steamed at full speed towards *Barmora* and led her away.

On reporting that Sollum was in the hands of the enemy, *Southern Isles* was ordered to take the transport to Tobruk. As they approached that harbour, a number of *Junkers* 87 dived without warning on the convoy and escort, letting go a considerable number of bombs, one of which scored a direct hit on the foc's'le head of the troopship. With her guns always manned at instant readiness, the South African whaler opened up such a rapid and effective fire that the enemy were unable to score further hits. Several of the attacking aircraft were damaged, and some of these were subsequently destroyed by R.A.F. fighters.

On 25th April, *Southern Maid* was sole escort to s.s. *Hanne*, carrying 527 prisoners of war and ammunition from Tobruk to Alexandria. When in the neighbourhood of Bardia, lookouts suddenly reported aircraft diving on *Hanne* from the sun. Turning round, *Southern Maid* immediately engaged the aircraft and the barrage put up, after the first plane had dived, prevented the others from pressing home their attacks. Furthermore, the Commanding Officer of *Southern Maid* successfully drew the attention of the enemy on to his own ship, thus saving *Hanne*. Although bombs fell within 20 yards, no damage was sustained by either vessel.

By their readiness to beat off air attacks, the *Southerns* undoubtedly earned the respect of the enemy who made repeated attempts to destroy them. On a certain occasion one of these South African whalers, when berthed alongside a wreck at Tobruk, was subjected to a six-hour bombardment with one shell falling every two minutes. Fortunately, she received no direct hit, though the decks were covered with splinters; but the unpleasant sensations it must have caused the ship's company only increased their aggressiveness.

EPILOGUE

THE success of the Syrian campaign produced a feeling of profound relief. After Crete, the Navy had felt naked: both flanks had been exposed and the realisation that, with little effort, the enemy could occupy Syria, march through Palestine and establish himself on the Canal had been uncomfortable. Now, at least, he could only do so by a major operation. The conclusion, then, of the fighting in Syria marked a definite phase in the Mediterranean War, and when the Germans failed to attack in the Levant the immediate issue was clarified —the expulsion of the enemy from North Africa. There were no diversions to confuse this object, and everything was now concentrated on its attainment. The Navy had two principle functions—to assist the build up of a powerful British Army and Air Force, and, by harassing his lines of supply, to prevent the enemy from strengthening his own position. The Syrian and Abyssinian campaigns had established the necessary conditions for troops to be transported in comparative safety to the Middle Eastern theatre, and the moral ascendancy achieved over the Italian fleet made harassing operations more fruitful.

Apart from escort duties, one task of the Mediterranean Fleet was to maintain the garrison at Tobruk and supply forward military units by sea. The formidable nature of this task has already been described, and it grew more expensive in ships and men as time went on. To harass Rommel's supply line, submarines carried out many gallant patrols from which some of them failed to return. But they were too few: the sea journey from Italy to North Africa was short, whereas that from Alexandria to the "hunting" area took four or five days. Hence it was a necessity to maintain Malta as a base not only for submarines, but also for a handful of light surface forces— cruisers and destroyers. The preservation of Malta was important both as a thorn in the flank of enemy supply, and as a stepping stone to assault the "soft under belly of the Axis" once Africa had been cleared.

The enemy now occupied too much of the Mediterranean coast, and commanded too much air over the sea to justify sweeps by the British Battle Fleet into the Central Basin merely for the fun of baiting the Italians, and naval operations were henceforth designed for the sole purpose of bringing supplies to Malta. Such operations from the east were usually combined with similar attempts from the west in order to divide enemy forces. Fast merchant vessels would be assembled and loaded in secret, then make the dangerous journey under the close escort of cruisers and destroyers, who would turn over their charges to the Malta based forces at a pre-arranged rendezvous. The battlefleet, meanwhile, provided more distant cover and discouraged any tendency in Italian surface units to interfere.

While thus covering a convoy towards the end of November, 1941, the battlefleet suffered a grievous blow. *Queen Elizabeth*, wearing the flag of the Commander-in-Chief, led the line, consisting of *Barham*, the flagship of Vice-Admiral Sir H. D. Pridham-Wippell, and *Valiant*, with a small screen of destroyers. During the afternoon there had been nothing to disturb the quiet sea, but at 4.25 the peace was suddenly shattered by four dull explosions. A U-Boat had penetrated the screen with unusual determination and had fired four torpedoes at point blank range into the unfortunate *Barham*. Black smoke poured from her funnels as the stricken ship heeled over, hauling out of line. The starboard bilge keel rose above the water, and men were seen leaping over the side because the rapid list foretold her imminent doom. From the fore top a man was observed in a perfect swallow dive. Then the whole ship was suddenly shattered by a great explosion which threw up a vast black cloud to hide her agony. Enormous pieces of metal performed weird contortions hundreds of feet in the air, then fell, splashing the sea in a wide circle. By 4.35 there was nothing left of this proud and historic battleship who had carried to her grave the majority of her company. Among the few rescued by destroyers was the Vice-Admiral.

A few weeks later another disaster occurred which put the two remaining battleships out of action, and the fleet was thus left without the cover of its heavy guns. War with Japan had rendered battleship reinforcement out of the question, and cruisers now had to perform the work of heavy ships and be prepared to stand up alone to the fire of the Italian battlefleet. Whatever happened, all knew that the Malta convoys must continue.

Thus, at the end of 1941, the naval position in the Eastern

Mediterranean was not encouraging, but two stirring actions in the Central Basin had proved most stimulating. One night in November, Force K operating from Malta and comprising the cruisers *Aurora* and *Penelope*, and two destroyers *Lance* and *Lively*, destroyed, without damage to themselves, an entire enemy convoy. Within the space of one hour, two merchant vessels were sunk, eight were left blazing furiously; two destroyers were sunk and a third badly damaged, later to be finished off by a submarine.

On the night of December 13th, a brilliant victory was won by four destroyers forcing the Narrows between Sicily and Tunis on their way to reinforce the depleted Mediterranean Fleet. About 2 o'clock in the morning, *Sikh*, *Legion*, *Maori* and the Dutchman *Isaac Sweers* were approaching Cape Bon from the west. Just before altering course to the S.E. in order to round the Cape, flashing signals were suddenly sighted ahead and powerful glasses disclosed to *Sikh* the presence of two enemy 6-inch cruisers. Within a few moments they both disappeared behind the land and *Sikh*, increasing to 30 knots, led the other destroyers in pursuit. Unaware of the proximity of British destroyers, the enemy turned sixteen points and proceeded to the north at 20 knots. Both forces were now closing at the alarming speed of 50 knots and quick action was required. Reducing speed, *Sikh* led the division close inshore so as to pass between the enemy and the land. Tense seconds elapsed —they seemed like hours—while numerous eyes strove to penetrate the darkness. Then two black shapes, moving swiftly, passed into the field of vision and the order was given to attack. The range was scarcely 1000 yards and it was impossible to miss such a perfect target, which was obviously unprepared for opposition. Projectiles hurled across the intervening space made a shambles of the cruisers' upper decks, and torpedoes, fired simultaneously, hit below their water lines with violent explosions which threw up dancing flames to illuminate the dramatic scene. Only the second ship in the enemy line fired one salvo, which burst harmlessly on shore. Caught by surprise and thoroughly disorganised, they were unable to do more, and a few minutes later the flames appeared to be dragged down as the cruisers took the final plunge.

A torpedo boat, like a frightened rabbit, darted out of the smoke—one salvo reduced her to a blazing bulk. A venturesome 'E' boat was also destroyed. Then, forming up his squadron, *Sikh* withdrew to the eastward. The whole action had lasted only five minutes, and the moment of withdrawal was scarcely sixteen minutes after the division had rounded Cape Bon—a fine tribute to a quick and correct appreciation.

Yet, in spite of these successes and the dashing initiative displayed by our submarines, supplies still filtered through to Rommel who was able to build up and re-organise an army that would carry him once more to the threshold of Egypt. But, in November, 1941, the 8th Army had struck and, by January, had pushed the enemy beyond Benghazi. This occupation of the North-African coastline had enabled Malta convoys to be run with less hazard, but such relief was only temporary. Rommel was able to advance and, by the end of January 1942, the coast of Cyrenaica was once more in enemy hands.

About this time Admiral Cunningham was relieved. When he left the station, no one imagined that the task for which he was detailed would bring him back again to the Mediterranean before the end of the year as naval commander of combined Anglo-American forces in an operation that was to transform the course of the whole war. The outlook for Malta was grim, but any idea that, because of the increased hazards, convoys should cease to run never entered the mind of the Navy. The "Club Run," as it was called, from Alexandria to Malta would continue at periodic intervals. It would prove expensive, without doubt, but some ships would get through to the beleagured garrison. The assembly and sailing of these convoys followed stereotyped lines—a few fast merchant vessels loaded in secret either at Alexandria, Port Said or Haifa; then, with all available cruiser and destroyer escort routed through "bomb alley." A few brief accounts of the more notable convoys will give an idea of the difficulties and dangers of this enterprise.

In the middle of March, 1942, it was decided to pass a convoy of four ships through to Malta, and the operation was distinguished by the way in which a greatly superior Italian surface force was driven off. Escorted by the A.A. cruiser *Carlisle* and six *Hunt* class destroyers, the convoy left Alexandria on the morning of March 20th, and at 6.0 p.m. the 15th Cruiser Squadron, consisting of *Cleopatra*, *Dido* and *Euryalus*, with a screen of four more destroyers, also sailed. The whole force was under the command of Rear-Admiral Sir Philip L. Vian, flying his flag in the *Cleopatra*. In order to reduce the scale of air opposition to be expected, the 8th Army launched a feint attack in Libya which so occupied the Luftwaffe that for the first two days the convoy encountered little opposition.

By 8.0 a.m. on March 22nd the entire force had concentrated in the Gulf of Sirte when the cruiser *Penelope*, with the destroyer *Legion*, joined from Malta. It was hoped that the good fortune which had so far attended the voyage would continue, but any idea that the enemy had failed to locate the convoy was dispelled by a signal received early in the morning. A strong enemy force, including heavy ships, was leaving Taranto.

It was estimated that the enemy could make contact in the late afternoon, and Admiral Vian was faced with two definite considerations governing his course of action—the convoy had to arrive at Malta within a few hours of daylight before enemy bombers could attack, and there was insufficient oil at Malta to fuel the cruisers who, therefore, could not proceed beyond a certain meridian. During any engagement, therefore, the convoy would have to steer west. It was also essential for the enemy to be driven off before dark; otherwise the fuel situation for the cruisers would become acute.

From 9.30 in the morning air attacks were continuous, but ships were unscathed. Suddenly, at 2.10 in the afternoon. *Euryalus* sighted smoke growing out of the northern horizon,

Within twenty minutes it had resolved itself into four enemy ships, but it was not before 2.44 when they could be identified as one 8-inch and three 6-inch cruisers. The British cruisers and attendant destroyers immediately concentrated and, at a suitable distance from the convoy, they turned east laying a thick band of smoke to hide it from the enemy. Then, turning towards the Italian ships, Admiral Vian opened fire at extreme range. The action was short, and the enemy, perturbed by these aggressive tactics, broke off the engagement shortly afterwards and disappeared into the northern haze.

But Admiral Vian was suspicious. The wind was blowing from the S.W. and it was possible that two of the enemy cruisers, which appeared to have detached themselves from the remainder, were trying to work round to windward of the smoke. So, with his own squadron, he made off in that direction leaving the destroyers to cover the convoy. But these two enemy cruisers were never sighted and, later intelligence indicated that they had been damaged earlier in the gun action from which they had retired early.

Thus *Cleopatra* was some distance from the convoy when disturbing news was flashed by Captain D.22 in the destroyer *Sikh*. Away to the north another and more powerful Italian surface force had been sighted, consisting of one battleship of the *Littorio* class, two 8-inch cruisers, three 6-inch cruisers and one other vessel. Without the support of the three British cruisers, the situation was critical, but in a remarkable and determined action *Sikh*, with *Havock*, *Lively* and *Hero*, managed to hold off the enemy who seemed swayed by indecision.

Exerting every ounce of speed, the British cruisers raced into action, but it was some minutes before they could join *Sikh*. Then, laying a smoke screen and following the same tactics as before, Admiral Vian's greatly inferior force turned towards the enemy. *Havock* was hit and stopped—though she later managed to get under way again—and a shell, bursting on the after end of *Cleopatra's* bridge, killed one officer and fourteen men, and wounded six others. But a palpable hit was observed at the same moment on the bridge of a *Bolzano* class cruiser.

For the best part of an hour the uneven gun action continued, but with masterly skill Admiral Vian kept the Italians at a distance. They seemed unwilling to risk coming through the smoke which lay in a heavy cloud hiding the convoy to the southward, and through which cruisers and destroyers emerged to hurl projectiles into the enemy battle line. About 6.0 p.m. Admiral Vian gave orders for a general torpedo attack to be delivered and, supported by gunfire from *Cleopatra* and *Euryalus* following close astern, the destroyers raced towards the enemy.

The smoke, a deteriorating visibility and rising wind and sea made conditions difficult, but the attack was pushed home with determination to a range of three miles. Columns of water tossed up by plunging enemy shells frequently hid ships from view. *Lively* was hit and stopped, but the remainder proceeded unscathed and at least one hit was certainly observed on the *Littorio* battleship. At the same time a fire was started on her quarter-deck as a result of accurate shooting by the British cruisers. This was enough for the enemy, who turned away to the N.N.W. and were lost to view at 7.0 p.m. The last sight of the retreating enemy were the flames from the burning quarter-deck of the Italian battleship.

It was a heartening and thoroughly deserved victory. Had the rôles been reversed, it is unthinkable that the convoy or much of its escort would have survived.

Meanwhile, the convoy had been subjected to no less than twenty-eight air attacks, but the volume of fire put up by the *Carlisle* and escorting *Hunt* destroyers was so effective that no damage had been sustained, and many of the enemy were destroyed.

Shortly after the surface action, Admiral Vian turned the 15th Cruiser Squadron and, parting company, shaped course for Alexandria. The convoy, meanwhile, scattered, each ship proceeding at its best speed for Malta so as to arrive as soon after daylight as possible. *Penelope, Carlisle* and eight destroyers afforded general support.

Shortly after 9.0 a.m. on the following morning, two of the gallant merchant vessels entered Valletta harbour, but the others were less fortunate. Daylight found the slowest about fifty miles from Malta. At 10.30 a *Junkers* swooped out of the sky and dropped a bomb which struck her amidship. A few minutes later she rolled over and sank, *Erridge*, who was in company, picking up 112 survivors.

Breconshire, after a long and arduous career in running stores to Malta, was only eight miles from the Grand Harbour when at 9.20 she, too, was hit and stopped. After unavailing attempts to tow, she was anchored close inshore. Powerful tugs were despatched to her assistance, but another attack developed; she was again hit, and, heeling over, sank on her side. During the efforts to salve *Breconshire*, the destroyer *Southwold* was mined and sunk.

But the tragic tale was not yet complete. The two ships which had managed to reach the harbour in safety were soon subjected to the fury of the *Luftwaffe*, and within a few hours nothing remained of them except shattered wrecks. Thus, of the large and valuable cargo which had been carried at such risk and price, only a small proportion was safely unloaded.

Galled by the irritation and threat of Malta, Hitler had assembled a vast air armada in a final and determined attempt to crush the island out of existence. Thousands of tons of bombs now fell in a most prolonged air assault of concentrated ferocity, and the gallant fortress reeled under the blows. Though it did not succumb, the harbours became no longer tenable for surface ships or submarines, and Force K, with so many brilliant exploits to its credit, had to be withdrawn. This bitter decision was softened by the knowledge that more than a thousand aircraft must have been taken from the Russian front in order to drive our ships from Malta.

The situation for Malta now appeared almost desperate and, during the next few months, it was realised that only a major naval operation could possibly bring relief to the hard-pressed garrison. The Mediterranean Fleet was too weak to undertake the task alone, and reinforcements were lent temporarily from the Eastern Fleet. To ensure a better chance of success and of confusing the enemy, the operation was synchronised with a similar attempt from the west covered by warships attached to the indefatigable Force H, and attempts were made to exploit every ruse and deception.

Forces left their ports in the Eastern Mediterranean on the 11th and 12th June, concentrating p.m. on the 12th. They consisted of 8 cruisers and 27 destroyers, and the convoy was composed of merchant vessels including tankers, which were packed tight with all kinds of stores, lorries, guns, tanks and ammunition. Submarines were stretched across the route in the Central Basin in order to deflect any attack from Italian surface units, and orders of a most detailed nature were drawn up to provide for every imaginable eventuality.

Air attacks began on 12th June and, by evening, one merchant vessel had been so damaged by near misses that she had to retire to Tobruk. But it was not until the afternoon of the 14th when they really became heavy and persistent. Two more merchant vessels were damaged, one of which had to be sunk by the escort as she could barely make way through the water. Towards sunset six 'E' Boats were reported to the north-west but, when they made their attack under cover of darkness, destroyers on the screen were able to drive them off. At dusk the air was filled with the angry hum of torpedo carrying aircraft, but skilful manœuvring and good luck enabled all torpedoes to be avoided.

But after dark an ominous signal was received. The Italian battlefleet was stirring in Taranto harbour, and two of the latest *Littorio* battleships with eight cruisers and a swarm of destroyers were reported proceeding to sea. A rapid calculation showed that they could make contact by dawn on the following day. With their higher speed, long range guns and greater manœuvrability they could, if properly handled, destroy the convoy and escape serious damage from the British forces. By some means they had to be stopped and driven off before they could get within reach of the convoy.

The Commander-in-Chief, ashore in Alexandria, had visualised this eventuality and had made plans to counter it. Ordering the convoy to turn sixteen points to the east, air striking forces were prepared in order to meet the menace of the Italian Fleet and, by attacks delivered during the night, try to dissuade it from advancing further. *Liberators* from Egypt and Torpedo bombers from Malta were flown off, found the enemy with the aid of flares and pressed their attack well home. Full results could not be determined, but one enemy cruiser was definitely crippled, and a submarine, which witnessed the attack, was able to finish her off. This same submarine later managed to score a hit with a torpedo on one of the battleships.

The night was not uneventful for the convoy. Soon after turning east at 2.0 a.m., 'E' Boats made another attack during which a torpedo struck the cruiser *Newcastle*, who was, nevertheless, able to continue with the remainder of the force. At dawn, the destroyer *Hasty* was sunk by a 'U' Boat.

Reports indicated a degree of uncertainty among the Italian warships, so the convoy was again turned to the north-west, but an hour-and-a-half later it was learnt that the Italian fleet was about 100 miles ahead and closing at high speed. Once more the convoy was ordered to retire until the result of another British air striking force could be examined. Insufficient aircraft were available to deal a decisive blow, but, in the subsequent attack, at least one torpedo struck an Italian battleship and one enemy destroyer was sunk. This, however, was insufficient to deter them immediately, though it must have reduced their speed, and the enemy continued the chase.

In addition to this disconcerting news, continuous attacks by *Junkers* 87 and 88 had made the position of the convoy far from enviable. British fighter protection was scarce. Rommel had suddenly launched his final great offensive which resulted in the fall of Tobruk and carried him many miles inside the

Egyptian frontier. This confused the task of British fighters over the fleet, because they had to operate from aerodromes which were continually moving back. During the course of that day two destroyers were sunk, the cruiser *Arethusa* and several other ships damaged. Scarcely a moment elapsed when one portion of the sky was not spotted with the bursts of shells; and the expenditure of ammunition was prodigous. Several enemy aircraft were destroyed, but there were always more to replace them.

As evening approached, the horizon to the west was viewed with more and more misgiving. At any moment the fighting tops of powerful warships might rise above the sea and complicate the situation, so it was with feelings of elation that news was eventually received that the Italian fleet had given up the chase, and were retiring to their base. Fear of another British air attack on their already damaged vessels doubtless influenced this decision.

Now was the time to turn and make the final dash for Malta, but before committing the convoy to this course the Commander-in-Chief enquired about the state of remaining ammunition. The reply received was disconcerting. Air attacks had been so heavy and continuous that all ships had insufficient ammunition to justify their continuing the voyage. On arrival at Malta they would have to meet more air attacks, and stocks of ammunition on the island were so low that it would be impossible to replenish their magazines. Thus, the return journey would be made by ships unable to hit back at a single aircraft. There was no alternative but to abandon the operation, and orders were regretfully issued—and as regretfully received—to return to Alexandria.

On the way back, the cruiser *Hermione* fell victim to a 'U' Boat torpedo.

Meanwhile, the attempt from the west was having more success, and the battleship cover given to that convoy enabled a battered portion to get through. As far as the Skerki Channel west of Cape Bon the seven supply vessels, in addition to their own close escort of the cruiser *Cairo*, nine destroyers, M.L.'s and minesweepers, had the battleship *Malaya*, the aircraft carriers *Eagle* and *Argus*, three cruisers and eight destroyers. Thus, they had their own air umbrella to break up enemy air attacks, and the force was sufficiently strong to dissuade any surface units from interfering—except during the final lap most of which would be traversed in darkness.

Up to June 14th the voyage had been peaceful, only a few reconnaissance aircraft indicating the nature of things to come. But soon after 10.0 a.m. on that day, when in a position south of Sardinia, enemy aircraft were detected gathering for attack. A few minutes later, a formation swooped down out of the sun while another attacked from astern. Many bombs were dropped, but no ship was damaged and two of the attacking planes were shot down by fleet fighters.

Half-an-hour later several groups of torpedo carrying *Savoias* 79 synchronised their attack upon the convoy with a high level bombing diversion. One group of *Savoias* attacked the port column; another swept up the starboard side from astern, then splitting up into three smaller groups concentrated on different sections of the force. The volume of fire they met was terrific, and friendly fighters patrolling overhead tore into the enemy, though hopelessly outnumbered. Five Axis planes were shot down by A.A. fire and another five destroyed by fighters, but the attack was so determined that the Force did not escape damage. An unlucky hit from a torpedo struck the cruiser *Liverpool*, reducing her speed to 3 knots, and one of the supply vessels was sunk. For *Liverpool* there was only one course of action—to limp slowly back to Gibraltar, where she eventually arrived after miraculous escapes from further bombing.

Several half-hearted attacks occurred during the afternoon, and towards dusk a heavy concentration of enemy aircraft was detected in the vicinity. Sixteen *Savoia* 79 with a fighter escort of twenty *Macchis* approached from the port bow, then split up and attacked columns from the rear; *Junkers* 87 screamed down in their well-known dive-bombing tactics, while a number of *Junkers* 88 plastered the force with bombs dropped from a high level. Due, both to the volume of fire maintained by the ships, and desperate efforts made by all available fleet fighters, these attacks were rendered abortive and several more enemy aircraft were destroyed or damaged.

At about this time the force divided, the six remaining supply ships continuing through the Skerki Channel with their close escort, and the heavier units of Force H with attendant destroyers turning round to the westward. The night was dark, and enemy attempts to locate both forces with the aid of parachute flares proved unsuccessful.

Up to this point, thanks largely to the presence of carriers, losses had been light, but a signal intercepted at 11.15 p.m. did not offer an encouraging prospect for the final day. Two large enemy cruisers and four destroyers had been reported leaving Palermo harbour in Sicily, and their probable objective was to cut off and destroy the convoy at dawn. For a variety of reasons it was impracticable to reinforce the escort, and it was clear that *Cairo* and her nine destroyers would have to meet the threat alone.

Dawn of June 15th found the convoy some 25 miles south-west of Pantellaria. It was clear and calm, and as the eastern horizon took form above the rising sun, the shapes of enemy vessels were sighted silhouetted against the sky. They were in two groups. A few miles ahead were two destroyers trying to work round the port flank of the convoy; astern were two large cruisers and three destroyers. Ordering the five fleet destroyers—*Bedouin*, *Partridge*, *Ithuriel*, *Marne* and *Matchless* to act independently, *Cairo* turned the convoy to the S.W. and, with four Hunts—*Blakeney*, *Middleton*, *Badworth* and *Kujawiak* (Polish)—endeavoured to hide it behind a cloud of smoke.

Bedouin led her division to attack at 30 knots, an action which proved so embarrassing for the three destroyers astern of the enemy cruisers that they retired rapidly to the north behind a pillar of smoke, and were not seen again. The remainder, however, opened fire as they pressed on, and endeavoured to work round the stern of the convoy. Shells fell thick and fast, straddling *Cairo* and the merchant vessels until the latter were hidden by the smoke-screen.

While the convoy retired with the M.L.'s and minesweepers to the S.W. a brisk action commenced between the rest of the forces. The four *Hunts* drove at the two leading enemy destroyers, and forced them to turn away, while the two enemy cruisers headed to the south at high speed, directing their fire at *Bedouin's* division, which was on a line joining the convoy and the cruisers. *Cairo*, having protected the flank of the convoy, hastened to support the fleet destroyers.

The Italian fire was accurate and soon began to take effect. *Bedouin* was badly hit and stopped; *Partridge* was on fire amidships and circling out of control, but forty minutes later the flames were extinguished and she was able to proceed at 12 knots. The range was still too great for torpedoes to be effective, but *Partridge*, seeing that she was unlikely to have another opportunity, fired her outfit, which the enemy managed to avoid.

For the next hour a running fight continued, *Matchless*, *Cairo*, *Marne*, *Ithuriel* and the four *Hunts* racing towards the south in that order between the enemy and the convoy. They did not possess the speed to close without dropping bearing, and it was of vital importance not to allow the enemy to draw ahead and cut off the convoy. Then suddenly the enemy turned to the east and broke off the action.

As the Italian cruisers disappeared over the horizon, *Cairo* and the destroyers closed the convoy, which was ordered to alter course back to the N.E., while the warship took station on the bearing on which the enemy had vanished. Touch with the convoy soon disclosed the motives prompting Italian tactics. The intention of the cruisers had been to draw off the A.A. protection afforded to the merchant ships by the guns of the escort, for while they had been engaged a swarm of *Junkers* 87 had dive-bombed the convoy, sinking one ship

R

and damaging the tanker *Kentucky*. Before the escort could get
into station another air attack developed, in which a third
ship was damaged. The force was still 150 miles from Malta—
too far to receive the benefit of continuous fighter escort, and
the enemy took advantage of those periods when there were
no *Beaufighters* overhead.

Towards noon, then, the situation was as follows. Two ships
out of the original seven in the convoy were intact, one large
tanker was astern in tow of the minesweeper *Hebe* and making
5 knots, another vessel was preparing to scuttle herself, and
Bedouin was in tow of *Partridge* approaching from the east at
8 knots, with the intention of trying to escape to the west.
Cairo was thus faced with two alternatives; proceed at 6 knots
with the damaged vessels or scuttle them and make the best
speed possible towards Malta. The first alternative risked the
whole force by making all ships easier targets and keeping
them longer in the dangerous area. No proper fighter protection could be expected until within 50 or 60 miles of Malta,
and there was still a threat from enemy cruisers, so the only
possible course of action was to sink the damaged merchant
vessel and *Kentucky*.

When this melancholy task had been accomplished, *Cairo*
turned back to cover separated units. Suddenly a look-out
reported a wisp of smoke to the north, and within a few minutes
the two enemy cruisers and some destroyers re-appeared
steaming fast towards the convoy. They first sighted *Bedouin*
and *Partridge* struggling gamely towards the west, and immediately opened fire, but when they saw the convoy they at
once shifted target. Their arrival coincided with the appearance of dive bombers and torpedo carrying aircraft over
Bedouin and *Partridge*, and *Cairo's* immediate reaction was to
speed to their assistance. But her first duty was the protection
of the convoy, so with great reluctance she turned to rejoin
the merchant vessels.

On sighting the enemy, *Partridge* slipped the tow so as to
give her greater freedom of manœuvre, and one of the torpedo

bombers, though hotly engaged by the gallant *Bedouin* who lay stopped and helpless, managed to launch a torpedo at close range, which caught the unhappy destroyer amidships. Within ten minutes she broke up and sank, but the aircraft did not witness her success. *Bedouin's* fire had been so determined that the plane crashed a few seconds after its torpedo had been released. Half-a-dozen dive-bombers then screamed down on to the unfortunate *Partridge*, deluging her with water thrown up by the explosions of near misses, but scoring no direct hits. The damage sustained, however, once more put the destroyer out of control, the rudder jammed and she chased her own tail for over an hour. She eventually managed to effect the necessary repairs, and three days later struggled into Gibraltar. Some time after the attack, two Italian destroyers were seen picking up survivors from *Bedouin*.

The enemy cruisers, meanwhile, kept their distance and did no further damage. Doubtless they were discouraged by two attacks made by small air striking forces from Malta. As the Malta based aircraft were also engaged in the abortive operation being carried out from the east, they could do no more. Four *Albacores* attacked the first time, and three the second. Both were carried out with great courage and determination in the face of heavy fire from the cruisers, and attacks by covering fighters. Two hits were claimed, but one *Albacore* was lost in the second of these strikes.

The remnants of the convoy steamed on. The safe arrival of even two ships might be sufficient to save Malta from disaster, and it was the firm intention of every officer and man that they should get through. More air attacks were delivered during the course of the afternoon, but all were frustrated, and as darkness began to fall this achievement was felt to be in sight.

But there was more misfortune in store. The action with the cruisers had delayed the convoy some five hours, with the result that when ships arrived off Malta it was dark. There were no lights to assist the intricate navigation required to avoid suspected and known minefields, with the result that the Polish destroyer *Kujawiak* was mined and sunk, two more destroyers, one minesweeper and one merchant vessel all mined but, in spite of damage, managed to make the harbour of Valetta.

Two months later it became apparent that, if Malta was to survive, another great convoy effort must be made. Though Rommel was held at El Alamein and the height of the Egyptian crisis had passed, too much of the African coast was occupied by the Axis to justify any attempt at getting supplies through from the east. Besides, there were still no heavy ships or aircraft carriers to counter the menace of the Italian fleet. So it was decided to concentrate on a big operation from the west, and it followed the same lines as the one carried out in June—but on a larger scale.

On the night of 9th - 10th August, fourteen fast merchant ships passed through the Straits of Gibraltar. Four cruisers and ten destroyers were detailed to take them through the Narrows to their destination, and the covering force, which would part company west of Cape Bon, consisted of 2 battle-ships, 3 aircraft carriers, 3 cruisers and 15 destroyers. Combined with this operation was one for flying thirty-eight *Spitfires* into Malta, and these were launched from aircraft carriers on the following day. During the process, *Eagle* ran foul of four torpedoes fired by a U-Boat and sank within a few minutes. The loss of this aircraft carrier which had a distinguished service to her credit, was bitterly resented by the fleet. That evening the first heavy air attack was delivered, swarms of dive-bombers and torpedo-carrying aircraft coming in from all directions. The spectacular barrage put up by the whole force was so effective that no damage was caused, and at least three enemy aircraft were destroyed.

The next day was full of incident. From first light the force was shadowed by hostile aircraft; numerous U-Boats were sighted and attacked, and from 8.0 a.m. onwards ships were subjected to the attention of large numbers of dive-bombers, high-level bombers and torpedo-carrying aircraft, who varied their attentions by dropping mines in the path of the convoy and launching torpedoes which had an unpleasant habit of taking circular courses. Ships' gunfire and fleet fighters were effective in destroying a satisfactory percentage of the attacking aircraft, but they were so numerous—in one attack alone more than eighty machines were involved—that some got through the barrage. Damage, however, was slight in proportion to the scale of attack, and, by 7.0 p.m. one merchant vessel had been near missed and damaged, *Indomitable* had been hit by three large bombs, and the destroyer *Foresight* had been unfortunate enough to receive a torpedo in her propellors.

By this time the force was approaching Cape Bon, and the moment for the heavy covering forces to part company had arrived. The Admiral commanding the 10th Cruiser Squadron in *Nigeria* began to re-dispose his ships for the night escort of the convoy, and this afforded an opportunity to a number of U-Boats in the vicinity. *Nigeria* was struck by a torpedo in the bow, and had to retire to the westward, the Admiral transferring his flag to the destroyer *Ashanti*: *Cairo* was torpedoed and so badly damaged that she had to be sunk, and two merchant vessels were also hit and damaged, though they were able to continue.

Soon after sunset more severe torpedo and dive-bombing was experienced with unhappy results. In spite of a thick smoke screen laid between the convoy and the light western horizon, two merchant ships were hit and blew up with terrific explosions. A short time later the cruiser *Kenya* was hit by another U-Boat torpedo, but she remained seaworthy and was able to continue.

Cape Bon was rounded at midnight.

But the night still held excitement of a disturbing nature, and groups of E-Boats attacked with unusual determination no less than four times. Results were tragic. The cruiser *Manchester* was hit by one or two torpedoes, which made her so helpless that she had to be scuttled, and five merchant ships were also hit, four of them subsequently sinking.

At 8.0 a.m. on August 13th, the convoy was some 35 miles north of Lampion Island when the first air attack of the day took place. Dive-bombers screamed down out of the clouds—and another of the merchant vessels blew up in a cloud of dense black smoke, tossing high into the air stores of vital necessity for the beleagured garrison of Malta. Long range fighters from Malta now began to put in an appearance, but it was not until towards noon, when the force was within 60 miles of its destination, that adequate protection could be made available. Previous to that time the convoy had been bombed with monotonous regularity, and another merchant ship sunk. So when, in the late afternoon, the time came to turn the convoy over to a small escort from Malta, there were only three merchant vessels in company—and two of these were damaged. Next day, however, two more who had fallen astern gallantly limped into harbour.

Although only five ships of the original fourteen reached their destination, they carried sufficient supplies to enable Malta to hold out for the two or three months before her final deliverance. This last convoy had been a terrific undertaking accompanied by serious loss, but the enemy had also lost heavily. At least sixty aircraft were destroyed, two U-Boats were sunk, four probably sunk and many more damaged.

Clouds were dark over the Mediterranean in the late summer of 1942, but in October a storm arose carrying the breath of victory to dispel them. It was as if the latent energy of Allied arms had suddenly burst in a blast of unprecedented fury. But this blast would not have been truly effective had it not been for the unremitting service in long and dangerous patrols given by the submarines based on Alexandria. Though their feats had been insufficient to prevent Rommel's advance into Egypt, once his lines of communication were stretched to their limits, British submarines could then starve his vital arteries. They thus prevented him both from delivering that punch which would have carried him into the valley of the

Nile, and from staging a counter-attack of sufficient strength to resist the indomitable thrust of Montgomery's army. Naval aircraft and light surface forces also played their part, and the complete destruction of a convoy of small tankers bringing fuel to Rommel's front line, was the final blow that softened his armour, causing it to dent and turn before the power of the Eighth Army.

During the final victorious advance from the east, devastating blows were dealt to Axis supplies in the narrow sea bases, with the result that Rommel was prevented from delivering any effective counter-attack or checking the inexorable progress of the Eighth Army. Then, in November, the whole world thrilled to the news of the Allied landing in North Africa, and the return of Admiral Cunningham to the scene of his earlier victories was regarded by friend and foe alike as a significant omen of importance. This invasion re-established Malta as a base, and light forces and submarines working from there, from the East and from the West gradually drew tighter the net which not only throttled the life lines of the Axis, but also caught any attempts to escape the clutches of the combined armies. All this "throttling" could have been rendered abortive if the Italian Navy had taken offensive action, but its earlier trouncing (by forces numerically inferior) had made it chary of doing so.

When Montgomery launched his offensive and scored the shattering victory at El Alamein, it was clear that the secret of complete success lay in speed. Speed to prevent the enemy from re-organising and making an effective stand; speed to inflict the greatest number of casualties on the retreating armies. Speed meant adequate supply, and the further the troops advanced across the inhospitable desert, the more difficult became supply problems. It was only possible for the momentum of the advance to be maintained if the Navy moved in step along the flank, opened up ports as they were captured, created landing places on the coast and transported by sea the enormous tonnages of different material required to support a modern Army. It was a terrific undertaking—something quite new in the annals of naval history. But, through bitter experience, a link had been forged during months of anxious waiting which made this possible. It was the realisation that, in war, there was only one Service, in which the Navy, Army and Air Forces were equal partners. So by October, 1942, a spirit of co-operation had been achieved which eighteen months, or even a year before, would have seemed impossible.

The governing administrative factor controlling the progress of the Eighth Army lay in the rate of build-up by the Navy in the advanced ports to supply it. Naval shore parties were organised to step into the ports as the victorious army marched into them, and their duty was to clear the harbours and prepare them to receive shipping at the earliest possible moment. All sorts of things conspired to hinder their efforts—embarrassing local populations, poisoned wells, booby traps, snipers hidden in drains or in the mud beneath ruined piers, wharves blown out, river mud silting on obstructions; no buildings, no water, no power, no lighting, no sheds, no stores, no drains, no bollards, no fire fighting equipment.

The tasks tackled by the naval authorities were legion, calling for the greatest display of initiative and determination in order to meet changing situations. They ranged from clearing harbours of obstructions placed by the Germans—blockships, sunken lighters, etc.; repairing wharves, floating cranes and lifting appliances; sweeping and buoying safe channels into harbour, erecting net defences, booms and other anti-submarine devices; arranging fuel for ships and convoy programmes; advising on A.A. defence as it affected the port; fixing the accommodation and victualling of naval shore parties and survivors; organising A.R.P.; evacuating by sea wounded and prisoners of war. The Naval Officer-in-Charge (N.O.I.C.) was also generally chairman of the Port Committee—a body representative of all three Services and civilians and dealing with all manner of problems.

SICILY INVADED

Prisoners of war marching along the beach to awaiting ships watched by Naval Commandos

By kind permission of the Admiralty

SURRENDER OF THE ITALIAN FLEET

[From H.M.S. Warspite with H.M.S. Valiant in foreground]

By kind permission of the Admiralty

Difficulties were stupendous and, in many cases, administrative experience was lacking, but the results—when the extent of enemy demolitions is appreciated—were more than satisfactory. Tobruk was entered on 13th November; two days later it was open to small craft and on the 19th could be used by shipping: Benghazi was captured on November 20th; small craft could use it on the 22nd and big ships could be berthed and unloaded alongside on the 26th. The harbour of Tripoli was more badly damaged than any of the other ports, blockships had been sunk in the entrance and it was heavily mined. In spite of this, it was opened for small craft on January 25th, 1943—two days after capture—and ships could anchor in safety in the outer anchorage on the following day. By February 2nd, a way had been blasted through the entrance, and ships could berth alongside in the inner harbour.

While Axis forces were being cornered in North Africa, plans for the biggest combined operation ever to be staged were maturing. At the Casablanca Conference in January, 1943, it was decided that Sardinia should be by-passed and that the conquest of Africa should be followed by a direct assault on Sicily. The magnitude and hazards of such an operation could not be minimised; nothing could be left to chance, and it had to be assumed that the Italians, who had sometimes fought well enough in North Africa, would resist fiercely any invasion and, stiffened by German divisions, make the enterprise most difficult. The attack had to be launched with all the power it was possible to exert, and the idea of failure could not be entertained. In the words of Admiral Cunningham, the attack was to be pressed home with relentless vigour, regardless of loss or difficulty. For that reason long and detailed planning was essential; a vast array of shipping had to be assembled and many hundreds of landing craft had to be built and transported to the Mediterranean. It was soon established when all factors had been taken into consideration, that no adequate assault could be made before July, 1943, irrespective of whether Africa could be cleared quicker than indications warranted. Towards the end of April, the day was fixed as July 9th.

It was decided that assaults should be mounted from the United Kingdom, Middle East and North Africa, the last including a powerful American force. For this reason, planning had to be carried out in London, Cairo and Algiers—by no means an ideal arrangement for an operation of such complexity. In spite of this, and in the face of obstacles which at times seemed insuperable, the terrific undertaking was set in motion. Although the Italian fleet had always shown reluctance to fight, it was imagined that they would make a great effort to resist actual invasion of their shores. Hence, powerful British naval forces had to afford cover to the vast concourse of shipping that moved in the Mediterranean during the second week in July, and, days before the operation, heavy air attacks were made on enemy warships in their harbours. A few months previous, that stretch of water between Sicily and the mainland of Africa had been controlled by the Axis— dominated by the *Luftwaffe*. Allied shipping had only forced its way through in the face of frightful hazard, and at great expense. Now, on July 8th, it teemed with vessels wearing the White Ensign and the Stars and Stripes, the flags of Holland, Poland and Free France. More than two thousand five hundred vessels and craft of all shapes and sizes were employed, and many of these were converging off Malta— from west and east, from North Africa and from the island of Malta itself. The air was filled with the noise of battle planes, wheeling and diving overhead. Whereas before such sounds had presaged death and destruction on the sea, an inferno of noise and fire, blue sky blotched with the bursts of countless exploding shells, now guns were silent and ships steamed on in safety. What a contrast! What a transformation! So complete was this display of Allied aerial might and so effective was the cover given, that not a single bomb dropped among that great armada as it steamed towards its destination.

With all these vessels concentrated in such a narrow area,

it was thought quite impossible to achieve surprise, which was essential for quick success. Another essential was for the weather to remain calm so that nothing would interfere with the swift landing of troops and stores on open beaches. Thus, anxious eyes watched a rising sea that caused some landing craft to labour and others to be late at different rendezvous. To withdraw at this advanced stage of the operation would be disastrous—on the other hand only the utmost determination and resolution could possibly obtain a foothold on the shores of Sicily in such weather. But so strange are the unaccountable factors in war that it was this adverse weather which enable surprise to be achieved. The enemy, satisfied that no landing attempt could be made under such conditions, slept and relaxed. When they awoke, invading forces were ashore—and the weather had eased.

By far the most difficult, though less spectacular, part of any overseas assault is the question of supply once the troops have established themselves ashore. To exploit initial success they must consolidate and push on rapidly, and this can only be done if the administrative machine of the "follow up" is highly organised. When the history of the Sicilian campaign is written, it will be shown that the "follow up" was a masterpiece of complicated organisation, which enabled such complete success to be achieved.

The expected action with Italian surface forces did not materialise, only a few E-Boats and submarines making spasmodic attempts at interference. This last opportunity for effective action slipped away as the Italian Fleet lay undecided in their harbours, and Allied naval units were free to bombard coastal positions, beat off air attacks and escort shipping to and from the beaches.

As in North Africa, so in Sicily, naval beach parties and port parties worked in the closest co-operation with the army, opening up ports with great rapidity and improvising with that initiative which is such a tradition of the Naval Service. So this spectacular campaign, born of a courageous conception,

moved to its glorious end, the three Services working as one
and in the closest spirit of comradeship with American allies.

As the first troops stepped ashore in Sicily planning for
alternative subsequent phases was already under way. Dates
on which further assaults on the mainland of Italy could be
made were dependent on the availability of shipping. Practically everything that floated in the Mediterranean under allied
flags was employed to supply punch for the armies in Sicily and
only as these ships were released with the development of that
campaign could they be made available for further operations.
Though ignorant criticism complained bitterly of what was
considered unjustified delay in carrying the war into Italy,
examination of what had to be done will reveal astonishing
speed in assembling and mounting another tremendous
operation. When the full extent of the collapse of Italian morale
could be appreciated, it was decided to launch the main assault
in the Naples area, and that this should be preceded by an
invasion of the toe of Italy.

In early September, British forces crossed the Straits of
Messina, and on September 9th the heaviest possible assault
was made south of Naples. Although it was known that an
armistice had been signed with Italy, it was realised that the
Salerno attack would be a tough proposition. German divisions
had concentrated in that area, there would be no surprise and
the attack would take place beyond the range of shore-based
air support. Fighter protection and bombing had all to be
provided by ship-borne aircraft, but it was hoped that the
confusion into which the enemy would be thrown by the
disclosure of the Italian armistice would sway the battle in
favour of the United Nations. History will decide how far the
armistice helped to establish a foothold in those first anxious
days.

But the most important feature of the armistice, and one
having a profound and immediate effect on the entire war,
was the provision for the surrender of the Italian Fleet.
Obeying secret instructions they left their ports. Though some

ships suffered damage from air attacks by the infuriated Germans, units converged on that gallant island which had played such a spectacular part in creating conditions for this dramatic climax. Fittingly enough the battleship *Warspite* and *Valiant*, veterans of Calabria, Matapan and other naval Mediterranean actions—met and led the Italian battlefleet, while, from the bridge of a destroyer, Admiral of the Fleet, Sir Andrew Cunningham, under whose inspiring leadership the whole Mediterranean campaign had been fought, witnessed this climax to his great endeavours.

"Be pleased to inform Their Lordships," he signalled on September 12th ,"that the Italian battlefleet now lies at anchor beneath the guns of the fortress of Malta."

GEORGE ALLEN & UNWIN LTD
LONDON: 40 MUSEUM STREET, W.C.1
CAPE TOWN: 58-60 LONG STREET
TORONTO: 91 WELLINGTON STREET WEST
BOMBAY: 15 GRAHAM ROAD, BALLARD ESTATE
WELLINGTON, N.Z.: 8 KINGS CRESCENT, LOWER HUTT
SYDNEY, N.S.W.: BRADBURY HOUSE, 55 YORK STREET

The Front Line Library

Lights of Freedom

edited by Allan A. Michie *and* Walter Graebner. *Illustrated with 58 action photographs. Second impression. La. Cr. 8vo. 7s. 6d. net.*

"We read first-hand accounts from men who have bombed enemy ships and towns, men who have fought enemy bombers, men who have been imprisoned and who have gone through such almost incredible adventures. . . . Every page has a story of resource and endurance."—*Times Literary Supplement.*

"Undeniably a thrilling, even fascinating book, depending for its gripping quality on the extraordinarily close transcript it gives of actual life. . . . Almost the best feature of the book is the multitude of photographs."—*Church Times.*

Their Finest Hour

THE WAR IN THE FIRST PERSON

edited by Allan A. Michie *and* Walter Graebner. *Illustrated with 32 action photographs. Sixth impression. La. Cr. 8vo. 7s. 6d. net.*

"There is shining action in every page of this unusual book, in which a varied selection of war stories are told in the first person by the protagonist of his or her little epic."—*Times Literary Supplement.*

Everyman to His Post

by Allan A. Michie. *La. Cr. 8vo. Illustrated with 22 action photographs. 7s. 6d. net.*

This book comes as a sequel to *Their Finest Hour*, stories of the war in the first person, which Mr. Michie edited with Walter Graebner. Their technique of first-person reporting was born out of the difficulty of vividly reporting for a picture magazine a war which they could not photograph. The authors' solution was to turn to the fighting men, draw their stories from them and record them as faithfully as possible in their own words.

With the new book the war has become global. The stories cover action in Crete, Malta, Libya, Occupied Europe, and Burma, as well as in Britain, and Lancaster pilots tell the story of their brilliant daylight raids on Le Creusot and Milan.

Hospitals Under Fire

BUT THE LAMP STILL BURNS

edited by George C. Curnock. *Fully Illustrated. Second impression. La. Cr. 8vo. 7s. 6d. net.*

"A most vivid realization of what went on as the bombs came showering down. . . . Here for once the authentic atmosphere of the blitz has been crystallized in print. . . . There are the makings of an epic in this Book."
—*Truth.*

Tsushima

by A. Novikoff-Priboy. *Translated by* Eden *and* Cedar Paul. *Maps.*
Royal 8vo. 16s. net.

Novikoff, paymaster's steward on the *Oryol* (one of the four most modern
battleships in Rozhestvensky's squadron), gives in this work a vivid
description of the greatest naval action in modern history, one which
decided the fate of two empires. A worker in "Underground Russia,"
aware that defeat of the squadron would favour the advance of the
revolutionary cause, he is nevertheless involved in the camaradie of the
fleet—such camaradie as was possible under the brutal regime that
prevailed in the Tsarist navy. His account of the start of the Dogger
Bank affair, the voyage round the Cape of Good Hope, the long stay
in Madagascan waters, the indiscipline and disorganisation of the Russian
Second Pacific Squadron under its stupid and ill-tempered admiral, are
like a Greek drama leading up to a fateful end—"the tragedy of
Tsushima"—when Novikoff witnessed "the complete destruction of a
floating city consisting of 38 ships with a crew of 12,000."

The Ship you will Command

by John P. Taylor. *Illustrated. Cr. 8vo. 7s. 6d. net.*

This is not "just another book about ships." It is a valuable guide
for all young men who want to go into the Merchant Navy as a career.
The author discusses ships, but he also explains the complicated financial
fabric which brought the influential shipping lines into existence to-day.
Everyone who aspires to command should know the background of
the great organizations and the great economic forces which brought
those ships into being. Otherwise he cannot understand the workings
of the shore end from which he is so long separated by the seven seas.
Nor can he discuss with confidence the problems of air competition
and the issues of state ownership or state control. The author draws
on his experience to discuss freely the future of shipping, and in simple
and straight-forward phrases explains the ships, the organizations and
the *raison d'être* of "The ship you will command."

LONDON : GEORGE ALLEN & UNWIN LTD

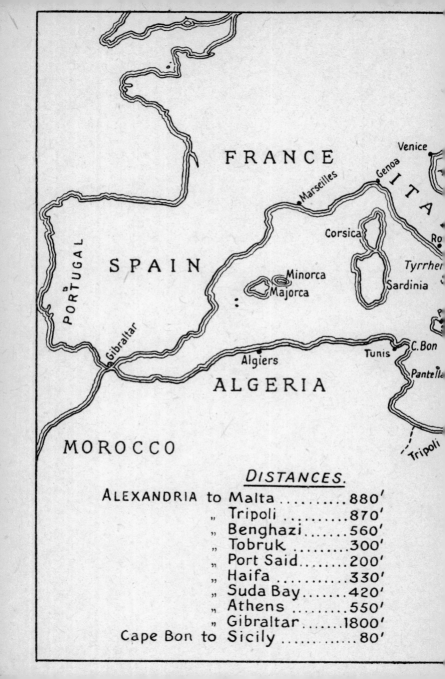

DISTANCES.

ALEXANDRIA to Malta ....880'
     " Tripoli ....870'
     " Benghazi.......560'
     " Tobruk ....300'
     " Port Said.......200'
     " Haifa ....330'
     " Suda Bay.......420'
     " Athens ....550'
     " Gibraltar ......1800'
  Cape Bon to Sicily ....80'

SMOOTHIES AND SHAKES

Elsa Petersen-Schepelern

photography by **Debi Treloar**

SMOOTHIES AND SHAKES

RYLAND
PETERS
& SMALL

LONDON NEW YORK

Senior Designer	Ashley Western
Editor	Maddalena Bastianelli
Production	Patricia Harrington
Art Director	Gabriella Le Grazie
Publishing Director	Alison Starling
Food Stylist	Elsa Petersen-Schepelern
Stylist	Helen Trent

Author's Acknowledgements:

My thanks to my sister Kirsten, my nephews Peter Bray and Luc Votan, and Luis Peral-Aranda in Madrid. In India, thanks to Prem Anand, Executive Chef of the Park-Sheraton Hotel in Madras (Chennai) and Shona Adhikari of the Welcomgroup. Particular thanks go to Debi Treloar for her wonderful photographs and to her sons Woody and Quinn who, as always, enthusiastically road-tested the recipes in this book. Thanks also to stylist Helen Trent for her usual beautiful work.

Thanks also to the Conran Shop in Fulham Road, and Purves & Purves in Tottenham Court Road, London, for lending us their gorgeous props.

Notes:

All spoon measurements are level unless otherwise stated.
Drinks in this book were made using a Waring Blender. Not all blenders are designed for crushing ice: if yours isn't, put crushed or uncrushed ice cubes in the glass, then pour the blended drink over them.

First published in the United Kingdom in 2001
by Ryland Peters & Small
Kirkman House, 12–14 Whitfield Street, London, W1T 2RP
www.rylandpeters.com

10 9 8 7 6 5

Text © Elsa Petersen-Schepelern 2001
Design and photographs © Ryland Peters & Small 2001

ISBN 1 84172 130 1

A catalogue record for this book is available from the British Library.

Printed and bound in China

contents

good health in a glass...

One of the best things about a smoothie is that it's actually good for you – but it tastes so good it seems positively sinful. Fresh fruit and fruit juice provide many of the vitamins and minerals our bodies need – doctors recommend we have at least five servings of fruit and vegetables a day. Add other good things, like yoghurt, nut milks and soy milk, and these drinks become vitamin powerhouses. Some recipes aren't so virtuous: chocolate and ice cream may not be exactly saintly, but they taste terrific.

To make these delicious drinks, all you need is a blender – and very often not even that. I like to start with ice cubes blended to a snow. However, not all blenders are designed to crush ice, so if yours isn't, put the whole cubes in the serving glass, blend the rest of the ingredients and pour them over the ice. Different brands of blender have different capacities. Most will make a one-serving smoothie, but to serve more people you may have to work in batches.

Many of the recipes have been written for one person – admittedly someone like myself with a large appetite – and can be made quickly and served for breakfast, for instance. Others can be made in bulk and served in big jugs for a party or brunch. After standing for a few minutes, the ingredients will separate into layers. Don't be alarmed – although the goodness is best just after blending, the smoothies will still taste just as good.

strawberry smoothie
with **lime juice** and **mint**

A marvellous way to be absolutely self-indulgent. One punnet of strawberries should last you two days – or one day if you're being generous and making a smoothie for someone else. The rule with strawberries is to wash them before hulling (removing the green frill and stalk) – otherwise they fill with water and you get a more watery strawberry.

about 6 large ripe strawberries (half a punnet)
4–6 ice cubes
juice of 1 lime
6 mint leaves, plus 1 sprig to serve
honey or sugar, to taste (optional)

SERVES 1

Put the ice cubes in a blender and work to a snow.
Add the strawberries and blend until smooth.

Add the lime juice, mint and sugar or honey, if using.
Blend again and serve, topped with a sprig of mint.

fruit smoothies

Make your version of this tropical smoothie, depending on what's good in the market that day. Starfruit, lychees, melons of all sorts – all are good. Take care with colours though: red and green make grey – not appetizing in the colour department.

tropical fruit smoothie
with **pineapple, watermelon, strawberries** and **lime**

2 limes
10 ice cubes
6 strawberries
1 small pineapple, peeled, cored and chopped
¼ watermelon, peeled and deseeded
your choice of other fruit such as:
  6 canned lychees, deseeded
  2 bananas, sliced
  1 custard apple, deseeded
  berries such as raspberries or redcurrants
sugar, to taste (optional)

SERVES **4-6**

Finely slice one of the limes and reserve. Grate the zest and squeeze the juice of the other.

Put the ice cubes in a blender and work to a snow. Add all the prepared fruit, in batches if necessary, and blend until smooth. Add the lime zest and juice and blend again. Add sugar, if using, then serve in chilled glasses with slices of lime.

pineapple ginger smoothie

A delicious fruit smoothie based on the sharbat – the beautiful sweetened fruit drink created for the imperial courts of Muslim rulers from Persia to Moorish Spain, from the Holy Land to Moghul India. Because Muslims don't drink alcohol and many of their lands are deserts, they have created an amazing array of non-alcoholic thirst-quenching drinks. This is, of course, the origin of our word 'sherbet'.

3 cm fresh ginger, peeled and grated
1 medium pineapple, peeled, cored
  and chopped
sugar syrup or sugar, to taste
ice cubes, to taste

SERVES **4**

Working in batches if necessary, put the ginger in a blender, add the pineapple and blend to a smooth purée, adding enough cold water to make the blades run. Taste and add sugar or sugar syrup to taste. Half-fill a jug with ice cubes, pour over the pineapple mixture, stir and serve.

Alternatively, add about 10 ice cubes when blending.

Bananas make very good smoothies – add them to almost anything else and they will reward you with a sweet creaminess. Bananas have a special affinity with nuts – so peanut butter is gorgeous.

banana and peanut butter smoothie

Cut the bananas into chunks. Put them into a blender with the remaining ingredients. Work to a purée. Thin with a little more milk or water if too thick, then serve.

2 large, ripe bananas
10 ice cubes
1 tablespoon sugar or sugar syrup, or to taste
125 ml milk, yoghurt or single cream
4 tablespoons peanut butter

SERVES **1**

Dried fruit smoothies make life easy when there isn't a single piece of fresh fruit left in the bowl. Just pop the dried fruit in a glass, cover with water and leave in the fridge overnight. Next morning you have your delicious high-fibre fruit hit all ready for the blender.

dried pear
and mint froth

6 dried pears
6 sprigs of mint
6 ice cubes

SERVES **1**

Put the pears in a glass, cover with water and chill for 4 hours or overnight. When ready to serve, put in a blender with the leaves from the mint. Add the soaking water and blend to a froth. If preferred, blend ice cubes with the other ingredients to make an icy froth, adding extra water if too thick. A marvellous cooler for a sunny summer morning.

breakfast shake
with dried apricots

6–8 dried apricots
6 ice cubes
honey, to taste
(optional)

SERVES **1**

Put the apricots in a glass and cover with cold water. Chill for about 4 hours or overnight. When ready to use, discard the seeds if any, then transfer the flesh and soaking water to a blender. Add the ice cubes and blend to a thick shake. Taste and add a little honey if preferred.

strawberry slush
with **mango** and **lime**

This is a very good way of making one mango go just a little further. You can also freeze the mixture into gorgeous frozen lollipops to have later in the day (see the recipe on page 26).

1 ripe mango, peeled, deseeded and chopped, or 1 small can unsweetened mango pieces
grated zest and juice of 1 lime
6 large strawberries, hulled and halved
6 ice cubes
sparkling mineral water
honey or sugar, to taste (optional)

SERVES **1-2**

Put the mango into a blender. Add the grated lime zest and juice and the strawberries. Add the ice cubes and blend to a froth. Add enough mineral water to make the blades run and make the mixture to the consistency you prefer. Add honey or sugar if using, then serve.

rose petal muneer

I tasted this gorgeous, refreshing drink in Madras, India, prepared by my friend, leading chef Prem Anand. If you live near an Asian market, you can buy cartons of sugarcane juice and coconut water (the liquid from inside the coconut, not coconut milk). If they are difficult to find, use all apple juice instead.

Chill all the ingredients except the rosebud. Put the coconut water and sugarcane juice – or apple juice – in a jug. Add the rosewater and honey to taste. Stir well and serve, sprinkled with rosepetals.

If preferred, you can add a little grated fresh coconut, and serve the drink in glasses half-filled with ice. This makes an impressive cocktail for non-drinkers.

250 ml coconut water or apple juice
125 ml sugarcane juice or apple juice
1 teaspoon honey (optional)
a dash of rosewater
petals from 1 rosebud
freshly grated coconut (optional)

SERVES **2**

thai papaya smoothie
with **mint, lime** and **condensed milk**

In South-east Asia, street vendors sell plastic bags filled with drinks – often luridly coloured. They are sealed and a straw provided to pierce the bag. Condensed milk is a common ingredient, used to add sweetness and creaminess to the mixture. Use plain cream if you prefer.

10 ice cubes
1 papaya, peeled, halved and deseeded
juice of 1 lime
3 tablespoons condensed milk
6 mint leaves

SERVES **2**

Put the ice cubes in the blender and work to a snow. Chop the papaya flesh and add to the blender. Add the lime juice, condensed milk and mint leaves, blend again, then serve.

summer fruit crush
with **peach, nectarine, apricots** and **raspberries**

Make this fruity mixture in bigger quantities for a party. I like it made with mineral water, but you could use cherryade for a children's party. If the fruit is sweet and ripe you may not need any sugar or honey.

1 ripe peach, skinned and halved
1 ripe nectarine, halved
2 ripe apricots, halved
a handful of raspberries
6 ice cubes
mineral water, to taste
honey or sugar (optional)

SERVES **2**

Discard the stones from the fruit. Put all the fruit in a blender, add the ice and enough mineral water to make the blades run. Blend to a purée.

Taste and add honey or sugar, if preferred, and enough extra water to produce the consistency you like. Pour into glasses and serve.

lollipops
with **mango, berry** and **passionfruit**

I discovered these lollipops when I was making a mango and strawberry smoothie one day and had just a little left over. A happy accident. Part-freeze them between each addition to keep the layers separate.

Put the strawberries in a blender, add the mango purée and blend until smooth, adding water if necessary to make the consistency of thin cream.

Scoop the passionfruit flesh and seeds into a bowl and break up with a fork. Add sugar to taste, and stir until dissolved.

Spoon a layer of mango and strawberry mixture into each lollipop mould, filling them about one-third full. Part-freeze.

Remove from the freezer and add a layer of passionfruit. Part-freeze. Do not freeze solid or it will be difficult to insert the sticks. Remove from the freezer and add a final layer of mango and strawberry mixture. Insert the sticks, then freeze until hard.

12 large, ripe strawberries, hulled and halved
500 ml canned mango purée or canned mango
   pieces, blended to a purée
4 ripe and wrinkled passionfruit
sugar, to taste

plastic frozen lollipop moulds, with sticks

MAKES **8**

icy treats

frozen watermelon, ginger and lime

Watermelon makes a delicious drink and it is terrific with hot, spicy partners like chilli and ginger – I use the lime zest and juice to point up the flavour. I find I don't need any extra sugar.

1 ripe, round watermelon, halved and deseeded
5 cm fresh ginger, peeled and grated
freshly squeezed juice of 2 limes
sugar, to taste (optional)
ice cubes, to serve

SERVES **4**

Put the flesh of ½ the watermelon in a blender, add the ginger and lime juice and blend until smooth, adding water if necessary. Taste, stir in sugar if using, pour into ice cube trays and freeze. When ready to serve, put the remaining watermelon in the blender and blend until smooth. Put the ice cubes in 4 glasses, top with watermelon juice and serve.

indian fresh frozen lime with soda

In India, a typical summertime drink is the juice of a fresh lime, topped up with soda water. I like to freeze the lime juice first.

freshly squeezed juice of 6 large limes and
**   shredded zest of 1 lime (optional)**
sugar, to taste
soda water

SERVES **4**

Mix the lime juice with an equal amount of water and stir in sugar to taste. Pour into ice cube trays and freeze.

When ready to serve, put the ice cubes into 4 glasses and top with soda water. Add the lime zest if preferred.

iced rosepetal tea

6 heaped teaspoons rosepetal leaf tea
sugar or honey, to taste
1 teaspoon rosewater

TO SERVE:
ice cubes
sparkling mineral water
rose petals (optional)

SERVES **8**

Put the tea and sugar or honey in a 4-cup cafetière and cover with boiling water. Let steep for 1 minute, then strain into a cup or jug. Let cool, then stir in the rosewater.

Fill a jug with ice cubes and pour in half the cooled tea. Add mineral water, then the remaining tea. Stir, top with rose petals, if using, then serve.

iced orange flower tea

6 heaped teaspoons orange pekoe leaf tea
sugar or honey, to taste
1 teaspoon orange flower water

TO SERVE:
ice cubes
sparkling mineral water
shredded zest of 1 orange

SERVES **8**

Put the tea and sugar or honey in a 4-cup cafetière and cover with boiling water. Let steep for 1 minute, then strain into a cup or jug. Let cool, then stir in the orange flower water.

Fill a jug with ice cubes and pour in half the cooled tea. Add mineral water, then the remaining tea. Stir, top with orange zest, then serve.

frozen grapes in pineapple juice

Frozen grapes are utterly delicious – the flesh turns to a sweet and scented snow. I think plain pineapple juice is sweet enough, but you may like to add sugar or honey to taste.

about 24 large, sweet, seedless grapes
500 ml pineapple juice

SERVES **4**

Arrange the grapes on a freezer tray and open-freeze.

When frozen, put into 4 chilled glasses, top with pineapple juice, then serve.

fruit juice ice cubes with low-fat yoghurt

The great advantage of fruit juice cubes is that they thaw very slowly. Children love them. Top up the glasses with yoghurt or buttermilk.

500 ml freshly squeezed fruit juice
or purée, sweetened with sugar
500 ml low-fat yoghurt

SERVES **4**

Freeze the fruit juice or purée in ice cube trays.

When ready to serve, put the yoghurt in a blender with 125 ml cold water. Blend to a froth. Fill 4 glasses with fruit cubes, then spoon in the yoghurt and serve.

frozen fruit juice granitas

Choose your favourite juices to make these granitas.
You might prefer one variety, or several. I find that thick
juices like pear, peach and apricot are especially good.
Serve the ices straight after crushing – they melt fast.

**1.5 litres fruit juice of your choice,
such as mango, cranberry, or
organic apple juice, or pear nectar
sugar, to taste**

SERVES **4**

Add sugar so that the juice is just a little sweeter than you like to drink it (freezing reduces sweetness). Fill ice cube trays with the fruit juice. Freeze.

When ready to serve, turn out into 4 small bowls and crush with a fork – you are aiming for an icy texture, not smooth like an ice cream. Serve in small glasses with spoons. Alternatively, fill each glass with frozen juice cubes and top with icy buttermilk.

ice cream smoothies

apricot ice cream smoothie
with **cream**

Essence of apricots! These fruit, like peaches and nectarines, are too dense to squeeze for juice – you have to purée them in a blender. The ice cream makes the mixture even more indulgent. I always leave the skins on – they chop up into little pieces and give pretty colour and interesting texture. However, if you're using peaches, skin them first.

3 ice cubes
2–3 ripe apricots, halved, deseeded and sliced
2 scoops vanilla or strawberry ice cream
1 small carton or can apricot nectar
milk or water
2 tablespoons cream or yoghurt, to serve
   (optional)

SERVES **1**

Put the ice cubes in a blender and blend to a snow. Add the apricot slices, ice cream and apricot nectar. Blend until frothing and creamy, adding enough milk or water to make the blades run.

Put the mixture into a glass, swirl in the cream or yoghurt, if using, and serve with a spoon.

Cherries and chocolate are a marriage made in heaven. When cherries are in season, pit them and stuff the cavity with a candy-coated chocolate button (I use Smarties®). Freeze and use straight away with chocolate ice cream and a smoothie made of pitted cherries – or keep them for later in the year, when you need to remind yourself of the taste of summer.

cherry-chocolate smoothie
with **frozen cherries** stuffed with **smarties**®

12 candy-coated chocolate buttons,
    such as Smarties® or M&Ms®
36 cherries, pitted
12 ice cubes
iced water or milk (optional)
12 small scoops chocolate ice cream

SERVES **4**

Press a Smartie® into the cavities of 12 of the cherries. Open-freeze on a tray in the freezer.

When ready to serve, put the remaining pitted cherries in a blender, add the ice cubes and work to a purée, adding a little iced water or milk, if necessary, to help the machine run. Make the mixture as thick or thin as you prefer by adding more water or milk.

Put 3 scoops of chocolate ice cream in each of 4 tall glasses and pour over the puréed cherries. Top with the frozen stuffed cherries, then serve.

strawberry ice cream smoothie

Strawberry smoothies are invariably the most popular with guests. Serve them made just with ice, or with yoghurt, ice cream or milk. Or (as here) with the lot: self-indulgence is a very good thing in my view.

12 ice cubes
4 scoops strawberry ice cream
12 large ripe strawberries, hulled and halved
125 ml low-fat yoghurt
low-fat milk

SERVES **4**

Put the ice cubes in a blender and blend to a snow. Add the ice cream, strawberries and yoghurt and blend again, adding enough milk to give a creamy consistency. Pour into glasses and serve.

blueberry ice cream smoothie

I love the ashes-of-roses blue-pink colour of puréed blueberries. Somehow, I always think of them as a great match for chocolate, especially chocolate ice cream (always providing of course that I don't eat them long before they even get to the blender!).

1 punnet blueberries, about 200 g, chilled
2 scoops ice cream, chocolate or vanilla
low-fat milk, chilled

SERVES **1**

Reserve a few blueberries to serve, then put the remainder into a blender.

Add 1 scoop chocolate ice cream and 125 ml milk, or enough to make the blades run. Blend to a purée, then add extra milk to taste (the less you add, the thicker the smoothie will be).

Pour the mixture into a glass and top with the reserved blueberries.

iced coffee

Some people prefer this frothy iced coffee made with instant coffee. Personally, I much prefer the real thing, frozen into ice cubes.

250 ml strong black espresso coffee, cooled
125 ml ice-cold milk, or to taste
3 scoops vanilla ice cream
unsweetened cocoa powder or chocolate
  sprinkles

SERVES **1**

Freeze the coffee in ice cube trays. When ready to serve, put the cubes in a blender, add the milk and blend to a froth.

Put 2 scoops of the ice cream into a glass, pour over the iced coffee, top with a second scoop of ice cream and sprinkle with cocoa powder or chocolate sprinkles.

mocha frappé

Dark chocolate ice cream and grated bitter chocolate make a marvellous mocha. If you don't have any bitter chocolate, use cocoa powder instead – it's also good, though not quite as sumptuous.

250 ml strong black espresso coffee, cooled
125 ml ice-cold milk, or to taste
1 tablespoon unsweetened cocoa powder or
  grated dark chocolate, plus extra to serve
3 scoops dark chocolate ice cream

SERVES **1**

Freeze the coffee in ice cube trays. When ready to serve, put the cubes in a blender, add the milk and cocoa powder or grated chocolate and blend to a froth.

Put 2 scoops chocolate ice cream into a glass, pour over the iced coffee, top with a second scoop of ice cream and sprinkle with grated dark chocolate.

leche merengada

Last summer in Madrid, a Spanish friend introduced me to this
wonderful traditional drink, half way between a milkshake and an
ice cream. I use a hand-held stick blender to beat it, but you could
also mash it with a fork and beat with a whisk.

1 litre milk
300 g sugar
1 curl of lemon zest, plus grated lemon zest to serve
1 cinnamon stick, broken

TO SERVE:
grated lemon zest
powdered cinnamon
cinnamon sticks (optional)

SERVES **4**

Put the milk, sugar and curl of lemon zest in a saucepan
and bring to the boil, stirring. Boil for 2 minutes, then
remove from the heat and let cool.

Strain into a freezer-proof container, cover and freeze.

When ready to serve, remove from the freezer. Using a
hand-held blender, beat the frozen milk mixture to a
creamy froth. Serve, sprinkled with powdered cinnamon
and grated lemon zest, with cinnamon sticks for stirring.

yoghurt and buttermilk

Yoghurt, whether low-fat or full-cream, is one of nature's wonder foods. It is one of the best ways to add calcium to the diet – especially important for women.

raspberry yoghurt smoothie

1 punnet raspberries, about 250 g
6–8 ice cubes
250 ml low-fat yoghurt
mineral water or low-fat milk
mild honey or sugar, to taste (optional)

SERVES **4**

Put the raspberries in a blender with the ice cubes, yoghurt and enough mineral water or milk to make the machine run. Blend to a thin froth, adding more mineral water or milk as required. Taste and add honey or sugar if using, then serve.

mango and ginger lassi
with **low-fat yoghurt**

Whenever I make smoothies, this recipe is always the most popular. Use very ripe fresh mangoes if available, otherwise canned mango pieces are often very good indeed. I use a variety called Alphonso, from India – regarded among aficionados as the finest mango in the world.

250 ml mango purée, fresh or canned
6 ice cubes
3 cm fresh ginger, grated
250 ml low-fat yoghurt
mineral water, ginger ale or semi-skimmed milk
sugar or honey (optional)
4 tablespoons diced fresh mango, to serve (optional)

SERVES **4**

Put all the ingredients except the diced mango in a blender and work to a froth.
Serve immediately, topped with the diced mango, if using.

fruit ice cubes
with **yoghurt** and **honey**

Fruit juice ice cubes melt more slowly than regular ice and inject a gradual essence of fruit into other ingredients, such as yoghurt, buttermilk or other juices. This recipe is especially delicious – yoghurt with honey is one of those marriages made in heaven.

1 litre fresh fruit juice, such as cranberry or apricot
sugar (optional)
750 ml low-fat plain yoghurt
honey, to serve

SERVES **4**

Sweeten the fruit juice if preferred, then freeze in ice cube trays.

Fill glasses with the fruit ice cubes and spoon in the yoghurt. Drizzle a few spoonfuls of honey over the top and serve.

soy milk, nutmilk and oatmilk

breakfast smoothie
with **banana, oatmilk** and **oatgerm**

If you're not a soy milk fan, but prefer not to use dairy, try oatmilk or ricemilk instead: both are sold in healthfood stores. Oatgerm provides fibre and is also recommended if you're watching your cholesterol. A thoroughly healthy breakfast.

Put all the ingredients in a blender with 4 ice cubes. Blend until frothy.

Taste, add honey if required, then serve.

1 large, ripe banana, chopped
juice of ½ lemon
1 tablespoon peanut butter (optional)
1 tablespoon oatbran or wheatgerm
250 ml oatmilk or ricemilk
honey, to taste

SERVES **1**

Horchata is a creamy Spanish drink made with tiger nuts. Since most of us can't easily buy tiger nuts, I have substituted cashews.

cashew nut horchata

350 g unsalted cashews or almonds
125 g sugar, or to taste
4 tablespoons rosewater or 1 tablespoon
  almond essence if using almonds
zest of 1 lemon, in long shreds

SERVES **4**

Put the nuts in a jug and add 500 ml water. Cover and soak overnight in the refrigerator. Next day, put the nuts and soaking water in a blender. Add 500 ml water and blend until smooth. Strain through a fine sieve, pushing through as much liquid as possible. Return the nuts to the blender, add 1 litre water, blend and strain again.

Stir the sugar and rosewater or almond essence into the nut milk, then chill. Serve very cold, topped with shreds of lemon zest.

almond sharbat

100 g blanched almonds
10 ice cubes
125 ml milk
rosewater or orange flower water
sugar, to taste

TO SERVE:
ice cubes
zest of ½ orange, in long shreds

SERVES **4**

Put the almonds in a blender or food processor and work to a fine meal. Add the milk and 250 ml water, blend again, then strain into a jug. Return the almonds to the blender, add 250 ml more water, blend again, then strain again, pushing as much liquid through the strainer as possible. Discard the nut meal (you can put through more and more water, and the milk will get thinner with each extraction). Chill. Stir in rosewater or orange flower water and sweeten to taste.

To serve, put ice cubes in 4 glasses, pour in the almond milk, then serve topped with shreds of orange zest.

coconut milk smoothie
with **vanilla, peaches** and **lime**

Peaches aren't tropical fruits, but they go very well with coconut milk. Other fruit such as apricots, mangoes, bananas or papaya may be used instead.

4 large, ripe peaches, skinned, halved, deseeded and cut into wedges
250 ml coconut milk
a few drops of vanilla extract
2 tablespoons sugar, or to taste
6 ice cubes
zest of 1 lime, cut into long shreds, and freshly squeezed juice

SERVES **2**

Put the peaches in a blender, add the coconut milk, vanilla, sugar and ice cubes and blend until smooth. Taste and add extra sugar if necessary.

Serve in chilled glasses, topped with shredded lime zest.

mango smoothie
with **strawberries** and **soy milk**

I love mango, but if you prefer other fruit, do use it instead. I think the strawberries are always a good idea though – their scent lifts the flavour of other fruits in a delicious fashion.

6 ice cubes
500 g fresh or canned mango pieces
12 large strawberries, hulled and halved
freshly squeezed juice of 1 lemon
250 ml soy milk, or to taste

SERVES **4**

Put the ice cubes in a blender and blend to a snow. Add the mango pieces, strawberries and lemon juice, then pour in the soy milk with the machine running.

Add extra soy milk or water until the mixture is the thickness of single cream. Transfer to a chilled jug and serve in small glasses.

raspberry smoothie
with **soy milk**

Soy milk is a popular alternative to dairy milk. Because it has a slightly sweet taste, I find it doesn't need a sweetener – but if your sweet tooth is incurable, do add a little honey.

1 punnet raspberries, about 150 g
about 500 ml soy milk
12 ice cubes
honey, to taste

SERVES **4**

Put the raspberries*****, soy milk and ice cubes in a blender and purée to a froth. Serve the honey separately so people can sweeten to taste.

* If, like me, you love raspberries, reserve a few and sprinkle on top of each glass before serving.

index